FOUR YEARS FOR THE RHINO

An Experience of Anti-poaching Operations

KAMAL JUNG KUNWAR

Save the Rhino Foundation Nepal

50% of all returns from the sale of this book will go to conservation activities and staff welfare.

First published in Nepali by Save the Rhino Foundation Nepal, 2009

Copyright © Kamal Jung Kunwar, 2009

This English edition published by Save the Rhino Foundation Nepal, 2012

Translation Copyright © Kamal Jung Kunwar, 2012

Translated from the Nepali by
Prof. Dr. Govinda Raj Bhattarai

Photographs Courtesy of
Chitwan National Park
(page no. 22, 79, 96, 97's 2nd, 105, 118, 139, 191, 275)
Author *(page no. 46, 91, 97's 1st, 166, 197)*
Bardia National Park *(page no. 82)*
Susheel Shrestha *(page no. 85)*
Bed Bahadur Khadka *(page no. 87, 88)*
Ram Chandra Nepal *(page no. 292)*
Amir Maharjan *(page no. 295)*

Cover Photograph
Kanchan Thapa

Published by
Save the Rhino Foundation Nepal
Kathmandu, Nepal

www.savetherhinonepal.org.np
savetherhinofoundation@gmail.com

Printed in Kathmandu, Nepal

FOUR YEARS FOR THE RHINO
An Experience of Anti-poaching Operations
(Non-fiction)

ISBN 978–9937–2–3350–7

Dedicated

to those people
who lost their precious lives
while trying to conserve innocent wildlife
and fellow conservationists who have given up everything
struggling for the challenging task
of wildlife conservation

Why I wrote

FROM THE FOURTH week of October 2006, when I began serving an unjust jail term, I kept asking myself: "What can I possibly do to conserve the rhinos? How can we stop the poaching of rhinos? How can we manage and conserve the rhino's habitat?" For weeks these questions haunted me.

I then made a resolve to write a book chronicling my experiences in conserving the animal. I told myself, in the book I would hide nothing of the incidents that took place while working in the field of conservation and reveal the complexities and importance of conserving rhinos in Nepal. I also made plans to establish an organisation, 'Save the Rhino Foundation', and provide half the returns earned from my book to it for the control of poaching activities as well as for the conservation and management of park and park resources. This book is the result of that resolution. I also made a resolve to use the rest of my earnings to improve the lives of officials and informers dedicated to the cause of conservation, and provide scholarships to their children.

The truth might be bitter to many, but I feel that telling the truth is my duty as well as religion. This book is an account of what I discovered, what I did, what actually happened. This book takes a firm stand against the destroyers and desecrators of nature. Many friends who went through my manuscript suggested that I not mention the names of smugglers to avoid danger. But my intention in naming everyone was to reveal the bitter truth. I have no enmity, prejudice, anger, jealousy or envy towards anyone I encountered in the process of rhino conservation. My sole intention is that they must repent for their actions and correct their mistakes, so that no child is labelled a smuggler's child, and no one of the future generation is ashamed of his or her forefather's deeds. If we intend to conserve rhinos, then rhino poachers and horn smugglers must be punished by law and boycotted socially.

I have tried to speak for the innocent and helpless animals that cannot speak for themselves. I have tried to give a voice to their painful cries. They all have the same opinion: allow us also to live and enjoy ourselves on the lap of nature in a small corner of the huge world. Every species should be allowed to live freely in the world, just like we humans. A rhino, pregnant or with a newborn infant, should be saved from being killed. An innocent baby doesn't know its mother has been killed and continues to suck on the dead mother's breast. Every animal in the world should have the right to live and reproduce freely.

I have tried to present events chronically and converted Nepali rupees into US dollars (at April 2011 rates) so as to make it easy for a foreigner to understand. The role of informers in anti-poaching operations is very important. To keep their identity a secret, I have changed certain incidents where they could possibly be identified.

The present work was published for the first time in the Nepali language in 2009. It sold well and was liked by thousands of readers. However, when I started to write it, I wanted it to publish into English. Finally, I managed to publish it into English. I hope some of the ideas, concepts, methods, knowledge and skills obtained in the course of rhino conservation will prove useful to the policy makers, planners and conservation activists of the world with regard to the conservation of rare and endangered wildlife species.

Acknowledgement

EVEN THOUGH I am the writer of this book, all active staff of Chitwan National Park, informers, helpers, conservers and conservation lovers have contributed equally to it. This book would not have come into existence without their help, good wishes, encouragement and inspiration. I am grateful to them all.

I am grateful to my late father Chitra Bahadur Kunwar for his love and inspiration in conserving the forest resources. I am deeply indebted to my loving mother as well. Likewise, I have recorded the love and inspiration that my wife Pramila has always preserved for me. She inspired me to write, always read my manuscripts and gave valuable suggestions. Also, I am truly grateful to my dear sisters, brothers and sons for their constant love, encouragement and blessings.

At this moment I express my deep gratitude to Dr. Govinda Raj Bhattarai, Professor of English at Tribhuvan University, for translating the book from Nepali into English.

I am also grateful to journalist Bijaya Lal Shrestha for editing the book.

Likewise, I would like to thank respected journalists Sharat Chandra Wasti, Paras Prakash Nepal, Bishnu Prasad Gautam, Ujjol Prasai and Denielle Preiss, and writer Ratna Mani Nepal for their valuable suggestions.

I would like to thank Sabin Shakya who designed the cover

and did the layout of this book. I would also like to thank Gokarna Jung Thapa who provided the map.

Unlike in the Nepali version, I have included some photographs in order to give the real picture of the time and space where the rhinos are struggling for their survival. At this moment, I would like to express sincere gratitude to the Chitwan and Bardia National Parks, Ramchandra Nepal, Kanchan Thapa, Bed Bahadur Khadka, Susheel Shrestha and Amir Maharjan for the photographs, and Ram Kaji Shrestha, Chaturlal Shreshta, and Kaushal Khaki for their computer support. I would like to thank Ajay Karki, Ananta Bijaya Parajuli and Bishwo Nath Kafley who provided me laptops to write this book.

I am thankful to my friends, readers, seniors, conservationists, tourism entrepreneurs, journalists, local people and intellectuals for their encouragement in bringing out this book in English. I hope my valued readers will provide further suggestions and cooperation for improving the forthcoming edition.

Kamal Jung Kunwar
kamalkunwar@hotmail.com

Contents

Jail Diary   244

The Struggle for Conservation

HAVING COMPLETED my tenure as officiating chief warden of the Sagarmatha National Park, I returned to Kathmandu in January 2003. The director-general of the Department of National Parks and Wildlife Conservation called me over and told me: "I am sending you to a good place. The rhinos in Chitwan are getting killed everyday, I am deputing you there, do a good job."

I answered in the positive. But I could not understand why the director-general called Chitwan a 'good' place.

My deputation papers were soon ready, and I was ready to start work as an assistant warden of the Chitwan National Park. I was to work as coordinator of the Anti-poaching Operation Unit there. My well-wishers were worried and told me about the high rate of rhino deaths in Chitwan and advised me to be careful since it was a risky job. I, however, had already made my resolve to carry out my duties to the best of my ability. I was glad to have had the opportunity to carry out the challenging and important task of conserving such a rare and endangered animal. I took my papers and left Kathmandu in the second week of February. Surya Bahadur Pandey, an officer from the Department of National Parks, a clerk and I left Kathmandu together in an office vehicle.

When we reached the park headquarters, it was already evening. We went to meet Chief Warden Puranbhakta Shrestha who was very pleased at having me there. "If I have an assistant like you, we can surely save the rhinos," he said.

The chief warden and Pandey briefed me about the work involved in anti-poaching. The chief assured me that he would soon give me all the necessary information, introduce me to the informers and tell me all that I needed to know about the work. At that point, I had no knowledge about anti-poaching activities. I had never undergone any related training or participated in any workshop. I just had with me my experience of working in the different protected areas and their buffer zones and ways of achieving active people's participation in managing the protected areas.

Pandey took me to see places like Sauraha and Khagendramalli of the park. The people, the places and even the job were all new to me, and yet the staff all seemed hopeful in having me. "Now that you are here, maybe there will be some progress," they said. I too told myself: one day I will control the poaching activities and not allow any rhino to die an unnatural death.

I was not familiar with the places and roads of Chitwan. Yet, I was motivated to accomplish this challenging task. The times were not good. The activities of the Communist Party of Nepal (Maoist) in the district were alarming, and everyday we got to hear of their growing influence. However, that made no difference to my resolution. I had no worries on that count, I was just worried about how I would save the rhinos.

When I first came to Chitwan, poaching was at its peak. My simple desire or my gentle requests would not be enough to stop the activity. Everyday I would just hope that no rhino would be killed that day or not have to hear of their deaths. But contrary to my hopes, the rhinos continued to be killed. I was discouraged. When a state of emergency was declared in the country in 2001, the 33 army posts in the park were merged for reasons of security and reduced to seven. Army patrolling was almost negligible. In the office, I found no network to control or monitor poaching activities. Neither was the surveillance network strong or adequate. We never understood from where the poachers came, who they were, how they killed the rhinos and where they went. We just got to hear terrible news of a rhino being killed, a horn or a hoof gone missing, the tail being cut off, a bleeding rhino on the run or of a gunshot in broad daylight. But we were unable to locate the dead body of the rhino even after hours of search.

At normal times, the army battalion in Chitwan has 850 soldiers. Besides, 300 civil servants are posted at the park itself, of whom 140 look after the elephants while the remaining 160 make up park technicians and administrative staff.

The park's technical staff comprise the chief warden, assistant wardens, rangers, senior game scouts, game scouts, veterinary doctors and compounders.

The locals are employed by the park as informers when necessary. Some of them are eager to help in the conservation efforts and work for the park voluntarily without payment. Many of the informers themselves must have previously been involved in some way in buying and selling rhino horns and tiger skins and bones. Some of them change their course after being penalised for smuggling and realise the wrong they have done. They begin to understand that conservation is the right approach and work as informers for a salary. However, some tend to be cunning. They work for the smugglers and the park at the same time, and the park has no way of suspecting them. The informers enjoy negligible facilities. Yet they must work all month long even though they might not receive a monthly salary. The park, however, pays for their food, lodging and telephone calls while at work, provided they are successful. If they are unsuccessful, the informers might, however, have to pay for these services out of their own pocket.

Since the informers receive minimum wages and facilities from the park, sometimes they could be tempted to act as double agents if the smugglers pay them more. Traditionally, they have always been employed as and when needed instead of on a permanent basis or on a contract basis. While they are given no training and there are no programmes to build their capacities, sometimes they are fired if the park officials do not like them and may not be paid for months. But they could be given bonuses if they worked well.

The informers are mostly managed by the assistant warden, rangers and other park officials. They are mostly answerable to the Anti-poaching Unit. Many a time, they come up to say what they have unearthed, while at other times, the park asks them to find out about individuals who have been named by the arrested poachers. The informers' responsibilities are assigned according to their location, situation, capacity and previous knowledge.

FIRST OPERATION

ON FEBRUARY 16, 2003, the chief warden opened his secret diary and asked me to note down the names of the people he wanted me to arrest. The list included 24 poachers and a few smugglers and brokers. I had all the names now, but I was worried as to how and where I would arrest them.

Shriranga Kandel, a *mukhiya* of our team, was very skilled in anti-poaching operations. He possessed deep knowledge besides long years of experience working on this job. He was also very diligent, brave and dedicated. "I have just asked a few informers to go after three persons," he said. "If you give me some money, I will meet the informers right now and make the arrangements."

I gave him Nepali rupees worth $21, and he sped towards Narayangadh on his bike.

At around 5 in the evening, we received a message: "The target is at home, we go at night to arrest him."

From Kasara, a team comprising army personnel and park officials left in two vehicles for the Laukhani post. Rangers Madhav Khadka and Rupak Maharjan, *mukhiya* Shriranga and a few others also joined our team. Also with us was poacher Nara Bahadur B.K. to show us where his friends lived. On February 5, Nara Bahadur had been arrested after five rhinos were killed in just three months in the community forest where he served as a forest guard.

Also in our team was the chief warden. The National Parks and Wildlife Conservation Act 1973 empowers the chief warden with discretionary powers to decide on lawsuits and cases within the park. In such circumstances, whether or not it was right for the chief warden himself to be part of the mission to arrest criminals is debatable. However, it was certainly not unethical for him to accompany us as the chief warden and not as a judge.

For the first time in my life, I was part of a mission to arrest a rhino poacher. At 9 p.m., we moved east from Laukhani towards Daldale. After proceeding a little further north from Daldale, we spotted a house on the left side of the road. My colleagues confirmed that this was the very house. They got off from the jeep and surrounded the house. They were obviously experienced in such operations. We all took our positions. Madhav and Rupak opened the door of the house. I, too, entered the house with them. There was no one on the ground floor. We climbed to the first floor where we found a boy of about 11, a woman and a small girl sleeping.

After waking up the woman, I asked her, "Where is your husband?"

"He has been in India since the past six months," she said.

"He was here in the afternoon, how can he be in India now?"

"Really he has gone to India," she said.

"Isn't this Mahato's house?" I asked her.

The boy answered, "No, this is our house, and I am not a Mahato by caste."

"Which is Mahato's house then?" I asked.

"It is that wooden house up there."

We got out in a hurry. In a flash, the rangers were on the first floor of the wooden house and had arrested a man - Buddhi Bahadur Mahato. His wife and children started crying.

We returned to Narayangadh at around 11 at night with Buddhi Bahadur. Our vehicle turned towards Kshetrapur area to arrest another smuggler there. When the house was ascertained, we surrounded it from all sides. We had information that the man we wanted lived on the first floor of the three-storied building. But its channel gate was locked. So we roused the person sleeping in a room next to the gate and asked him for the key. He handed over the key without any objection, probably because he was scared to see so many of us. In our team of over 20 people, many were soldiers. The rangers too were of heavy build and had loud, fearsome voices.

We opened the lock and went upstairs. We searched all rooms. The door of a room facing east was closed. Before opening the door, we tried to see if a person might be able to escape from there. After that, we forced it open. Inside was the man we had been looking for.

We addressed him by his name: "Are you Prem B.K.?" On hearing our query, he suddenly got up in a furious manner.

Startled, his wife started crying, "Why, what has happened?"

Prem consoled her while he wore his pants. "Don't cry, leave me alone, let me die, I will go, let whatever must happen, happen." He understood why we had come for him in the middle of the night. His kids too woke up and started wailing, wanting to know what was happening. One son, however, stood quietly without any reaction. Probably he was aware of his father's illegal activities. We searched the whole room, including the cabinet and bed, but found nothing.

We took Prem along in the vehicle and went to Kasara.

"Our operation was 100 per cent successful," said Madhav.

I too was overjoyed to think that the first mission of which I was a part had been successful.

After we had crossed the Bharatpur Cancer Hospital and were heading towards Kasara, Madhav started questioning Prem.

"Yes, I sold a horn," he opened up.

"You sold five of them."

He denied it, and Madhav delivered a tight slap.

"Yes, I sold three of them," he admitted.

Madhav was not satisfied. "No, you are still lying about the other two horns."

He refused to admit it for quite some time, but after more questioning and threats, he confessed to having sold all five of them.

At that moment, I felt very proud at having nabbed such a dangerous criminal in my very first attempt with the help of *mukhiya* Shriranga. Actually Prem B.K. was nabbed on the basis of information provided by Nara Bahadur B.K. Nara Bahadur had accused Prem of taking away the horns of all the five rhinos that had been killed while he was the forest guard of the buffer zone community forest.

At Kasara, we again started questioning Prem. He revealed that the owner of Atma Glass Centre in Narayangadh had introduced him to a man from Manang, Gyamjo. His testimony revealed that Gyamjo, who used to stay at the Rhino Hotel in Narayangadh, was the one who used to smuggle the rhino horns.

However, Prem informed us that Gyamjo had died of a heart attack six months ago and that his brother came periodically to collect the horns. He even gave us the person's description, address and phone number. Prem had previously lived in his flat in Kathmandu upon learning that we were keeping track of him. He had returned from Kathmandu on February 15 when Gyamjo's brother had assured him there would be no one to bother him.

Prem claimed that this brother of Gyamjo was the one who spearheaded the business, and we would know everything if we arrested him. As he apprised us of the dangers of the situation by informing us that Gyamjo's brother knew a lot of bigwigs, he seemed very scared. He pleaded for his life as Gyamjo's brother had threatened to kill him if he ever mentioned his name to the authorities.

We decided to send two rangers to Kathmandu to find out about this smuggler. They had with them his personal details, address and phone number. But after a few days, they returned empty-handed.

Prem Bahadur had mentioned that he had given a horn to Chandrakanta Pandey from Dhading, Chhatre-Deurali, who owned a vegetable shop at Kalimati, Kathmandu. Chadrakanta frequently came to Kawasoti to buy vegetables. So an informer obtained Chandrakanta's address from a vegetable dealer at Kawasoti and went to Kathmandu with a friend. There, he met Chandrakanta on some silly pretext, arrested him and brought him to Chitwan in a reserved microbus. An informer who takes such initiatives must be rewarded. However, whether an informer should be given such authority is something one should decide for oneself.

News of Abduction on Radio

On March 12, we received news that the owner of Atma Glass Centre, the broker who did business with Gyamjo's brother, was in his shop. At 6 in the morning, I, *mukhiya* Shriranga and a few army personnel set off for Narayangadh. We parked our jeep near Shahid Chowk, and we decided that I, the *mukhiya* and an army man would go to see if the man was in the shop. The market was quite busy. When it was ascertained that the man was there, we signalled to the other colleagues to come closer. I went inside and asked the man, "Are you the owner of this shop?"

"Yes, why do you ask?" he replied.

"I want to buy some corrugated sheets," I answered.

"How many?"

"Four or five bundles."

"Sure, I will give them to you at a good price."

"By the way what is your name?" I asked him at this point.

"Why do you ask?" he queried.

"My friend knows you, and he told me that you would give me at a reasonable price."

I conjectured this to be the person Prem B.K. had indicated. But still, I was making small talk to make sure he was the person. Should we apprehend an innocent man by mistake, the criminal might elude arrest forever. So it was very important that we were sure we were arresting the right person.

"Come with us for a while," I requested.

"Why?"

"Just come," I insisted.

I had instructed the driver to have the vehicle near the shop once I entered and its engine running, as I would be there only to get the man.

The shopkeeper was resisting our efforts to take him. So I told him frankly, "We have come to take you. Don't resist if you do not want to lose face in society." And so he came quietly with us.

It was not good for us to hang around the place for long. I was a stranger to Narayangadh and did not know the sentiments of the locals. So we left immediately. On the way, we started questioning him. The man denied everything at first. "I am sick, please don't harm me," he kept repeating.

Immediately upon leaving, FM radios began blaring news that a shopkeeper had been kidnapped in such and such a vehicle. There was even an investigation from the administration office. We later found out that a motorcycle had tailed us from Narayangadh to Prembasti village and had given our vehicle number to a FM station.

The rhino horn broker's name turned out to be Nagendra Shrestha. After we had handed him over to the park office, the park officials started getting phone calls saying that he was a sick man. The chief warden too received such phone calls. As a result, he instructed us not to be very strict with him. I myself was busy with my work and could not interrogate him.

I later learnt that *subba* Uttam Prasad Kharel had changed Nagendra's statement to the court (park office) more than three times, which is illegal. According to the National Parks and Wildlife Conservation Act 1973, there is provision for a semi-judicial authority in the Park Offices and District Forest Offices. My legal knowledge was limited to the 30 credit hours of a law course that I had undergone at the Institute of Forestry, Pokhara at the intermediate level. We learnt about the legal investigation and other court procedures through experience.

A lot of noise was made over the arrest of Nagendra. Many people were happy that finally a dangerous criminal had been apprehended. Several people were of the opinion that he was the ringleader of the horn business in Narayangadh and that must have been how he had been able to earn a lot of money and build such a big house.

Different people said different things, but in his statement, Nagendra only owned up to receiving $413. I, too, had felt that we had nabbed an important criminal, but we couldn't get much information out of him. I was new, had no knowledge of the methods to make criminals confess and, besides, could not interview him properly as he was not well.

One fine morning, an uncle of mine visited me. After chatting for a while, he said, "Sita *didi* has asked to see you."

The next day I went to Narayangadh to pay her a visit. Her son, my nephew, had just opened the Munch Time Café. In the cafe, my sister introduced me to Nagendra's brother-in-law. There was no need to object, and we chatted over coffee.

"I have heard that you decide everything in the office, and your word is all that is needed for a decision. People did offer to resolve the problem for $13,774, but I wasn't convinced and decided to meet you instead," said Nagendra's brother-in-law.

I got the idea - he was trying to send me two messages: first, that he was willing to spend any amount of money to free his brother-in-law, and second, he was expecting me to do the job. I, however, would never accept a bribe and let a rhino horn smuggler go free.

I warned him against mentioning anything like a bribe to me so casually and told him, "I cannot do this. Do not try to meet me from now on. Your brother-in-law must suffer his fate as per the law."

He did not try to meet me after that. However, that one meeting clearly revealed how conspirators bribed officials into freeing smugglers. Also, why would someone be willing to spend $13,774 to free a person who had just "once received $413?" That just went to show how deeply Nagendra was involved in the rhino horn smuggling business.

SOLDIERS WITHOUT GUNS

MARCH 18 HAPPENED to be *Fagu Purnima*, or *Holi*, the Festival of Colours. Our informer from Makwanpur district informed us that the man wanted by us was in his house that day. We started from Kasara in a Land Rover with a few army men. When we got to Bastipur, a few of my friends went over to check if he was indeed at home.

We stopped to buy *abeer* as we were going to the house pretending to play *Holi*. We parked our jeep at a distance from the house, and I started for his home with two army men. We came to a building under construction where a man was overseeing the work. The workers were quite busy. We were nearly 20 metres away when he turned around and looked towards us. He was a tall man with a beard. He was in a shirt and pants, and around his neck he wore a silver necklet with a pendant. He was startled when he saw us and began descending fast. The soldiers and I jumped over the terraced beds, one after another.

After giving chase for about half a kilometre, the soldiers caught up with him. I, too, was beside them. "I will stab you if you run," a soldier threatened with a knife in his hand.

"No, I won't run," the man pleaded.

I was surprised to find the soldier carrying a knife with him. I had expected him to carry a pistol. Apparently they were without firearms.

The poacher's name was Ramsharan B.K., and he had been exposed by Nara Bahadur and Prem B.K. When all our colleagues had gathered, we pushed him down through the maize fields towards our jeep. However, before we could get him in, Ramsharan's sister arrived on the scene. She started to pull Ramsharan, and the soldiers pulled him back, so there was a bit of tension. Amidst the confusion, I asked everyone to get into the jeep, and we got Ramsharan in, too. Some villagers had arrived by then and were enquiring as to what had happened. The chief warden was alarmed and drove ahead. However, two elderly colleagues from Sunachuri village were left behind. If we did not take them with us, the villagers would surely beat them up. I, therefore, dismounted and got them into the jeep.

But before I myself could get in, Ramsharan's sister had grabbed me. I pushed her with some force, and she fell. I ran and grabbed hold of the running jeep and hung on to it. The jeep was speeding away on the rough road. My other friends were sitting on its hood. When I was about to get onto the hood, the chief warden suddenly put on the brakes. Both my legs banged against the iron netting of the hood, and I was hit with spasms of pain. In fact, my trousers were torn, and my knees were bruised and bleeding profusely. When the jeep got to the highway, I descended and sat inside. I was in great pain and could not even move my legs.

The police tried to stop the jeep at Bharatpur, but the soldiers in the front seat reprimanded them for trying to stop us, and they let us go. The police had tried to stop us because they had been informed that a man had been kidnapped and was being taken away in a white jeep.

We stopped to have cold drinks in Narayangadh and then moved on to Kasara. I had my legs checked up at a pharmacy and bought some medicines for my knees that were still hurting badly.

Ramsharan B.K., who was now in the park's custody, had in a statement said that Hiralal Shrestha of Khairahani, Chitwan had given him a gun to kill a rhino and promised to buy its horn. Ramsharan had even provided his phone number.

Hiralal was arrested on the basis of this statement when he came to the Park Office on April 10, 2003. He was at the Park Office as asked to appear in a horn smuggling case. There was no way we could file a case against him based merely on Ramsharan's statement. The laws do not provide a basis for filing a case just for planning to kill a rhino. Furthermore, a case cannot be filed even if one shoots at a rhino and misses it.

Apart from Ramsharan, Prem B.K., too, had named Hiralal as a broker in the horns trade; however, no one could tell us from whom he bought the horns. Unable to produce stronger evidence, he was released on May 5, 2003 on guarantee.

BETRAYED BY A WOMAN

LOK BAHADUR RAI and Riphal Rai, who were arrested by our Sauraha team on February 27, 2003, did not reveal anything particularly important in their statements. We received information that they would reveal all secrets provided Chature Rai, a friend of theirs, was present. On March 26, we were ready to arrest Chature and so started for Pyaridhap, a village to the east of Sauraha. We parked near the embankment of the Rapti River and walked along the rice fields. We walked in the dark, without so much as switching on our torchlights, and reached his house. We entered after surrounding the house from all sides. We did not find the man on any of the floors. There were just two teenage boys sleeping. We did, however, find a few deer horns on the first floor.

We woke up the sleeping boys, and asked, "Where's the house owner?"

"We don't know," they said. Suddenly from outside, we heard shouts of, "Catch him," and sounds of people running in the rice field. The man we were looking for was apparently sleeping in the kitchen built next to the house. He was trying to sneak away when he got wind of the search party inside the house, but he was unable to do so as we had surrounded the house. His wife tried to stop us from taking him away and came crying after us. However, we talked to her and convinced her into going back.

Once Chature Rai, Riphal Rai and Lok Bahadur Rai were together, we started questioning them. They told us that they had found a dead rhino in the jungle and had cut off the horn. They had brought it home hidden in a roll of dry grass. They had then tried to sell it to a *Bhote* woman of Gorkha district.

The woman had promised to pay them in Kathmandu, but when they got to Kathmandu, she had instead set people after them and beaten them up. They also told us that, together with Tika Bahadur Pun, they had tried time and again to look for rhinos to poach but were unsuccessful. On May 2, all three were sent to jail for the theft of a horn and attempt to sell it.

ZERO RESULTS

ON APRIL 15, 2003, we received news from an informer that a few people had gathered in downtown Parsa bazaar to the east of Chitwan with the intention of poaching a rhino. We talked with the army and decided to go after them at night. We went to the informer's house as we wanted to take him along, too. He was reluctant in the beginning as he was scared that the poachers might see and recognise him.

We assured him that he would not have to face the poachers. He would just need to point the man out to us.

We reached the home of Ramchandra Praja aka Mudha Sainla at Magani Chowk of Parsa. There we arrested Ramchandra Praja, his brother, his youngest son Buddhi Praja and another individual Raj Kumar Praja. We searched the whole house but found nothing.

Our informer had told us that rhino poachers also lived in a house to the south of the East-West Highway. We entered that house, too, and asked the house owner for his name.

"Karma Lama," he replied. We wondered if he was the same Karma Lama that Prem had mentioned.

We went through his phone diary and photographs, and searched the house, too. Six or seven boys were sleeping on the terrace of the house. They turned out to be sculptors who made statues. We did find a few suspicious numbers in Karma's phone diary, but on analysis, concluded that this was not the same Karma mentioned by Prem. So we left without arresting him.

Among those whom we arrested, Ramchandra Praja, or Mudha Sainla, had already been jailed once in a rhino poaching and horn smuggling case. His youngest son was a drug addict. Raj Kumar Praja kept repeating that he had been staying in Mudha Sainla's house for his studies. We had no proof against any of them, just information that these people were involved in rhino poaching at some point of time. Since we could not file a case based on just that, we released them with a former Village Development Committee (VDC) member of their village acting as surety.

On the list of names that the chief warden had given me on my first day in Chitwan, there was a man called Thagu Praja, also called Taakule. On May 10, he had come to the park to meet his father Mudha Sainla, who was in custody. The chief had told me several times that Taakule had hair coloured in the front. The boy in front of me had hair like that, but when I asked his name, he replied, "Mangal Praja."

I asked him again, "Aren't you Taakule, son of Mudha Sainla?"

"Yes," he replied.

"Arrest him, too," I instructed my staff.

There was no proof in hand against this boy. We did ask him a lot of questions, but he revealed nothing. In a few days, his father, brother and Raj Kumar Praja were released for lack of proof. Taakule knew that he too would be released if he did not reveal anything. In the end, he, too, was released on guarantee. Though we knew they were involved in poaching activities, we had to release them as per the law.

WAITING FOR POACHERS IN THE WETLANDS

I HAD PURCHASED an official cell phone for anti-poaching activities. There was no budget in the office for such expenses. I had bought the phone from the money left over from the Terai

Arc Landscape (TAL) Programme fund meant for repairing a repeater tower on the Churia hill near the Tamor Lake, which had been damaged by the falling branches of a tree during a storm the previous year. On April 23, I received information on the phone that poachers were about to enter the island jungle at Bhagedi in Dibyanagar village and that a Bote was leading them.

We were told that before 4 in the afternoon, we had to get to the wetland, beside the Island Hotel's old watchtower, with soldiers.

I was at Rajahar of Nawalparasi at that time with some friends. From there, we went to the Nandapur barracks at Amaltari. The captain himself got ready to go on this operation with us. I drove the vehicle fast, and soon we were at the Laukhani post. We entered the island jungle on a boat along with Ranger Rupak and Game Scout Gopal Bote. We reached the described location at the right time. Sure enough, there was an old watchtower and a wetland nearby. We took our positions and waited for the poachers.

Though we hid in the bushes, we would climb trees at times. Occasionally, we heard splashing sounds as the oars hit the water, and we became alert. It was very hot in the jungle, and we were not supposed to speak or move. We were thirsty but did not have any water with us. We could have gone to a waterhole for water but were scared that the poachers might arrive and see us. We stayed there for nearly two hours, and we returned when we finally realised that no one was coming. We had expected to catch the poachers red handed and were disappointed. Either we had received wrong information or the poachers got wind that we were coming.

In mid-April, a new battalion - the Purano Gorkha - replaced the Devidutta Battalion in the park. Soon, temporary army posts were put up at Baghmara and Dumariya, too, where rhinos were often poached in the past.

BIG CASH HAUL

I HAD GONE to my home village of Hemja in Kaski district. At this time, we received information from Kawasoti, Nawalparasi district, that a horn smuggler was coming from Kathmandu. I had handed over my cell phone as well as my duties to Ranger Madhav, and he had received the information on it.

I called up Madhav from Pokhara and asked him if my presence was necessary. But he assured me that they would be able to handle the situation themselves.

On May 2, Madhav told me that two people had been arrested and detained at the Island Hotel, Bharatpur and that more people were to arrive from Kathmandu. However, when no one arrived for a long time, they started for Kasara. When they were at Patihani village, they again received a message by phone: "They are here."

Immediately Madhav and his team returned to Narayangadh and arrested two people at the Gulmeli Hotel at the Pokhara Bus Park, Narayangadh. They then took Tanzing Nima, a Tibetan, and Chhiring (aka Dogla), a man from Humla district, to Kasara. They seized cash worth $10,331 bound around the waist of one of them, and this arrest was considered a huge achievement then.

That day, after arresting the two horn smugglers - Sundarsingh Thakuri and Bijay Malla of Chitwan - Madhav had first offered them a deal: if they could get the horn buyers to come, he would release them.

Sundarsingh had then called Dogla in Kathmandu and said, "I have the horn, come with the money." Dogla and Tanzing had left Kathmandu the same day and walked straight into Madhav's trap. Gaja Bahadur Phaalmagar of Deurali village of Nawalparasi - the man whom they in turn had named - was arrested by the patrolling unit the next day.

I returned to Kasara on May 4. Everyone was glad to have arrested a notorious smuggler and his whole gang. The head of the army battalion then was Lt. Colonel Prabhuram Sharma, and he too had come to congratulate our team and express his happiness. On the other hand, my colleagues were discussing whether to allow me to investigate the case. They were of the opinion that one of the rangers should do it, as I would "undeservingly take credit for someone else's work."

When Madhav told me about this, it saddened me. I had no wish to take credit for anyone else's work. My intention was simply to put a stop to poaching. I was of the opinion that we should work as a team, and the credit should go to the team, not individuals. I regretted not being present during such a significant and successful operation.

I later met the informer who had given us the tip-off about this gang. He insisted that half of the money seized should be given to him as a reward. "The chief warden has assured me that I would get it," he told me.

"That amount is recorded in our deed of recognisance of recovery. That money cannot be tampered with," I told him.

He kept asking for the prize money, repeatedly referring to the chief warden's word. Later, I gave him $344 from the prize money I received from the International Trust for Nature Conservation (ITNC), but he kept complaining time and again.

The ITNC was established to use the money donated by tourists staying at the Tiger Tops Hotel or collected from charities for anti-poaching activities. Conservationist and tiger specialist Chuck McDougal and the management of the Tiger Tops Hotel had an important role to play in the establishment of the ITNC. This trust provides $344 per month, or $4,128 every year, to pay 10 informers. It also periodically purchases necessary materials like torchlights and binoculars essential for anti-poaching operations. When poachers and smugglers are arrested and convicted with proper evidences, the trust also provides cash rewards to increase the morale of all those involved in the operation. This time, the trust had awarded us $344 for arresting Tibetan Tanzing Nima and four other poachers, brokers and smugglers. My colleagues did complain that I had given the whole amount to an informer.

Sundarsingh had once told me, "There is a *Jeri* shop at Parsa bazaar. Dogla buys tiger skins from there, too. There is a man called Hari Shrestha at Bal Kumari Chowk in Narayangadh, he too is engaged in the smuggling of horns."

I called Dogla and enquired, "Did you buy tiger skins from the man who owns a *Jeri* shop in Parsa?"

"No," he replied, "I just go there because the *Jeris* are tasty, I haven't done any trade with him."

Tanzing Nima apparently would take the horns to Kathmandu and give them to a man. That man in turn would get the horns to another man called Tasi in Lhasa, Tibet through some bus driver going to Tatopani on the Sino-Nepal border.

They were all sent to jail on May 30, 2003 to stand trial, and their mug shots were taken.

Sometime later, we received information that Om Bahadur Rana Magar, a man wanted for selling horns to Dogla and Tanzing Nima, was coming to Narayangadh. Captain Bishal Bahadur Shah and I led a team to Narayangadh at 9 in the morning, where we waited for him. He arrived with a few people, and we tailed him.

Going close to him, I said, "Hello, Mr. Hari Kumar."

"I am not Hari Kumar," he replied.

"What is your name then?"

"My name is Om Bahadur."

He was wearing a hat. He looked like a retired soldier in his fifties and seemed gentlemanly. We arrested him right there and then put him in the jeep as his friends watched bewildered.

THE INFORMER WHO had tipped us off about Nima and Dogla was thrilled by his success. He informed us that another horn smuggler would be arriving on May 17. In the evening, we went to Kawasoti where our informer took us to a hotel. A man was having dinner there, and Madhav arrested him. He was Ram Bahadur Ghale, also called Rabindra Ghale, from Baseli, Dhading district. We brought him to Kasara. Upon enquiry, he revealed that Sonam Lama, a smuggler from Kathmandu, had sent him to check whether the horn at Kawasoti was genuine.

When we were informed that Sonam lived at Dallu, Kathmandu we got ready to leave for the capital. Upon reaching Kathmandu, we called him, and his mother picked up the phone.

"Sonam has gone to Delhi," she told us.

We stayed at a hotel that night. We raided Sonam's house the next day, just in case his mother was lying. His mother put up resistance for a while, but she kept quiet after a soldier threatened her with a gun. Only Sonam's brother and mother were at home.

Our repeated failures told us that it was useless arresting people without evidence. We had no evidence against Rabindra, and we had to release him. Until this time, I had no concrete plans or programmes to control poaching. We were unable to strengthen our network of informers. When I joined work, we had three or four informers, and they did not seem very capable or effective. We were unable to penetrate into the core of the poachers and smugglers' network.

CHAINED GHOST

THREE WEEKS AFTER arriving in Chitwan, in the first week of March 2003, I, Chief Warden Puranbhakta Shrestha and the *mukhiya*, Shriranga Kandel, had visited a former forest staff member. He took us to a relative of his, who told us that if we employed a *Chepang* (an ethnic group) from Padampur village as an informer, we could get hold of all the rhino poachers.

So I went to Padampur with a friend. It was evening by the time we reached the bank of the Rapti. Since it was the month of March, we were able to wade across the river. Darkness had set in by the time we crossed the Rapti and got to the village. This was where my friend and I had to part ways. I was supposed to go to the park post at Amrite, in old Padampur village, and he was to go to the village.

"Be careful, there are bears in these parts," he told me while parting. There were no human settlements in that area - just a few scattered huts - because the government had only recently translocated the settlements to new Padampur village in order to increase the park area.

Since it was my first time there, I had no idea about the place. In the dim light, I made out the tin roof of the post. I was not scared of the wild animals, as we, who work in conservation, consider them friends. I kept the tin roof in sight as I walked along the bushes and berry trees. When I had walked about a kilometre, I heard some strange noises - those made by chains.

I paused midway. I tried guessing what could be making the noise, but my mind went blank. I then started wondering if it might be a ghost or spirit of some kind. I was scared, but there was no way I could turn back. There was no option other than to keep moving forward. I kept wondering how I could avoid that thing - whatever it was - and reached the post in time. I broke off a small piece of a stick and started walking in the other direction of the noise. But I got caught in the middle of a thorny bush. I cleared it out of my way and was about to reach the post when I heard the noise again ... closer and clearer it seemed to come this time. I decided to be strong, and with determination looked in the direction of the sound. There stood two elephants with their legs tied with heavy chains.

I laughed at myself in relief and breathed deeply. I did not know that elephant chains rattled like this. At the post, I met Senior Game Scout Gopal Giri, who had worked with me at the Rara National Park in 2001, and other staff members. They were surprised to see me. "How come you are arriving at such a late hour?" they asked. I told them about my journey, and they too had a hearty laugh.

After having our meal, we walked towards the village with a stick each so as to chase away any bears that we might meet on the way. In the village, an old woman ran a shop from a hut. We sat on wooden seats on the floor, and she offered us drinks in steel glasses. Two of my friends took the drink, but I declined as I did not drink liquor in those days. Some children had seen me in the evening while arriving. By now, the whole village was abuzz with talk that a new man had arrived at the post. I was introduced as the brother of a staff, who had come to visit the place.

Only children and elderly people were about, and we wondered where the rest of the people might have gone. When we enquired indirectly, we found that they had gone to the jungle to steal wood. We also learnt that they would be taking the timber to the next village across the Rapti River the same day.

When we returned to the post, I instructed the staff to get the two elephants ready to cross the Rapti.

While crossing the river, we noticed that the headlights of our vehicle parked on the other side of the Rapti, were on. We signalled with our torchlights. But on crossing the river, we saw no vehicle. We went up to Janakpur village of Kumroj but found no trace of the vehicle and returned disappointed. The following morning, we again went to the old woman's hut for some tea. There we were again met by the same children and elderly people that we had seen the previous night. We learnt that the smugglers had ferried the timber across the river the previous night. They asked us why we hadn't arrested them. We returned to the post without giving them an answer.

Two boys were waiting for us there - Rajan Praja (Chepang) and Chandra Bahadur Praja. I asked Rajan to work for us. The Chepangs are a simple and marginalised ethnic group. Rajan requested that I make an official identity card for him. So I asked him to bring a photograph. Meanwhile, Chandra Bahadur cooked for us at the elephant keepers' kitchen, where we had food together. I gave Rajan $1.37 to make phone calls and bade him bye.

On returning from the post, the chief warden and the *mukhiya* were waiting for me on the other side of the Rapti. They had slept in the jeep without eating anything. The previous night, they had seen us signal by torchlight and had waited for us all night. Had we been able to meet that night, then surely Dambare Praja, Dhidara Mahato and others would have been arrested right there and then.

The following day, I had an identity card made for Rajan Praja. However, for the next two months, he neither phoned me nor brought me his photo. I sent messages asking him to come and see me, but he didn't show up. I grew suspicious of him when I started hearing rumours that he was involved in poaching activities. So I made up my mind to arrest him instead. In the third week of May 2003, he asked me to come and meet him at the old Parsa bazaar at 4 in the evening, but he did not turn up.

In those days, folk song programmes would be held at different places in Chitwan every Saturday. One Saturday, there was one such programme at a school near the Birendranagar VDC office. Rangers Rupak and Madhav and others were together with me, and we met our contact person. He informed us that Rajan and others would be coming to the programme that day. Our plan was to try and identify the leader among the rhino poachers and have him arrested with the help of the army. However, the leader of the gang did not show up. Among the folk singers was Rajan Praja who sang a song about the monsoon rains. We, however, decided not to arrest him that day.

NOTICE TO FLEE

ON MAY 30, people were gathering to attend a folk song programme at the highway bus stand near the Belsi bridge of Tandi bazaar in east Chitwan. *Mukhiya* Shriranga and I got there on a motorcycle. We smoked and had some cold drinks to pass time. The audience was starting to get restless as the artistes hadn't arrived when I spotted Rajan Praja. Our informer had told us that he would be accompanied by Mangale and Raj Kumar Praja. There was one person accompanying Rajan who seemed familiar and looked like Mangale to me. But soon they were lost in the crowd, presumably, they had seen us and made good their escape.

We spent the next few minutes puffing at our cigarettes, waiting for them to show up. And soon enough, the two arrived on a motorcycle from the direction of Tandi bazaar. At the same time, two girls also arrived from the east on bicycles. Upon meeting on the East-West Highway, they chatted for a few minutes before heading west for Tandi together.

Our motorcycle was parked some distance away. So by the time we got on our motorcycle, Rajan's bike was pretty far away. The *mukhiya* said to me, "The girls are still here on their bicycles. For sure, they will be meeting the boys, so let's keep a watch on them instead."

We started following the girls. They entered a restaurant at Bakulahar, Tandi. By this time, we had telephoned Sauraha and asked for army backup. A few soldiers in civil dress but armed arrived with Lieutenant Ganesh Mahat. It was around 3 in the afternoon when we entered the restaurant. The two boys and the girls had ordered cold drinks. Rajan recognised me immediately. "*Namaskar*, sir," he said.

"Come with us," I said to the two boys. The girls were dumbfounded. Since we did not see the motorcycle that the boys were riding outside the restaurant, I asked them where it was. They said it was being repaired. We had been looking for that motorcycle for days. We had information that Birman Praja, the most deadly rhino shooter in Chitwan, was using a YBX motorcycle with number plate 'Na 1 Pa 5973'.

We took them with us from Tandi to Sauraha in a rented vehicle. Upon questioning them at the Sauraha barracks, Rajan Praja admitted to accompanying Birman Praja to poach rhinos a few times. He confirmed that Birman was the leader among the poachers. We gathered more information about Birman from Rajan. The other person we had assumed to be Mangale turned out to be Chandra Bahadur, who had cooked for me at the elephant keepers' kitchen. He had recently been released from jail after being convicted of rhino poaching. Rajan kept requesting us to release him as he was innocent. "Yes, yes," we assured him.

Rajan also gave us information about Birman's other friends. He told us that Bijay Lama of Padampur village worked closely with him in the poaching and smuggling business. We already were aware that Birman had a second wife, a Magar woman, in a settlement called Onegroup in Birendranagar VDC of Chitwan, though his house was in Korak, Somitar. We also regularly heard rumours of parties being thrown where deer meat was served. One day the *mukhiya* and I had gone to Onegroup in our jeep. On the way, we had seen the motorcycle with the number plate 5973. But when we returned, it wasn't there.

We decided to go to Birendranagar that very night to arrest Birman. Since we knew there were no Maoist combatants in that area, we went straight in with the soldiers. We parked a little further away so that he wouldn't run away at the sight of the jeep. His wife and her sister were sleeping outside the house. We went inside and looked around, but Birman wasn't there. We looked at their photo albums and asked his wife to identify the people in the album. We found a photo of Birman and Bijay Lama.

We then left for new Padampur. Rajan was our guide. We reached Bijay Lama's house and surrounded it from all sides. His elder brother's wife and a few children were sleeping inside, but he wasn't there. In the outside, we found his old parents sleeping.

"Where is Bijay?" we asked.

"He does not come here very often. He lives with his uncle at Narayangadh," they replied.

Bijay's uncle, Chyangba Lama, was also a notorious rhino horn smuggler. We asked Bijay's sister-in-law to take us to his house. "I do not know his house, I just have the phone number," she said.

We planned to take her to the Bharatpur Hospital from

where she would call Bijay to come to the hospital soon as his mother was ill. We planned to arrest him there. When Bijay's sister-in-law came with us, Bijay's old mother too climbed on board forcibly.

We gave a telephone call to Bijay from the pharmacy at the Bharatpur Hospital and asked his sister-in-law to talk to him. We had asked her to speak in Nepali and not in her native Tamang language. We were scared that she might help Bijay escape, so we had also stationed a Tamang speaking colleague nearby.

She started speaking on the phone, but the other side replied in the Tamang language. She too said a few words in Tamang and then hung up. "He said Bijay is not at home, he has gone out," she told us. We got her to call again, but the phone was not received. We suspected that she had given a hint to Bijay to flee, but there was nothing we could do. We dropped them off at Padampur again and returned to Sauraha. Though our operation went on the whole night, there was no achievement. On top of that, we seem to have helped the smugglers flee rather than arrest them. This is what happens when you go to arrest people without precise information. We arrested Rajan Praja during the day time, and the two girls and restaurant operator might have informed his friends - Birman and Bijay - about the arrest.

SHOT WHILE RUNNING

FROM RAJAN PRAJA'S statement, we concluded that Birman Praja was the most dangerous of the rhino poachers. On June 9, we received news that Birman had been to Onegroup the previous day. Again our team went to his house. But this time, not even his wife was at home. We enquired with her neighbours about her. "The brother of her former husband will know where his wife is," they told us. We went looking for him and came to a place where a recent death was being mourned. "I don't know where Birman has gone," he told us. "But I could help you arrest another poacher."

"What is his name?" I asked.

"Tiku Pun," he replied.

Tiku Pun was a man who poached rhinos with Chature Rai's team. We walked nearly half an hour with that man to reach Tiku Pun's house. The lights were on in the house, and Rupak and I entered. A young couple sat chatting on a bed. I asked the man where Tiku was. He said there was no one by that name. I tried climbing up the ladder to find Tiku, but an old couple sat drinking liquor there. I pushed them aside and went up. A man was sleeping on the bed.

I woke him up and asked, "Aren't you Tiku?"

"No, I am not," he replied.

"Which of the sons are you?"

"I am the eldest."

"What is your name then?"

"I am Rame."

"Where's your brother?"

"He is downstairs."

Rupak was talking to the boy downstairs. The boy was waving his citizenship papers at him, exclaiming, "I am not Tiku, I am someone else."

I came down and asked him, "Aren't you Tiku? Your brother upstairs says you are, why deny it?" As soon as I said this, Rupak punched him on the nose, and it started bleeding profusely.

"What's going on?" clamoured the old couple as they climbed down. We walked out with Tiku.

I carried his shirt with me as he walked ahead of us dressed only in his pants. He was not even wearing shoes. He was the first in the line, followed by Lieutenant Ganesh Mahat, another soldier, Rupak and me at the end. After walking about

10 metres, the boys in front shouted, "He's running away." The three of them started chasing Tiku through the corn fields. I lagged behind as I did not have a torchlight with me. After a few minutes, I heard a loud gun shot. I was shocked and wondered if someone had been killed! I went running to the spot: the man had been shot in the hand.

"How dare you run away?" my friends were shouting at him.

We crossed the stream in a hurry with him and walked towards our jeep. We asked him to wash the blood away at a tap on the way. I gave him his shirt. I had pity on him at that time and asked him, "Why did you run?"

"I was scared that you would beat me up," he replied. This was the first time I was part of an operation in which my colleagues had to shoot someone.

Tiku told us that he had gone to poach rhinos with Riphal Rai but had met no success. We could find no evidence against him. Since he was actually shot in the hand, we all took care of him and didn't really bother to question him. It was only later after arresting other members of his team that we learnt of his involvement in killing rhinos. He disappeared soon after being released on bail, and he could not be found when we had the evidence.

The elderly couple who were drinking on the ladder in Tikule's home were his parents. His father's name was Chamka Jetha and had earned notoriety for poaching rhinos. In fact, he was the person who taught everyone how to poach rhinos in the area. We arrested only his son that day as we did not know he was a poacher, too. Chamka also fled from Chitwan to a village near Guleriya in Bardia district in western Nepal and returned to Chitwan only to poach rhinos. And he apparently killed rhinos in the Bardia National Park, too. He is still at large.

THERE WERE WHISPERS that Chief Warden Puranbhakta Shrestha was being transferred as there were a lot of problems with the office management as well as poaching in the Chitwan National Park. At the same time, I heard rumours that Nagendra Shrestha was going to be released on bail. We had arrested him in the second week of March, and he had been sent to jail for allegedly being the right hand man of Gyamjo, the notorious horn smuggler. He claimed being unwell and was to be released as he had the necessary papers to prove him so. The District Attorney General, Rajendra Shrestha, was present at the Park Office to seek his release on bail.

I asked the chief warden, "Why are you releasing him?"

"Whether to release him or not is my prerogative, mind your own business," he retorted.

I was not happy with his reply.

"We had to face a lot of dangers to capture him, how can you just say it's your prerogative?" I shot back.

At this, he got angry.

The chief warden had shown such happiness when I first arrived in Chitwan. But in the latter days, he was not happy with me and my work. To be fair, I was new to the work and lacked the basic knowledge, experience and skills required in anti-poaching work. I had several weaknesses that surfaced while on the job. For example, I got very angry at times, and at times I did whatever I pleased. I tried to do a good job. On top of that, we did not have enough resources while our staff and informers were not very effective. The few informers that we had were always complaining about not being paid. We seldom received the correct information. We would hear of rhinos being killed, but not about who killed them. But still, I was working day and night, putting all my heart to my job.

I returned in an angry mood following the chief warden's rude behaviour. A few days after the incident, I learnt that *subba* Uttam Prasad Kharel hung around with Nagendra's brother-in-law every evening and would party on meat and beer before returning to his quarter. "What does it matter if we are friends?" he replied when I asked him about all this.

Nagendra was released on bail. And I told Uttam, "People will talk and say that you helped free him for a bribe."

He took offence at that and replied, "I don't make those decisions, do I? I just do what the boss tells me to do."

In the third week of June 2003, Puranbhakta Shrestha, the chief warden, was transferred, and a new chief warden was appointed in his place. I was happy. I could not please my former boss but I intended to appease my new one.

GOLD FOR THE INFORMER

IT WAS MONSOON, and the rains were heavy. On July 30, I went to Sunachuri (eastern part of the national park) to meet an informer. While I was there, I took time out to inspect the posts at Khagendramalli and Sunachuri. While returning to Kasara late in the evening, the water in the Rapti was rising. It had rained heavily the whole night, and when I woke up the next morning, on July 31, the river was flooded. The way to Jagatpur, a village to the north of the park, was blocked. Four people had lost their lives in the floods in Ghailaghari village of Jagatpur. The phone lines, electricity, roads all were obstructed.

We received news from the elephant breeding centre at Khorsor, Sauraha that 15 elephants had gone missing and could not be found, and several had drowned. We also heard that the flooded Narayani had swept the rhinos to Triveni of Nawalparasi. The staff of the posts at Baghmara, Dumariya and Ghatgai had to climb onto the roofs and trees to save their lives after the posts were flooded. Helicopters arrived to rescue the soldiers, but left our staff to be stranded on the roofs and tree tops. They came into contact only after the water receded. It was the last week of July, during which many senior level staff members often take leave. I was the only one in the office, and I was under heavy stress.

I dispatched the details of our losses to the Department of National Parks and Wildlife Conservation (DNPWC), Kathmandu on August 1. The chief warden was also in Kathmandu. I went to Gauriganj of Bharatpur on a motorcycle after learning that a rhino had been stranded there. Also, three of the lost elephants were found in the jungle of Barandabhar. When the river started flooding, the elephant keepers were scared that the elephants might drown, so they had unlocked the chains and set the elephants free. Many FM stations had reported, with the authority of the District Forest Officer, that the elephants had been set free following the floods, and as a result, there was a huge uproar in town.

On August 2, the remaining 12 elephants were also located in the Barandabhar forest. That day I went to meet our informer at Sunachuri. Since arriving in Chitwan, I had been looking for Bam Bahadur Praja, the notorious rhino poacher, who had been named by the Dibyapuri Buffer Zone Community Forest guard, Nara Bahadur B.K. Bam Bahadur had killed five rhinos in the Dibyapuri area. He would go poaching with Ramsharan B.K., Buddhiram Mahato and others, and sell the horns to Prem Bahadur B.K.

I worked very hard to arrest him, and also spent a lot of money and resources to track him. Just the fuel for the jeep, cost around $21 to make the Kasara - Sunachuri round trip. I also had to give nearly $689 to the informer as demanded. At one point, I even had to pay for his marriage. We bought clothes and jewellery for the bride as well as fish, meat and other delicacies to take to his in-law's home. Even a vehicle was provided to take the groom's party to the marriage site.

I had expected these expenses to be reimbursed through the financial assistance provided by the Tiger Rhino Conservation Project (TRCP) for anti-poaching operations. Bimal Kandel, the accountant, did question me, "What is this Mr. Kunwar, you have billed us for gold, too." I narrated the whole story to him, and he did not object. Such is the nature of anti-poaching operations.

After meeting the informer at Sunachuri on August 2, Rupak, Shriranga and I finalised a plan to arrest Bam Bahadur. Our informer would invite him over and take him to an empty house. There, they would party over chicken and liquor, and when they slept, we would surround the house and arrest him. According to the informer, other friends of Bam Bahadur too were planning to come with him to poach rhinos. I gave the informer $13.77 to buy meat and liquor for them. We were also going to arrest the friends of Bam Bahadur. The plan looked foolproof.

But on the designated day, there was no trace of him. Later we learnt that it was all a hoax. The informer from Sunachuri had taken us for a ride. He had never met Bam Bahadur. He kept telling us how he would bring Bam Bahadur to us, and we kept believing him, while all the time it was just a ploy to get money from us. The simple person that I was, I trusted him and spent a lot of resources on him, which all went to waste.

POACHER OF 17 RHINOS

MEANWHILE, I INVITED an informer from Birendranagar to come and see me. He came to Tandi, and we had beer together at the Manakamana Hotel. I had stopped drinking while working at the Sagarmatha National Park. In fact, things never turned out well for me when I drank. Shriranga Kandel too did not drink on account of his health, but he drank that day.

Right from my childhood, I had harboured a desire to join

the civil service. Actually while waiting for my School Leaving Certificate (SLC) Examinations in 1987, I had worked for the Mardi River Drinking Water Project in Kaski, carrying huge iron pipes. I was 17.

It was no easy task for 16 people to carry the huge iron pipe over the difficult roads above the confluence of the Seti and Mardi Rivers. When that job was accomplished, I picked up a shovel and a pick to dig the earth to lay the pipe.

The results of the SLC Examinations were soon announced. Among the 57 students who had appeared in the exam from our school, only I made it in first division. In February 1990, I completed my Intermediate in Science in Forestry from the Institute of Forestry, Pokhara Campus. After that, I looked for work as a forest ranger, but no such opportunity was available. After the re-establishment of democracy in 1990, the Public Service Commission announced vacancies for the post of rangers, but the interim government scrapped it. In July 1990, I worked as a temporary teacher at Mahendra Secondary School at Lahachowk, Kaski.

To reach school, I had to walk 45 minutes after crossing the Mardi River. The fresh *asala* from the Mardi are very tasty, and some of us teachers, who came from Hemja, always stopped at the eateries along the bank of the Mardi River while returning from school. One day, the teachers had arranged to have fish and beer. At that time, Nepal produced only one beer - Star beer. It was the first time, I had tasted beer and found it very bitter. It was difficult for me to finish even the half glass of beer they offered me.

But later, when I went looking for work in different places, I took to drinking. But alcohol did me no good, it only ruined me. So I stopped drinking. However, I could not hold on to my resolution for long. In Chitwan, I found drinks were necessary to create an atmosphere of bonhomie with spies, informers and almost anyone to obtain information for the anti-poaching operations. Liquor is a business for some people, and they are willing to provide information about smugglers and poachers if you frequent their restaurants.

That day, over drinks we made good friends with the informer. He was ready to provide us the necessary information.

However, in the subsequent days he faced a lot of trouble trying to get the information across to us. Every time he met poachers and smugglers, he would immediately call us. But our office phone was constantly out of order. He would call the army barracks and ask them to relay the message, but they would declare their inability to do so. This way, his attempts to contact us failed many times. As a result, though I had been looking for Bam Bahadur and Bir Bahadur (aka Birman) since February 2003, I could not arrest them until August 2003. During this time, they had killed several rhinos, and due to lack of proper communication, we could not stop them.

Bam Bahadur Praja, the poacher, was arrested on August 3. A special team from the District Forest Office, Chitwan arrested him at Adhavar with help from the Parsa Wildlife Reserve Office, Adhavar and the army barracks.

The District Forest team had been tipped off that a tiger skin was being hidden in the house of Bam Bahadur's neighbour. By chance, they got to know about Bam Bahadur when they arrested the neighbours. After learning that he was heading for his newly-built house at Chandranigahapur in Rautahat district that same day, they immediately set out and arrested him at Adhavar.

At the District Forest Office, Bam Bahadur admitted killing 17 rhinos: 16 in the park and one in a national forest. It would have been great if the District Forest Office had handed him over to the park. He was wanted for several cases in the park, and we could have extracted a lot of information from him - much more than what his friends Nara Bahadur B.K., Ramsharan B.K., Prem Bahadur B.K. had already revealed after their arrest. But the District Forest Office decided to pursue the case itself since it had made the arrest.

Bam Bahadur had been on the run ever since his friend Nara Bahadur was arrested on February 5, 2003. However, he did not stop killing rhinos. After Rajan Praja's arrest and our attempt to nab Bijay Lama, Bijay had advised him to flee. Bam Bahadur had bought a house and land worth $11,708 at Chandranigahapur with the money he made smuggling rhino horns. He had made nearly $66,116 from killing 17 rhinos, and after sharing the spoils with his friends, he had invested his share in the house.

We can estimate the existing market price of the horns from the statements made by those arrested. In areas near Chitwan, like Narayangadh, Kawasoti, Bhandara and Triveni, horns sell for $826-$964 per 100 grams, which means $8,264-$9,642 per kilo. A rhino poachers' team can consist of up to 10 people. According to their performance, each person is paid from $69 to $2,066. Bam Bahadur received more than $1,102 in one poaching mission. Since he was a sharp shooter, he was the one who usually shot the rhino. According to Bam Bahadur, he used to kill monkeys in his village, and the skills he thus developed came handy to the rhino horn smugglers.

After my plans to nab Bam Bahadur failed, I realised how necessary it was to evaluate the information we were receiving. If we kept following useless leads, we would just be wasting our time, energy as well as resources. And on top of that, we would be making a mess of our job. While you are busy weaving worthless plans in one place, things could be going severely wrong in another place. The smugglers distract you with insignificant things while they accomplish their task. Putting full trust in the informers and spies can be unproductive and at times even counterproductive. I don't know for how long I would have been fooled by the informer if the District Forest Office hadn't arrested Bam Bahadur in time.

AFTER NARA BAHADUR'S arrest, members of Bam Bahadur's team started fleeing the village. Among them were Ashok Bote and Bed Bahadur Bote. One day, we received information that Ashok was walking past the Dibyapuri post to fish in the Narayani River. While he was returning from the river, we arrested him at the post on the charge that he did not have a fishing license. But he did not reveal much, and since there wasn't much evidence against him, we released him.

Two months earlier, one of our informers had got Ashok's elder brother Bed Bahadur arrested with help from the Kawasoti army barracks. "I have not done anything… I just killed a rhino once and got $689, that is all," he had confessed to the army. At that time, the army had released him, assuming that Bed Bahadur was not the person they were looking for. In fact, they were looking for Maoist cadres. The army did not inform us about this incident.

We were told that the best time to arrest Bed Bahadur would be when he was drunk. That day was to arrive when we received information that he was drinking at a local restaurant. After arresting him, he revealed that Bam Bahadur Praja had lived in his house when they went rhino poaching, and that Bed Bahadur had been given $689. He was sent to jail.

PRISONER MAKES GOOD HIS ESCAPE

ON AUGUST 16, 2003, *mukhiya* Shriranga and I were in Arun Khola bazaar of Nawalparasi on our way to Tamaspur village. Our staff from the Tamaspur post were there also to buy goods in the weekly market. While talking to them, we learnt that a poacher had come home. We then gave a motorcycle to our staff to bring Game Scout Jange Shrestha, who knew everything about the place. When he arrived, he further corroborated the information. We had with us our informer from that area, but he revealed nothing about the poacher. Instead, our staff informed us that the informer hung around with the poacher in his home. So we prevented this informer from going home lest he give us away to the poacher.

We returned from there to the Laukhani post and asked for army backup from Sauraha. An army team led by Captain Bishal Bahadur Shah as well as our park staff arrived in two vehicles. It was around 10 p.m. when we again started out for the Arun Khola bazaar on the East-West Highway to go to Tamaspur. By the time we got to Chormara, it started raining heavily, and the roads were flooded. We were unable to see the road clearly and made wild conjectures. A tree had fallen on the gravelled road to Tamaspur, to the south of the highway. Since we were unable to lift the tree, we tried going around it. But my jeep got stuck on a stump instead, and we were unable to move in either of the directions. The rain showed no signs of stopping. I was very worried that we might get stuck and not be able to arrest the criminal. However, our colleagues lifted the front of the jeep straight up and pushed it behind, and it started moving forward again.

At Tamaspur, we went to a house and woke the people who were sleeping there. We found that the person we were looking for had gone to the bank of the Narayani River, where the flood victims were being settled. So we started looking for another criminal instead. We parked some distance away from his home. I and the informer stayed in the jeep while the soldiers along with Rupak, Madhav and Shriranga went in. In a few minutes, they were out with a man.

"This is Thulo Kanchho Bhujel," said Shriranga and punched him in anger for having avoided arrest for so long. He was a notorious poacher of that area and his friends were active in Nawalparasi. We expected him to give us all information about his network of smugglers, which included Chhakka Kumal. Afterwards, we also arrested Hasta Bahadur Kumal, a member of Thulo Kanchho's gang. That same night we also arrested Pancha Bahadur Gurung.

We returned with the three. It was still raining, and the roads had turned into rivers. Luckily, our jeeps did not get stuck anywhere, and we arrived at the Arun Khola bazaar safely. We were tired from having worked all night. Yet at Tandi, we headed towards Siddhigaun of Chainpur VDC, Chitwan, to arrest Nar Bahadur Gurung. Nara Bahadur was a distant cousin of Pancha Bahadur, and our informer had told us that he was involved in buying and selling horns. However, the floods had damaged the bridge over the Ladari stream that day. So we returned to Sauraha without going to Siddhigaun.

I was driving. The jeep would at times lurch to the side as I tried to fight my sleep and fatigue. It was 4 in the morning when we reached Sauraha, and we only got to sleep for a little while in the morning.

Coincidently, Thulo Kanchho was released three years later by the Appellate Court, Hetauda on the very date he was arrested. Govinda Prasad Parajuli was among the judges who acquitted him. He was the very judge who had acquitted the notorious poacher, Lekh Bahadur Rayamajhi, without even being present in court. He was also the one who acquitted Dinanath Mahato, a rhino poacher who had escaped from the Bharatpur Jail.

How did Dinanath escape? He professed being unwell and was given a motorcycle to go to hospital, with a policeman on the pillion. The policeman accompanying Dinanath was, in fact, a relative of his. The Bharatpur Hospital is just 500 metres from the prison, but instead of going there, both the prisoner and the policeman headed westwards towards Nawalparasi.

When they got to Kolwa village to the south of the East-West Highway, Dinanath said, "The bike engine is not functioning properly, so I will go and get it repaired." The policeman let Dinanath go and later returned to the police station alone.

Dinanath's escape on a motorcycle was politically motivated, and it could not have happened solely on the strength of his links with the prison administration and policemen. It is said that his boss was a landlord and a member of the Nepali Congress party from Rajahar area, Nawalparasi. Many people claim that leaders of the Nepali Congress Party got him freed by presenting his case to the then home minister. It is not unusual for poachers to be so confident when they have such strong protection.

Thulo Kanchho Bhujel, Chhakka Kumal, Lekh Bahadur and other poachers had gone poaching in 1996/97 with Dil Bahadur Karki and Dil Bahadur Chhetri, junior army officers of the Nandapur and Seri posts of the park, respectively. The more enhanced security became with the addition of posts, the more ingenious the poachers became. While in 1996/97 they made use of the junior army officers, in 1998/99 they used the park staff (elephant keepers) Mandal Mahato and Bhadai Mahato.

Jeri, Horn and Tiger Skin

On August 25, 2003, we received information that Thagu Gurung, who owned a *Jeri* shop in Parsa, had a rhino horn for sale in his closet. I suddenly remembered the conversation I had with Sundarsingh Thakuri four months ago. He had informed me that Chhiring Lama, called Dogla, took horns and tiger skins over to Thagu. I immediately called the Battalion Commander Prabhuram Sharma for a support team. Prabhuram was a very helpful and amiable person who had all the qualities of a leader: skilled, foresighted and decisive. Whenever I told him

I was going to nab poachers, he would immediately accept my request for soldiers.

Ranger Madhav, *mukhiya* Shriranga, I and Captain Bishal Shah's team headed towards Parsa bazaar. We reached there at around 3 in the afternoon. I entered the sweets shop first. I looked around: two women and a few boys were working. The customers were having tea, soft drinks and snacks.

I asked for tea and headed for the backyard as if to go to the loo. As portrayed by the informer, a man of around 60, thin and short, in a vest and pants, with hair swept upwards was sitting on a bed sorting and cleaning vegetables. Immediately it struck me that this was the man we were looking for. He was smoking and mumbled something when he saw me. On returning from the loo, I signalled to my friends to come inside. After they entered, I ordered tea again and went to the back with them.

"How are you, Thagu," I asked him.

"I am fine, sir," he replied.

We told him that we were from the park and were looking for him. We asked him to come quietly with us. The *Jeri* shop had a room at the back. We searched the whole room, including the closet, but found nothing. Then we asked him to come with us to his rented room to the south of the highway. He was stunned. The informer had told me that he had rented a room and hidden a horn in a closet there. I warned Thagu against mentioning anything to his family. "Do exactly what we say or else you will have to lose face in the community," I said.

He took us to a house to the south of the highway, near the road to a cinema hall. In the room was a steel almirah. We asked for its key, but he said he didn't have it.

"Who has it?" we asked.

"I don't know," he replied. We guessed then that the informer had told us the truth. With the belief that the horn was in the almirah, we pressured him into producing the key. He still feigned ignorance. A woman descended from the floor above, wanting to know what was happening.

"What's going on? How can you enter someone's room just like that," she fumed. She turned out to be Thagu's eldest daughter-in-law. We asked her to give us the keys. She refused at first but relented when we threatened to break it open.

We unlocked the closet but found nothing. Thagu watched all this in silence. We started to go out, but his daughter-in-law continued to shout at us, "What evidence do you have to search someone's house?"

We brought Thagu with us to Sauraha for interrogation. He revealed that Mudha Sainla, his brother-in-law Raj Kumar Praja, Kalu and Payamarang Kainla had given him a horn nearly 15 days ago. He had already sold it to a person by the name of Karna Bahadur Ranamagar of Kusunti, Kathmandu and had even paid the poachers. Also, he had given a tiger skin to Dogla. Dogla visited Thagu not just for the delicious *Jeris* but also for the rhino horns and tiger skins. Thagu gave us the contact number of Karna Bahadur. I dispatched Rangers Madhav and Rupak to Kathmandu to locate that man, but he could not be traced.

Tanzing Nima and Dogla had appealed to the Appellate Court of Hetauda, claiming that they were being detained without cause. On August 27, the court ordered their release on bail.

By good fortune, we had arrested Til Bahadur Gurung. He admitted to giving a tiger skin to Dogla. As per the court's order, we released Dogla and Tanzing Nima, but rearrested them as soon as they had crossed the Rapti River bridge at Kasara. They were elated to be released and dumbstruck to be arrested again. We again started our investigation into the tiger skin. This time, Dogla did not admit giving Til Bahadur's tiger skin to Tanzing. Previously, he used to name Tanzing as the buyer in every deal, but this time he refrained from doing so. We again filed a case against Dogla, but having no proof against Tanzing, we were forced to release him on guarantee.

When we arrested him on May 2, 2003, we hadn't been able to gather proper evidence. We had only seized the money intended for the purchase of the horn, but not the horn itself. Similarly, one person had recorded the prisoners' statements, both during our investigation and the judicial proceedings in the court (park office). Both statements were exactly the same, which shouldn't have been that way. We were unable to arrest Sitaram Chaudhari from Madi, the person who was supposed to sell the horn. Instead of making our position secure with more evidence, we arrested people based merely on our convictions. Tanzing's case taught us this big lesson.

Later, a doctor's report was presented to us, which stated that Tanzing had died in a private nursing home in India. However, that document did not have his photo or a report of a post-mortem or any description of how and of what cause he had died. He might have really died, but it was equally possible that the report was a fake. First of all, releasing him on bail was a wrong decision of the Appellate Court of Hetauda, since Tanzing, being a Tibetan citizen, could flee. Since he was supposed to be dead, we had to return all the money that we had confiscated from him.

During that period, I was officiating as the chief warden and though I had marked his documents with "not enough evidence of death, seek further evidence", *subba* Uttam Kharel overwrote on it: "When a person dies, his case dies with him." Later, in the court (park office), Chief Warden Shivaraj Bhatta decided the case based on Uttam's statement.

Tanzing Nima would be arrested in Kathmandu in October 2011 through the joint efforts of the Chitwan National Park and the Central Investigation Bureau (CIB) of the Nepal

Police on the charge of smuggling rhino horns. According to his statement, after his release from jail, he had sold dozens of rhino horns.

ESCAPE IN THE MIDST OF BULLETS

AN INFORMER INFORMED us on October 22 that poachers had killed a rhino and was hacking away the horn. I talked to Colonel Prabhuram Sharma. A team of 22 soldiers led by Captain Bishal Shah got ready to go on the mission. From the park, in the team were Rangers Bishnu Thapaliya and Pramod Yadav, Game Scout Laptan Tharu and others. There were nearly 30 of us, including one informer.

We got ready to go, but our destination was quite remote. The way was not easy, and there were chances of crossing Maoist insurgents.

"We will not go if there are chances of running into the Maoists," I told the informer. "Should we happen to open fire, it will not be good for us. The army will blame us for bringing the Maoists into the picture, and the Maoists will be angry for setting the army on them. Rhino conservation will lose its focus, and our relations with the army will sour at a personal level."

"I guarantee you that no such thing will happen," he assured me.

It was 11 at night when we parked on the highway near the Pampa Khola bridge at Birendranagar and started northwards on foot. There was a high chance of ambushes being laid along the dirt and gravelled road. We were also blindly following the informer. None of us had any idea of the road, the time it would take, the destination or anything. We did not even switch on our torchlights as we walked, sometimes along the edge of the fields and sometimes along the streams. After walking for more than an hour, we reached Kalikhola, a village in Korak VDC.

The informer pointed from afar, "That is the house."

The house stood on the southern face of a slope with just a few houses around. We first climbed down the hill, crossed a small stream and started climbing. The informer stopped at a *tauwa*, a haystack, on the way. A few soldiers also stayed with him. Dogs started barking as we neared the house to surround it. Some old people were sleeping in the yard in front of the house. We woke Ram Kumar and Raj Kumar Praja, who were sleeping inside, and brought them out into the courtyard. Ranger Bishnu Thapaliya's team arrested Mangale Praja from a shed nearby as pointed out by the informer.

We were there on the basis of information that Mangale and Ram Kumar had killed a rhino and were hiding its horn. The informer had asked us not to arrest Raj Kumar as he was not part of the poachers' team. We had called Raj Kumar outside simply because he was a young man. We were questioning both Ram Kumar and Mangale about the horn when suddenly Raj Kumar darted down the slope.

As he ran, the soldiers opened fire.

"Don't fire," I shouted at them, terrified.

"He must have been the head of the operation, that's why he fled," said the captain.

"He was not on our list of suspects," I told him.

There could have been two reasons why Raj Kumar fled. One, he had been arrested once already and had spent 25 days in custody in April-May, and he might have been scared. Secondly, since we were persistently asking about the horn, he might have thought it best to flee as he could be jailed, too. Even when we arrested and brought him out of the house, he was making excuses to go to the backyard for some drinking water. But we did not allow him for fear that he might run away.

The soldiers fired at him as he ran, but due to the darkness and his speed, he managed to escape. The soldiers could have switched on their torchlights and fired, but he would have fled far away by then. Five or six of the soldiers fired more than 25 rounds from their M16. Some of them went to look for Raj Kumar after the firing stopped. I was relieved when they found nothing. We came back to Sauraha with Mangale and Ram Kumar Praja.

In our previous attempt, we had tried to nab them on *Ashtami*, the eighth day of the Hindu festival of *Dashain* that falls in September-October. We had received information that they would be coming to Parsa, and we had waited between Khairahani and Parsa all day. Had we been able to arrest them then, we could have been spared the trouble of going to Kalikhola at night.

RHINO ELECTROCUTED

THE PREVIOUS YEAR, an adult rhino had been found dead in the fields belonging to Kedar Bahadur Basnet in Kumroj village in eastern Chitwan. The post-mortem revealed that it had died of electrocution. The people who were sharecropping his fields, Kujuwa Chaudhari and Palat Chaudhari, had fled the scene following the rhino's death. As a result, we assumed that they were the ones who had electrocuted the rhino. However, our moles informed us that Kedar was the one who had given them money to flee, and both were currently working as labourers in Dibyanagar village.

Upon their arrest on October 24, 2003, they both stated that Kedar had bought the necessary wires and taught them how to electrocute a rhino. So we arrested Kedar, too. "Kujuwa and Palat must have electrocuted the animal to scare it away, I have done nothing, it is them," he insisted.

Upon investigation, it was found that they regularly electrocuted animals, not for the horns or skins, but for the protection of their fields. Apart from the rhino, they would also eat the meat of other animals such as the wild boar and deer when electrocuted. A case was registered against them for killing a rhino by electrocution. After this incident, there was a slight drop in the number of electrocuted rhinos.

ON NOVEMBER 4, I was in Tandi bazaar. At 1 in the afternoon, we were to arrive at Tandi on our way from Sauraha to Kasara. Our informer had informed us that a poacher from Kathar village was in Tandi. I stopped the jeep at the *chautari* of Bakullahar bazaar. Bikram Chaudhari was sitting there with his wife, and our game scout, who knew him, held him by the arms and brought him to us.

"Why?" asked his wife to me.

"We have business in Bharatpur regarding the land," I lied.

We interrogated him in Kasara but did not get much information. A lot of rhinos had died in eastern Chitwan and also in Devisthan Buffer Zone Community Forest of Kathar. His home was near this jungle. The informer had told us that he had a gun, but we were unable to locate it. We felt as if we had arrested an innocent man and released him on guarantee. Nobody admits to killing rhinos without solid evidence, and such cases are difficult to investigate.

RED CHILLI POWDER IN CASE...

IN THE MORNING of November 8, an informer told us by phone, "Come immediately to Parsa." *Mukhiya* Shriranga, driver Dillijang Tamang, Game Scout Mahendra Thapa and I left for Parsa immediately. At Parsa bazaar, he pointed to a shop and said, "Dawa Lama is drinking in there."

The informer described Dawa's appearance, the colour of his clothes, age and everything. We could identify him by the severed thumb of his left hand caused by exploding gun powder. I knew that Dawa was a dangerous person. There were only three of us besides the driver. I was tense because he was a poacher, and he might have a pistol or a knife with him, and we didn't know what he would do if we tried to arrest him. Something came to my mind while trying to decide what to do with Dawa.

It was February 18, 1990, the day the movement for democracy in Nepal had started. I was at Nalamukh of Pokhara at 11 in the morning, the appointed time. However, I didn't see many activists, though there were a lot of policemen around. Slowly, around 25 people came into view, shouting slogans. However, a group of policemen faced them and arrested them. I was just looking around and loitering from one side of the street to the other when I met Dhirendra Prasad Singh, president of the students' union at the Institute of Forestry, Pokhara Campus. He was a man wanted by the police.

Dhirendra had changed his appearance. He had a handkerchief tied over his mouth and was wearing a big coat. He signalled me to come towards him and shook my hands firmly. From the right pocket of his coat, he took out a bottle and said, "This is acid to throw at the police if they come."

From his left pocket, he took out a packet of red chilli powder.

"This is to sprinkle it in their eyes."

I was stunned by his readiness. He really looked like a guerrilla fighter ready to go to war.

So I too thought of sprinkling chilli powder into Dawa's eyes should he try to run away. From a nearby grocery, I bought three packets of chilli powder and gave one each to Mahendra and *Mukhiya* Shriranga. "Bring the jeep near as soon as you see us arresting the man," I told the driver.

Mahendra stood guard outside the restaurant while Kandel and I went inside smoking. Two people were having hard drinks at one table. The owner was cooking on a stove. I looked for the person matching the informer's description and made a guess.

"How are you Dawa?" I asked him.

"I am good, sir, please sit," said he. As he kept moving his glass on the table, I saw that he didn't have a thumb. Now there was no doubt that he was Dawa. Since I had gone in smoking, he had perhaps assumed that I had come for some hard drinks. I wasn't dressed very smartly either. But I don't know why he continued to address me as 'sir'.

"Come with us Dawa," I asked him.

"I am not Dawa," said he.

"What is your name then?"

"My name is Toram Bahadur Baju."

"Aren't you from Padampur?" I asked again.

"No, I am from Dhusel in Lalitpur district," said he and showed me his citizenship card.

But I was sure he was Dawa. So we took both Dawa and the man who was sharing the same table to the jeep. While we were taking him to the vehicle, a lot of people had gathered and were asking what had happened. "Nothing," we told them. The lady of the restaurant was bewildered.

On the way, we asked Dawa who the other man was, but it turned out the two were unknown to each other. We dropped him off immediately. I was glad that just the three of us had arrested Dawa without having to use chilli powder. But the chilli powder had built up our morale, and we were convinced that he wouldn't run away.

We interrogated Dawa at the Sauraha office, but he didn't reveal much. We were busy with other jobs the whole day. In the evening, we took him to Kasara, through Tikauli and the Bis-Hajari Lake jungle on the road along the Khageri *Nahar*. On the way, we started to pester him mentally, threatening to leave him alone in the middle of the jungle if he didn't tell us the truth. He then promised to reveal everything, and we again returned to Sauraha. He told us he had been waiting for one Lahure and his brother-in-law from Birendranagar, Onegroup village, as they had planned to kill a rhino that day.

Upon receiving this information, we decided to go to Onegroup village. A joint team consisting of me, Captain Bishal Bahadur Shah and others left at night. We parked quite far from our destination under a *Pipal* tree that had a Maoist party banner. We left Mahendra and driver Dillijung in the jeep, and proceeded to surround the house of Lahure's in-laws. We also surrounded a smaller house where his brother-in-law lived.

Lahure's father-in-law was sleeping outside his house.

"Where is Lahure?" we asked.

"I don't know," said he.

We opened the door and looked inside. Lahure wasn't in there. We climbed upstairs where his wife was sleeping.

When we woke her up and asked her, she told us he had gone to India.

"A man we met in Parsa says he was here today, and you tell

me he is in India?" I shot back.

"How am I to know what crime he has committed? Is it my fault?" she retorted.

We searched the house but did not find him. In the house of Lahure's brother-in-law, there were no men, only his wife was sleeping. In the bright light of the electric bulb, we could see everything clearly from outside.

"Where is your husband?" we asked her when she woke up.

"In India," came the ready reply.

Birman Praja, another man on our most wanted list, also lived nearby, so we decided to pay a visit to his house, too. The house that he used to live in was locked. From the environ we sensed that nobody lived there. We then went to his father-in-law's house, surrounded it and searched the building. We found only Birman's wife and sister-in-law. In the adjacent house, we found his father-in-law Chhabir Pun Magar.

"Where is your son-in-law?" I asked.

"I don't know," said he.

"Where is the gun then?"

"I don't engage in such work. I have asked my daughter to leave this house, and I have told Birman also to stop coming here if he continued to engage in such work."

However, we were told that Chhabir supplied guns and ammunition to Birman. Hence, we arrested him and took him with us. Next on our list were Surya Pun Magar and Kumar Pun Magar. But nobody knew their houses. We asked Chhabir, but he refused to tell us as they were his brothers' sons.

"If they find out, I will be accused of getting them arrested," said he.

"We won't let them know you informed us," we said.

He pointed out the house from afar. In our usual approach, we surrounded the house and arrested Surya. There was a 20 inch LG colour television set.

"Let's take the TV, too. We know that he bought it with the money gotten from poaching rhinos," said Game Scout Yam Bahadur Khanal, a member of our team.

"We shouldn't tamper with other people's stuff," I said. In fact, it was an expensive TV set and did not quite suit the house he lived in. It was probable that it had been bought with money earned from horn smuggling.

The other guy Kumar Pun Magar was in a room with his newly married wife. He was quite embarrassed when we woke him up from outside. "Just a moment, sir," he said, and we waited for him outside until he had his clothes on. Then we went in and arrested him. Though we could not arrest Lahure - our target for the day - we were glad to have nabbed three others.

TORTOISE IN THE WELL

ON NOVEMBER 16, we were informed that Birman Praja had crossed the Rapti River in a boat to come to Kathar village from old Padampur village. "Birman was in the boat with me and is right now sitting on a *tauwa*," said the informer.

Hurriedly we left for Kathar at 9 in the evening with Captain Bishal and his team. After parking, we walked towards the field where many *tauwas* were standing and surrounded the area. Several people, including couples, were sleeping in small thatched huts. We woke them up, and it was clear that they were scared by the sight of guns. We searched all the *tauwas* but found no Birman.

The informer too was with us. "He must have gone to his relative's house nearby, let's go there," he said.

"He will not be found if we go without evidence, let's not go," I insisted. So we returned empty handed.

Our team then went to the Devnagar post, where our staff always had heaps of complaints about a person. "This man is a menace," they told us. "He troubles us and threatens to beat us up. He cuts trees in broad daylight and takes away the wood. He has poisoned the Bis-Hajari Lake and Khageri Irrigation Canal and killed the fish there. He catches tortoises and takes them away."

The man's name was Rakesh Adhikari, and we arrested him. "Where is the tortoise that you caught yesterday?" we asked him.

"In the well," he replied. We sent him to the well to get the tortoise. He went inside the well and looked around but found no tortoise.

Rakesh Adhikari was charged with stealing wood and tortoises. But later, he was released on bail. He was a local bully who drank, beat his wife and parents, troubled the park officials and members of the community forest user group by stealing the wood.

We were unable to locate Rakesh's friends, so we left for new Padampur village. There we arrested rhino poacher Chandra Bahadur Poudel after being tipped off by an informer. We then went to arrest his friend Purna Bahadur Tamang, but without luck.

LIKE TALIBAN'S TORA BORA

ON NOVEMBER 20, an informer tipped us off that Dambare Praja, Devraj Chhetri and other rhino poachers were smuggling logs from old Padampur village that day. We were in Sauraha, attending a small party at the Tiger Rhino Conservation Project office. We ate in a hurry and got ready to go.

"I don't know when I will be eating, so let me have some food before coming," said the driver. But he failed to return even in half an hour. He had a weakness for liquor and was apparently drinking at the party. The informer was becoming impatient, as our targets had already returned. We too were worried that the criminals might escape if we did not leave in time. When you do not have a driver who is particular about time schedules, then anti-poaching operations are at risk. Criminals do not wait to be picked up.

We left as soon as the driver arrived. It must have been 9 in the evening when we reached the post at Janakpur. We woke the staff and left our jeep there before proceeding for Padampur village. After walking for 10 minutes, we heard people's voices. There were women's voices, too. Since the voices were coming towards us, we set up ambushes on both sides of the road and hid in the bushes. The voices would rise and then fade away. We waited for nearly an hour, but nobody appeared. We moved slowly to the bank of the Rapti River, but no one was there.

We decided to go to Padampur itself. At Jitpur *ghat*, we saw that a boat had just left for the other bank. So we also took a boat to Padampur. But we had no idea where to secure the boat. There was no place from where we could get onto land. So we climbed with great difficulty the sandy slopes to reach land. The soil was all sandy, and it just did not support our weight when we stepped on it. Had we fallen from there, we would have landed straight in the Rapti.

There we asked a Bote, "Did you take the people with wood across?"

"Yes, I did row them across, but they must have returned on their own," he replied.

"Point out their houses to us," we told him. But there was no one at home. Then he showed us their hiding place. It was a sort of tunnel, covered by a variety of stubborn shrubs. We walked in about 40 metres. It formed a perfect shelter from the rains. Also, there were beds of hay to sleep on. We were stunned, it seemed like a Tora Bora cavern used by the Afghani Taliban to hide. But no one was there.

On a hunch that they might have gone to the hut of Dambare Praja's sister for a drink, we went to her place and roused the people from their sleep. One of them was our staff - an elephant keeper. He was married to Dambare's sister. No one we were looking for was there, and we returned like defeated soldiers.

The informer again told us, "There are two furniture factories in Janakpur village, that's where they must have taken the logs, let's go."

We started for the house of Jamuna Mahato who ran the furniture factory. The smugglers had left logs at his courtyard and banana farm. We surrounded the house and entered. We woke up the sleeping Jamuna and asked him, "Whose wood is this? Who brought them?"

He told us everything.

There was a boy in his late teens sleeping on the ground floor. His name was Man Bahadur Praja, and he was also part of the team that transported the wood. He told us the names of everyone on the team. We raided the house and confiscated all the wood as well as ready-made furniture.

Man Bahadur turned out to be a gifted folk singer. The staff would ask him to come out of his custody and sing for them. One day, they asked me to come too to hear him sing. He mesmerised us with his beautiful voice.

Our informer had told us that Man Bahadur was also involved in rhino poaching, but he denied it. No one interrogated him strictly, as everybody loved listening to his songs.

One day, Man Bahadur's parents happened to meet United Nations Development Programme (UNDP) team at Padampur village and had wept, requesting the country representative, Matthew Kahane, to free their son. When Mathew Kahane came to Kasara, the park headquarters, to inspect a participatory conservation programme (operated with financial and technical support of the UNDP) at the park, he mentioned about it to Chief Warden Shivaraj Bhatta, who, in turn, released Man Bahadur. I found out about this a few days later.

Meanwhile, I learnt from an informer that Man Bahadur kept two guns belonging to Birman, and Birman was desperate to get him released to lay his hands on the guns. After his release, Man Bahadur returned the guns to Birman. I was disheartened by the action of the UNDP country representative.

THE SEARCH FOR A LIFE PARTNER

FOR THE PAST few years, there had been talk in the family to find me a bride, but each time something did not click. After I was posted in Chitwan, I tried several times to find an appropriate life partner. I had been to my home village Hemja in this regard many times, but I couldn't find the type of girl I was looking for. My uncle, Surya Bahadur Kunwar, and Dal Bahadur *dai* worked hard to find me a wife. One day, a classmate from my school days, Jit Bahadur Karki, mentioned a girl who was studying at the Master's level with him.

Subsequently, the marriage date was fixed - well almost. But before the wedding, it was decided that the bride and groom would meet once. When we met, I told the girl that we would be married in a temple, and I would not accept any dowry. However, she was adamant that we could not get married in a temple, and that there could not be a marriage without any dowry. I tried to persuade her, but she wouldn't agree. I was firm on my stance, and we broke up.

My friend Deepraj Sapkota got to know of my unmarried status. During a chat one day, he mentioned that a friend of his, Hari Adhikari, had a niece. "Sure, let's see the girl," I told him.

After a few days, I, Deepraj, Hari Adhikari and another friend, Umakanta Gautam, headed for Chainpur, Chitwan. Since it was the month of August, streams had risen everywhere. There was no way we could cross the streams in our jeep. We tried doing so from three places, but we had no luck given the condition of our old vehicle. We then found a slightly easier point to cross the

Ladari stream, and with great difficulty we arrived in Chainpur. Having walked for hours by the river trying to find an easy crossing, we were dog tired by the time we reached the place.

In Chainpur, we were offered tea by the girl we had come to see. I liked her, and since we had arrived there with great difficulty, I assumed that the fruits of labour were always sweet. The girl's father, Ganesh Bahadur Adhikari, was present, too, and we had a pleasant chat with him.

A few days later, just before *Tihar*, the Festival of Lights celebrated in October-November, Surya uncle and Dal Bahadur *dai* arrived from Hemja. Again we went to meet the girl in Bharatpur at Hari Adhikari's home.

Later, my brother Ram Kumar of Chitwan and I went to see her for the third time.

Finally, our marriage was fixed for December 9, and we were married at the Harihar Temple of Narayangadh, Chitwan.

Our marriage was a simple affair. There were just 12 members in the groom's procession, including just two or three people from the office. At the wedding site (*jagge*), I gave my mobile to Madhav. "If he gets a call that Birman has been sighted, Kamal sir will take off his wedding garland and run after him," he joked.

Everyone laughed.

And so, Pramila Adhikari became my wife, and no dowry was accepted.

POACHER ESCAPES

I HAD GONE to Hemja on personal business on December 16. Ranger Madhav was in Sauraha. An informer informed us that a group of poachers, including Raj Kumar Praja, were staying at Ramchandra Praja's (aka Mudha Sainla) house at Magani Chowk in Parsa bazaar. I informed Madhav and he set out and arrested Raj Kumar Praja aka Kalu, Mangale Praja aka Taakule, and Padam Bahadur Praja. Among them, Kalu managed to escape after being caught.

They released Mangale immediately since he had already been arrested before. Padam Bahadur was arrested and taken to Kasara, where he was interrogated over 25 days. However, since we could gather no evidence against him, we released him with the vice-chairman of Shaktikhor VDC acting as surety.

I was out of Chitwan. The *mukhiya*, Shriranga Kandel, told me how he had received information from New Padampur village. So a team consisting of Ranger Bishnu Thapaliya, Captain Bishal and others had gone to Padampur at night on January 3, 2004, and arrested Krishna Bote, Dambar Bahadur Praja, Dhidara Mahato and Ramkrishna Mahato.

We had tried to arrest a few of them on November 20 the previous year, but we were late. Then I did not have the money at hand to give the informers and had rewarded them only a year later.

Dambar Bahadur used to work in Birman Praja's gang. He also told us about Birman Praja. One evening, *mukhiya* Shriranga Kandel, Bishnu and others had brought him out for interrogation, and he had used the opportunity to run away. However, Buddhinath Lamicchane and other staff were able to nab him in the jungle again.

FATHER-IN-LAW GETS SON-IN-LAW ARRESTED

THOUGH WE HAD arrested Toram Bahadur Baju, known as Dawa, we were unable to arrest the main poacher of the gang, Lahure. One day we received information that Lahure was sighted at a wedding in the village. We decided to go at night on February 4, 2004, and a team including Captain Bishal, Ranger Bishnu, *mukhiya* Shriranga Kandel and I left for Onegroup village. We went to the house of Lahure's in-laws but found only his wife. We asked his father-in-law to point him out to us.

This was the second time that we had been there to arrest Lahure. Apparently, his father-in-law was fed up with our repeated presence because he said, "I better get this man who brings such shame to the family arrested."

We walked along a stream towards the Dudhpokhari Community Forest. Among the few thatched huts near the jungle, one belonged to Lahure's brother-in-law. His father-in-law pointed out the house to us. We surrounded the house and went inside, but he wasn't there.

"Where is he?" we asked his brother-in-law.

"I will show you," he said.

He took us to a shop on the way to Korak village. This was a shop that we too used to frequent for tea. The owner was a tall, fair and cheerful woman. This was also rhino poacher Bam Bahadur Praja's frequent hangout, and she knew we were looking for him.

Lahure had frequently asked the woman to buy his land. Accordingly, his brother-in-law assumed that he must have stayed there after getting drunk in the day. We surrounded our familiar tea shop and commanded, "Open the door."

The woman refused, probably scared that we were Maoists or army men. One soldier kicked the door open, and we entered and searched the house.

Lahure wasn't there. He had left after drinking in the day. The woman was angry at us. We were all quiet, ashamed of our mistake. However, we had acted on the tip that a notorious criminal was hiding in there.

Again his brother-in-law decided to lead us to another shop where Lahure frequently stopped to drink. There we found only the landlady and her 3 teenage daughters, but no Lahure. When we failed to locate him once again, we turned to a third place. The hut of his *mit* stood nearby, beside a stream. We searched it too but only found a person with speech impairment there.

"He was walking around drunk in the evening, but he's not there now," said he. We returned to Sauraha disappointed. It was nearly 4 in the morning. We were exhausted from the whole night's operation, searches, walking, thirst and disappointment. People were slowly waking up. The sun was turning the eastern sky red.

In Sauraha, everyone started for their rooms. I too rested for a while in the guest house. I was to take Pramila to Hemja that day. I left for Chainpur in a jeep. I was tired and hadn't slept, so I wasn't fresh at all.

"What happened?" asked everyone.

"Probably he was chasing crooks all night and hasn't slept," Pramila answered

I hadn't eaten, and everyone was waiting for me. But suddenly I got a call from Parsa: "You must come immediately, something important has turned up." I assumed that Lahure had been sighted, and I immediately left, telling everyone I would be back from Parsa soon.

The woman from the shop of the previous night's operation and another person had arrived in Parsa. The lady was very angry with me. I apologised to her and asked her to put the matter behind us and reiterated that it wouldn't happen again.

While returning, when I was about to reach Chainpur, I met my father-in-law. He had come looking for me on a cycle. Maoist combatants were very active in Chainpur, and he was worried that I had been kidnapped by the Maoists or something else had happened to me. When I reached Chainpur, I found my mother-in-law, Jagan uncle and my wife Pramila worried and waiting for me. My mother-in-law wept when she saw me.

I consoled everyone.

We ate and left for Hemja.

Arrested while Selling Land

When we learnt that Lahure was trying to sell his land, we sent an informer acting as a purchaser. Lahure had asked the chairman of the community forest to sell his land. I sent our informer to contact the chairman. He called Lahure over and finalised the land deal. The informer pretended to agree on the price and even gave him some advance. Accordingly, I gave him $3,444, the price of the land, borrowed from the Buffer Zone Management Programme of the Chitwan National Park.

On February 16, 2004, a few of us left for the revenue office in Bharatpur. We reached there even before the office opened and talked to the security guard commander (police) there. "Please help us should the need arise," I told him.

We were in continuous contact with our informer. We learnt that Lahure was staying in a hotel in Narayangadh. When the office opened, he arrived in a red taxi which bore the plate number of Pokhara. His wife, daughter and brother were with him. We had made arrangements to complete all documents regarding the sale of the land inside the office while money would be handed over later outside. I had instructed my team to scatter around and sit in different shops, and come only when I signalled.

After a few moments, Lahure appeared alone unaccompanied by our informer and prepared to leave in the taxi. I immediately sensed that things weren't going according to plan. He had apparently received the money inside the office. Hurriedly, I signalled my team to come closer. The taxi driver had already started the engine. I stood fidgeting in front of the taxi. As soon as my colleagues arrived, I switched off the motor engine and removed the key. My colleagues then pulled Lahure out. Our jeep arrived, and we shoved everyone in except the driver. Our colleagues sat in the red taxi, and we left for our office at Kasara.

The locals assumed it was a kidnap case. Some of them had even thought of informing the police about how thieves had looted money from a man. Thus we nabbed a rhino poacher the way a kidnapper would abduct someone. However, the informer who had acted as the buyer began assuming the land now belonged to him. In February 2006, when I told him we needed to sell that land as I had to return the money to the Buffer Zone Management Programme, he refused, insisting that the land was now his. This matter took a long time to resolve. He sold that land and bought land in Nawalparasi. It was only in 2007 that the property registered in his wife's name was duly transferred to the Buffer Zone Management Committee.

Lahure's real name was Gadar Purja Pun. He was from Banau VDC in Parbat district and lived in Onegroup village with his second wife. He told us everything about his activities. We learnt of his horn dealings and of the other members of his team. He admitted to killing 13 rhinos in two years. Out of the 13 rhinos he had killed, one was pregnant. According to his statement, he first shot the rhino. Although the rhino was wounded, she managed to walk slowly. So with a sword he cut the back leg. She could no longer walk but was still alive. He then hit her on the backbone. While she lay on the ground still alive, he cut off the horn.

When he narrated this incident to me, it reminded me of the rhino I had seen at the Khoriyamuhan area of the park. I was shocked by Lahure's statement but very happy to have arrested such a notorious poacher.

We brought him to Sauraha from Kasara in the evening. From there, our team, including Captain Bishal, headed for eastern Chitwan.

OPERATION IN WEDDING HALL

THE PREVIOUS DAY, on February 15, I had gone to Simaltandi village to learn about a Chepang in Onegroup village. There was a concrete house to the north of the highway on the left side. A groom's party was about to leave from that house. It was clear from the looks of the groom's party and the presence of Lamas that it was a Tamang wedding. Suddenly it just dawned on me that such a big and attractive house in this village could only belong to a horn trader.

On the night of February 16, we planned to raid the house where the wedding had just taken place. Lahure had mentioned that he used to give horns to Buddhiman Tamang of Simaltandi. That attractive house belonged to Buddhiman, and his son had just gotten married. According to Lahure's statement, Buddhiman had been smuggling horns and tiger skins since 1984-1985. He had returned from the Indian Army after contracting tuberculosis and was currently working as a Lama. His two sons were still in the Indian army.

It was already 11 at night. There were no public vehicles on the road because of a curfew that was imposed on the highway every evening. Only our two jeeps were speeding from west to east. Usually, I myself used to drive. As we neared Simaltandi, we could see the wedding house clearly from afar. Twinkle lights adorned the house. A few youths had lit a fire on the terrace on the top floor and were singing and dancing around it.

When we reached the house, the channel gate at the entrance had already been locked. The people inside would not hear our shouts from outside. There was no way we could enter. I looked around and saw that the poles of the welcome gate, erected in front of the main gate, extended to the balcony of the first floor. With help from friends, I climbed the pole and got onto the balcony. Captain Bishal climbed after me. Now we were inside the house. The rooms were closed, some were sleeping while others were talking among themselves.

We both headed for the terrace. The people who were dancing had probably seen us parking, so they quietened down. "Where are Sonam and Buddhiman?" we asked. They replied that both of them were not present. We had to use force on some of them who were trying to be rude by speaking in a loud voice, probably sensing that there were just the two of us. But they got scared when they saw Bishal's pistol.

We went downstairs and roused the people who were sleeping. Relatives who had come for the wedding showed us where Buddhiman was sleeping, and we arrested him. We then ordered the people to open the channel gate, and our friends came inside. As we started looking for Sonam, everyone in the house was shocked. As we searched the house, we also happened to open the room where the newly married couple were sleeping.

The bride was badly shaken and asked the groom, "What is this, why?"

The groom too failed to understand what was happening. "I don't know," he replied.

Later, we learnt that the bride had wept and complained to her parents for getting her married into such a house. She was innocent, her misfortune was the result of her father-in-law's crimes, not hers.

SMUGGLER WHO COUNTED THE ROSARY

WHEN WE WERE about to leave with Buddhiman, we asked his wife to bring his clothes. Buddhiman asked her to bring his rosary, too. What hypocrisy - on the one hand, he counted the prayer beads and chanted "*Om Mani Padme Hoom*" and on the other, he killed and smuggled innocent wild animals.

"Where is Sonam?" we asked Buddhiman, and he pointed to a nearby house. We entered the house. There too, a couple was sleeping, but there was no Sonam.

From there, we headed for Onegroup village. On the way, Lahure showed us Sonam's house. It was a small house, and certainly no comparison to Buddhiman's residence, maybe his involvement in the smuggling business had only just begun. Sonam was Buddhiman's brother-in-law. The lights were on both inside and outside the house, and we could see him sleeping inside.

People in Chitwan's villages mostly sleep with their lights on. They do not even switch off the lights outside their homes. The people here are experts at stealing electricity by tapping onto the power lines. Poultry farm owners collaborate with the Nepal Electricity Authority personnel to steal power, while villagers just chase away the people who come to remove the wires. They do not need to switch off the electricity because they are neither billed for it nor will they ever pay for it. Chitwan is one of the districts where electricity is widely stolen by the locals.

The door opened easily from outside, and I shouted, "Sonam." He was deep in his sleep and got up only after a lot of shouting.

"How are you, Sonam," I asked him.

"I'm fine," he said, rubbing his eyes.

He tried to go back to sleep. I shook him. His breath smelled of liquor. When he finally opened his eyes, he was shocked to see us. Both his sleep and intoxication abandoned him. We asked him to come with us and instructed him to get dressed quickly. He understood immediately, asked no questions and walked quietly with us. We also took his cycle with us. His wife was in Simaltandi attending her nephew's wedding. Otherwise, we might have had to arrest a man while he was in bed with his wife. Thank God we did not have to violate human rights to arrest a man who had violated animal rights!

Actually, Sonam turned out to be quite a simple guy. He had gotten into the business attracted by the smugglers' luxurious lifestyle. He told us how Birman had said, "Come with us if you want to earn money." It seems the intention of smugglers is to lure as many people as possible into rhino poaching. The lure of money attracts a lot of unemployed and poor youths into this vicious circle. As the gang members increase, so does the smuggling business.

A LINE OF SMUGGLERS

BUDDHIMAN TAMANG told us that Chet Prasad Kharel had given the horn to him. I had heard that in the mornings, he came to Bairahani Chowk in eastern Chitwan. On February 18, when Game Scout Mahendra Thapa and I were going from Tandi to Bhandara, I saw a man who matched Chet Prasad's description going to Khurkhure on a cycle. We stopped our jeep and asked a man sitting under a tree, "Is that Chet Prasad Kharel?"

"Yes," the man replied. We followed and arrested him. We took him to Tandi in our jeep, and when I asked him who had given him the horn, he named Chhetra Bahadur B.K. We asked for backup from the Sauraha office, and with two more Game Scouts Laptan Tharu and Nageshwor Chaudhari, we went to arrest Chhetra Bahadur. He was busy in a smithy a little further from Bairahani.

Afterwards, both of them named Gore, the son of Mudha Sainla, as the one who had given them the horn. It was my guess that this Gore was Buddhi Bahadur Praja, whom we had arrested the previous year and set free for lack of proof. I took our jeep to Magani Chowk in Parsa and asked Mahendra to get that man. Gore was at home and asked no questions when we told him to come with us. "Is this the man?" I asked Chet Prasad.

"Yes," he said. Then we took him also with us to Kasara in the jeep.

"Where did you get the horn?" we asked him, and he told us everything.

We had arrested Mangale and Ram Kumar Praja in Korak village in October 22, 2003. Although we were unable to find it, they had a horn with them that day. Following their arrest, they had asked Buddhi Bahadur to sell the horn. He had given that horn to Chhetra Bahadur, who gave it to Chet Prasad, who, in turn, gave it to Buddhiman, and Buddhiman to Tamling (a Tibetan refugee).

IN KATHMANDU LOOKING FOR SMUGGLERS

LAHURE USED TO sell horns in Pokhara and Kathmandu. In Pokhara, he sold it to a man from Manang who dealt in medicinal plants, and in Kathmandu, he was introduced to Tamling by Birman, who lived at Bouddha. On February 20, we decided to take Lahure to Kathmandu. We consulted with the army, too. They assured us that, if necessary, soldiers would be there to support us in Kathmandu. We set off in a Land Rover. From a petrol pump in Bharatpur, we got Lahure to call Tamling in Kathmandu. We were scared that if we called him from our office in Kathmandu, it would arouse suspicion as the phone would reveal the caller ID.

Lahure placed the call. It was received by a lady. "*Sahuji* is not here," she said.

"Where is he?"

"He has gone to India."

"When will he return?"

"Tomorrow."

Then it was her turn to question, "Who are you?"

Lahure spoke with a Mongoloid accent, "I am Birman's brother. I have the stuff, I will bring it."

"How much?"

"Eleven hundred grams."

"OK, come."

"When will Tamling arrive?" he asked again.

"I will buy it," said the lady.

According to Lahure, he sometimes handed the horn over to Tamling, and sometimes to this girl who worked at his place. The girl would weigh and check the horn, and they would settle the price before she called Tamling. He would come and pay for it in the end, and sometimes his sons did the job.

Our Land Rover had just been repaired in Kathmandu for $3,444. But the driver had to take it to a workshop since it was again giving trouble. Though the mechanic said it would take just 15 minutes, it took more than two hours. When it was finally repaired, we received news that the road in Jugedi village was closed due to a strike called to protest the murder of a man. It was the day of Shivaratri, and the army had shot dead a person who was collecting money for the Shivaratri festival, assuming he was a Maoist. We had no option but to take the longer route to Kathmandu via Hetauda and Daman. We backtracked and headed east. When we were near Birendranagar village, we received a phone call. The chief warden asked Ranger Bishnu Thapaliya to return to the park office, Kasara.

As the rhino translocation programme from Chitwan to the Bardia National Park had been cancelled, we would be tying the radio collar (a transmitter around a rhino's neck which tells us where the animal is at the moment) around the rhinos' necks and releasing them in the forest. Television crews from around the world had arrived in Chitwan to film the operation. Also, special guests, including Director-General of the DNPWC Tirthaman Maskey, would be arriving. Bishnu would be managing the event.

We proceeded after sending him back. I was obsessed with catching the ring leader of the rhino horn smugglers. According to Lahure, Tamling had bought and sold more than a hundred horns. The horns in the possession of Bam Bahadur Praja, Gyamjo, Birman Praja, Jhalendra Gurung, Anil Ghising and several other notorious poachers and brokers all found their way to him. On these grounds, we could easily estimate that he had bought and smuggled more than a hundred horns. I wanted to nab this dangerous smuggler and take him to my bosses while they were still in Chitwan.

When we were heading towards Kathmandu through Hetauda, Lahure confirmed that Chhabir Pun (whom we had arrested but released for lack of evidence) was the man who provided the poachers with guns and ammunition for poaching. He was released on general bail and was supposed to make his presence on the date summoned at the park office, Kasara on February 22. I instructed the staff to arrest him when he arrived.

We reached Naubise, 26 km from Kathmandu, when it started getting dark. The headlight failed to switch on, and all the hours of repairs in Bharatpur did not help. I asked the driver to proceed in dim light, but he refused. We asked Lahure to call the lady again and to tell her that he wouldn't be able to make it that day.

The repairs took about two hours, and it was 10 at night when we reached Bouddha. We made a survey of Tamling's flat on the top floor of a three-storied house. We could clearly hear voices of people talking in the house.

We discussed amongst ourselves when we should arrest him.

"The man we want has not talked to us on the phone. If he is coming tomorrow, then let's do it tomorrow," I suggested.

"No, let's do it tonight," said *mukhiya* Shriranga.

We then called the army at Kasara. They, in turn, called the army in Kathmandu, and soon a team from the Bhairabnath Battalion arrived with Captain Milan Tulachan. I gave them a short introduction of our mission.

The main gate was locked, and the compound walls were high. With great difficulty we climbed up. A few soldiers were stationed on the ground. There was another channel gate before we could get to the flat. Since it took some time for us to reach there, people inside had gone to sleep.

We woke them up by banging on the channel gate.

A girl with Mongoloid features, aged about 20, came out and asked, "Who is it?"

We gave her our identity and asked her to open the gate, but she refused. The captain showed her his ID. When she still refused, he showed her his pistol. She then relented and opened the gate.

We asked Lahure if this was the girl who had talked to him on the phone.

"No," said Lahure. He entered the flat timidly. He had been scared the whole day and had begun crying when we started heading for Kathmandu after having tea at Daman in Makwanpur.

"Why are you crying?" I asked him, but he would not reply.

"Are you scared of Tamling? Are you crying because he will kill you?" I asked him again. But he would not reply and just kept weeping.

"Well, you were the village bully until we arrested you. You used to chase your friends with a *khukuri*. Everyone used to be scared of Lahure, and you used to say that you would teach us an appropriate lesson. But you seem to be a coward. You are gutless," I told him.

And then he opened up. "Sir, he will kill me. He is a very dangerous man, he knows all the big shots. The generals, colonels and heads of the police are all friends of his, he will surely kill me." He assumed that his poaching partners Anil Ghising, Jhalendra Gurung and other friends were killed by the Nepal Army after their arrest at the bidding of bigger smugglers.

"We have you in our custody, we won't let him kill you, don't worry," I assured him.

He stopped crying after a lot of consoling.

Finally, we entered Tamling's house. A plum, fair man of about 25 was sleeping in there. Lahure had told us that Tamling's son too was a smuggler. But when we pointed to the sleeping person, Lahure could not identify him. A few Lama *gurus* were sleeping in the other room. They pretended not to understand Nepali.

We searched the house but did not find the man we were looking for. We went through the photo albums, confiscated the photos, citizenship cards and passports, and asked the girl working there to call on the mobile number that we had previously contacted.

She called the number, and Lahure talked to her. "I am at your place, I have the stuff (horn), come soon," said he.

"Didn't you just say that you won't be able to make it today?" she asked. She was probably suspicious, and told Lahure that she would arrive in 15 minutes. We took our positions, ready for her to come.

She called a few moments later and asked for the girl working there. "I want to talk to my own people in there," she said. I signalled the girl to refuse.

"Then I am not coming," said she.

Assuming that Lamas are honest and will tell the truth, I asked a Lama to speak to her on the phone in Nepali and ask her to come. But the Lama spoke rapidly in Tibetan and put the receiver down.

We waited for more than half an hour, but she did not turn up. Then we started wondering if the Lama had informed her about us. It was poor judgment on my part to trust a Lama and ask him to speak to a criminal, but I only did it out of respect for and faith in the Lamas.

Since we did not find the horn smuggler in the house, we took a Tibetan boy along with us. We also confiscated a pair of scales used to weigh horns and a phone set.

Lahure further informed us that Tamling could be in his other house, so we raided another house at Mahankal, too. The house had high gates. When we called from outside, no one received the phone. With great difficulty, we climbed to the first floor, broke the ventilation window of the toilet and roused the people sleeping inside. But still we didn't find the person we were looking for.

We then went to the telecommunication office at Chabahil to find out from which house the woman had made the call. We woke the guard on duty and sent a jeep to the house of a telecommunication officer to get him. It was already 2 at night. The telecommunication officer arrived and looked up the phone catalogues. After a while, he gave us a rough map of the house.

We located the house and called from outside. The phone rang, but no one picked it up. We surrounded it and entered. There was just a domestic worker inside. We found neither Tamling nor the woman called Buti, who apparently had left that house at night. That house belonged to a man called Marche from Mugu district. Later, when a man called Aidey from Mugu was arrested, he informed us that Marche was a smuggler of rhino horns.

We returned empty-handed from that place. I was depressed and humiliated by that incident. That was the result of trying to decide as a group rather than imposing my decision. Even today that failed operation saddens me.

Dejected, we headed for the Bhairabnath Battalion. It was nearly 4 in the morning when we got there. Captain Milan arranged for me to sleep in the officers' barracks. My friends slept in our jeep. On the one hand, we were tired from our long journey; on the other, I was humiliated by our failure. But I managed to fall asleep.

The following morning, we interrogated Nima, the Tibetan boy we had arrested from the house. "I don't know anything," he said. Later the army interrogated him, but he was stubborn. They covered his eyes and mouth, and poured water into his nose. Terrified, he would shout, "I will tell," but when they removed the gag, he would again say, "I do not know anything, brother," in Hindi. He would say a few words in Hindi and pretend not to understand Nepali.

This was how I learnt to pour water into the nose while interrogating. To tell the truth, after that we used this method many times in Chitwan. This method was useful in obtaining information. But I would always be careful not to suffocate the person I was interrogating. In some cases though, not even this method worked. The people we had arrested without preliminary evidence admitted nothing and were rather prepared to die. "Kill me," they would say rather than reveal the truth. But once they opened up, they usually told everything.

"Why didn't you tell us before, you could have avoided a lot of misery," we would tell them, and they would say they were trying to save themselves for as long a period as possible.

I went to meet the Commander of the Bhairabnath Battalion. Actually he had been the Company Commander at the Shuklaphanta Wildlife Reserve while I was deputed there for three months from July to September in 2000, and we were meeting after four years. We formulated a plan to keep watch of the airport.

We got information during a telephonic conversation between Buti and Lahure that the smuggler we hadn't been able to arrest the day before was arriving from New Delhi, India that day. Based on this information, we contacted the security at the airport and started scanning the list of passengers coming from Delhi. We were at it the whole day but to no avail. We stayed the night at a hotel in Thamel. The next day we got a friend to call Tamling's girl. She, however, refused to disclose her location. So we returned disappointed.

The previous night, we had confiscated some documents from Tamling's house. These documents were strange: there was a fake Nepali citizenship card, a reference letter from the Indian Embassy, an identity card and an UN-given ID of a Tibetan refugee, among others. The passport read T. Chhiring. We were amazed that this man had several ID cards!

On our way back to Chitwan, I received a call on my mobile. It read: "Your maternal grandmother is on her deathbed and wants to meet her grandson once." From Muglin of Chitwan, I veered towards my grandmother's home in Kaski, Sarangkot.

We were forced to release the Tibetan boy, Nima Khamba, since the interrogations revealed nothing. By this time, the Tibetans had taken the matter to our Chief Warden Shivaraj Bhatta through Taranath Dahal, president of the Nepal Journalists' Association. We had released him for lack of evidence and not on Taranath Dahal's insistence, but the Tibetans thought otherwise.

Tamling had connections with international gangs. He used to trade in not just horns from Nepal but from India, too. He smuggled them from the Kaziranga National Park of Assam, India. He was also wanted in India.

THE CHITWAN NATIONAL Park, listed as a world heritage site in 1984, was selected among the top 10 national parks of Asia in 2004 by United Nations Educational, Scientific and Cultural Organisation (UNESCO), and Manoj Mishra (former chief conservator and head of the anti-wildlife trafficking body in India) was in Nepal to make an evaluation of the park. He was a consultant with the Wildlife Institute of India in Dehradun, and while on the subject of smuggling, he mentioned T. Chhiring. I was elated to think that this notorious criminal

I had been tailing would be nabbed by the Indians. I took Manoj to my room and showed him all the evidence I had. He took pictures of them with his camera.

But after a while, we realised that the T. Chhiring he was referring to was a different person. India hadn't been able to arrest the T. Chhiring who lived in Kathmandu and bought tiger skins from Sansar Chand, a notorious Indian smuggler of tiger skins and bones. Detectives from the Central Bureau of Investigation (CBI), India had even come to Nepal, prepared a detailed report on him and submitted it to the Nepal Police as well as the DNPWC. They had even sent out a red corner notice against him. It was clear from their report that they were emphasising that he held Nepali citizenship when in reality he was a Tibetan refugee. If we were to start an investigation, we would probably find along with letters of reference from the Indian Embassy, fake Nepali citizenship papers and an UN-given Tibetan refugee ID card, as with the case of Tamling.

He was finally arrested by the DNPWC in Kathmandu with the help of the Nepal Police, when tiger skins and bones despatched from Kathmandu were confiscated in the Langtang National Park.

For a long time, I communicated with Manoj Mishra by email about the horn smuggler T. Chhiring aka Tamling. In the beginning, he told me that a CBI officer was working on it, and he too had an informer who was especially working on the case. But later, he did not furnish any information on the developments.

WE LEARNT THAT rhino poachers would be going to Devghat on bicycles on March 2. At 9 in the morning, *mukhiya* Shriranga, Game Scouts Laptan Tharu, Mahendra Thapa,

Nageshwar Chaudhari and I went to the Aaptari checkpost in Chitwan, which is on the way to Kathmandu. We talked to the duty officer at the army checkpost and secured his help should the need arise. As informed, the poachers came from Devghat on bicycles. We arrested Likharam Mahato from Kawasoti and Shivanarayan Chaudhari from Dibyanagar, Chitwan. They were members of Anil Ghising and Jhalendra Gurung's gang. They had run away from the village and were in hiding after Anil and Jhalendra were killed.

RHINO POACHER OF A DIFFERENT KIND

ON MARCH 25, we received news that poachers that included Birman Praja were getting ready to kill rhinos and were staying at a house at Sundi in Kathar village. Immediately, a team from Sauraha that included Captain Bishal, *mukhiya* Shriranga, Ranger Bishnu Thapaliya and I left for Sundi. We parked on the Rapti River embankment and surrounded Kajiman Tamang's house. However, his bed was empty. A man was sleeping on the first floor, but he did not match Kajiman's age or description. A teenage girl was sleeping alone in the yard. Shriranga and I sent everyone outside, and we approached the girl. She was in deep sleep.

We woke her up and said, "We are friends of your father, where is he?"

"He was gone to the fields to water them," said she after looking around for a while.

We then asked her to sleep and went to the fields with our team. Our informer had seen Kajiman working in the field earlier in the day, and that is where he took us. We walked like cats, but our legs kept slipping into the muddy fields. But he wasn't there. We sat there waiting for him. We occasionally saw the flash of a torch. The light seemed to be coming towards us but after sometime, it stopped on its track.

Nearby, we found two people in deep sleep. So we went to hide a little further away so as not to disturb them. After a while, *mukhiya* Shriranga Kandel and I decided to find out who they were. They turned out to be a man and a woman. The light from the torch did not seem to near us even after an hour. Then *mukhiya* Shriranga and I again went to have a look at the people sleeping there. The *mukhiya* lifted the blanket to have a look at the man's face and declared, "This is Kajiman." He was able to recognise Kajiman as he had previously been jailed for killing rhinos. We arrested him, and the wife began weeping and wailing.

We then headed for Hathana Darai's house and surrounded it, but he was not there. We were told that he too had gone to water the fields. By this time, it was starting to get noisy. We went to the canal to look for him, but he wasn't there either. Hathana, whom we couldn't find that day, has not been arrested to this day.

We then woke the man who had been sleeping in Kajiman's house and brought him outside. He was Sher Bahadur Tamang who lived in Bartunchet village of Nuwakot district. "I have come from India," he kept telling us.

"How do you know Kajiman Tamang?" we enquired.

"I got to know him in jail," said he.

"Why were you in jail?" we asked.

"It was a rhino case."

We arrested him, too, sure that he was also preparing to poach rhinos.

We interrogated Kajiman at the Janakpur post. He told us nothing. However, when we applied the new interrogation techniques recently learnt in Kathmandu, he started talking. "We have hidden two guns in the jungles of the Amrite post area inside the park. I will show you," he said. We then returned to Sauraha.

Early morning the next day, we started out to look for the guns. We crossed the Rapti River and walked eastwards along the bank past the Amrite post. After walking for an hour, he stopped near a fallen tree and said, "It is here somewhere." We looked around for a while but could not find them.

"Show us the guns or else we will kill you," we threatened. Then he started uncovering the leaves at the base of a small tree. After a layer of sand, we found a plastic package. In the bag, we found guns, ammunition, matches and the like. Since they were wrapped in plastic, they were not damp.

This was the second time I had confiscated guns. The first time was in March-April 2000 while working in the Makalu Barun National Park in Sankhuwasabha district as an assistant warden. Game Scout Harka Bahadur B.K. and I were on our way to the Tamku sector office from Khandbari, the district headquarters of Sankhuwasabha. When we were about to reach Tamku, we heard a gunshot just above the road. We put down our bags on the road, and from two sides tried to approach the place. After climbing a short distance, we saw a man loading his gun. We climbed a little higher and approached him from behind. He was concentrating in the act and was quite shocked when we pounced on him. We first snatched his gun and then took him to Tamku. But his village lay on the way. The villagers, including his daughters, all gathered around. One of his daughters turned out to be a student of Sagarmatha Secondary

School in the village, where I was a volunteer teacher. The little girl wept copiously, but there was no way we were going to release him.

WE INTERROGATED Sher Bahadur at Kasara. He had been jailed previously in a strange case. He had gone to work in Saudi Arabia, where through friends he had learnt that killing rhinos in Chitwan was very profitable business. He then returned to Nepal and headed straight for Chitwan without even going home.

In Narayangadh, he asked all and sundry where rhinos could be found. When he learnt that they were aplenty around the Tiger Tops area, he left for Meghauli village near the resort in a bus.

At Meghauli, too, he had asked the people where rhinos could be found.

"On the banks of the Rapti River and in the national parks," came the reply.

He then started for the Rapti banks.

He asked the cattle herders, "Where do the rhinos come?"

"Right there," they showed him.

"How is a rhino killed?" he had asked.

"Dig a ditch, and when it falls into the ditch, attack it with a spear," they had said.

He then used a pick and a shovel to dig a ditch on the bank of the Rapti and waited for a rhino to fall into it. A good Samaritan who knew of these activities informed the park post at Bhimle. From there, the information was relayed to the park headquarters at Kasara. The team from Kasara found Sher Bahadur along with his shovel. He was arrested and a case was filed against him.

He was jailed for three years, and on release, he thought, "Why go home now?" and left for India instead. His family did not even know that Sher Bahadur who had gone to the Middle East to work was spending his days in a jail in Chitwan. He wasn't able to earn much in India, and while returning, he got stuck at Sunauli (Nepal-India border) due to a week-long strike. He then took the train and walked through Thori of Parsa district (border between Nepal-India) to finally arrive at Kathar, Chitwan.

He and Kajiman from Kathar had been together in Bharatpur jail for rhino poaching. As they had become pals, Sher Bahadur had come directly to Kajiman's house. The week-long strike was still on when we arrested him. He had been there for a few days only, and the two had planned to go rhino poaching already after the rice planting season. Birman was supposed to come from Thori of Parsa to shoot the rhinos.

When we tried to take a statement from Sher Bahadur, he just repeated his old story in a Tamang tone. His story seemed like something out of a movie, and the staff time and again asked him to narrate it. Though there were plans to go rhino poaching, no animal had been killed, and so no evidence could be produced against him. Since the legal provision prohibits filing cases in the park against anyone without evidence of poaching, he was released on guarantee.

Before he left, our staff teased him: "The next time you come to Chitwan, don't even get off the bus. We will arrest you even if we just see you peeping at the national park from a window of a vehicle. Don't even think of poaching rhinos in your dream."

Kajiman was, however, jailed since the confiscated guns had already killed rhinos.

ECOSYSTEM

DURING THE *KHARKHADAI* (cutting and collecting of thatch for roofing and other purposes) period in February-March

2004, a group of villagers from Dibyanagar village landed up in a bush where a tigress was resting with three of her cubs. When the tigress panicked and attacked to save her cubs, one woman was killed. Having tasted the blood of a human, the tigress then began attacking others again and again, and earned the tag of 'man-eater'. The tigress needed to be darted (shot to lose consciousness) for proper investigation. A team that included American scientist Dave Smith darted her after several attempts over days. But the tigress died a day after being darted.

A few days after the tigress died, there were reports that a cub of the tigress had been killed and hung from a tree. A team from the park headquarters, Kasara, went to fetch it.

Again a few days later, I got a call from Kasara while I was in Bharatpur, the district headquarters of Chitwan. It asked me to bring another dead cub that had been found at Gajapur of Dibyanagar.

I went to the Gajapur army post all alone. The villagers had beaten the cub to death even though it had been exhausted from lack of food. Fresh wounds could clearly be observed on its body, and it was clear that it had bled from the nose and mouth. I took the dead cub in my jeep and returned to Kasara, alone. I don't know why, but to me the dead cub felt like my own son. Even today, that little cub's dead body still haunts me, and I keep seeing it. At that moment, I felt like a father whose young son had been mercilessly killed. I was very angry with the villagers, and in that moment of anger, I don't know at what time I reached Kasara.

From Kasara, I phoned Prabhakar Ghimire, a reporter with the *Kantipur* and *The Kathmandu Post* dailies. Two days later, a news item was published in *The Kathmandu Post* which read: Trespasser Kills Tiger in Chitwan Park. The news story named me as the source. Immediately I began getting phone calls. The DNPWC demanded an official explanation for making such a statement to a newspaper. The people who knew me, however, congratulated me for doing the right thing.

What had actually happened was that after a pursuit of several days, the tigress had been finally found at noon, when the team of tiger experts darted her. She had been left in the jungle where it had been found after being examined, her blood sample taken and an antidote given. However, the tigress never regained consciousness and died in her unconscious state. Her cubs, barely 10 months old, had not learnt how to hunt. The hungry cubs would enter the nearby villages and chase the dogs and goats. But they could not kill their prey since they had not learnt how to attack their throats. However, the villagers noticed that they were tigers and killed two of them, ignoring the fact that they were not yet fully grown.

The remaining female cub had survived simply because she had gone to Meghauli village. The villagers of Meghauli too had seen her wandering hungrily in the village. However, they did not kill her like the villagers of Dibyanagar. Instead, they trapped her in a gunny bag and informed the park. A team from the park rescued her. The cub was reared first at Sauraha. That cub, lucky enough to get a new lease of life, was named Narayani and kept at Kasara. She was the centre of attraction for tourists visiting Kasara. However, she had no ecological value anymore. She had only educational, scientific and recreational value and lived just as a tigress. She has now been handed over to the Central Zoo in Kathmandu.

Darting a mother of three cubs at noon in the month of April was actually the cause of the death of the two cubs. Darting rapidly raises the body temperature, and cold water must be poured over the tiger to lower the temperature. However, Dave Smith, a renowned tiger expert, and his team, had not taken any water with them. So much so that they did not even have a thermometer to measure the body temperature. Hurriedly, they had taken the blood sample they needed, performed the necessary examination and left her after a shot of an antidote. They did not wait for her to regain consciousness. As a result, not just the tigress but her cubs too lost their lives for no reason.

Even Nepalese people need permission from the park administration to enter the park. Actually darting endangered wildlife species like a tiger requires permission from the Ministry of Forests, but this team had taken no such permission. Accompanying them was a team of veterinary doctors from the park itself. However, the foreign team had not even allowed them to dismount from their elephants and had insisted on doing everything themselves.

I, as a park official and wildlife technician, was incensed by the irresponsible behaviour that left a tigress dead for no reason and her cubs helpless. I felt it my duty to inform the newspapers of the truth, and for this, an explanation was sought from me. Losing three tigers is a huge loss in terms of conservation.

If national parks were to be managed along the line of community forests, thousands of villagers would go to the forest to collect different products everyday. The above example is enough to predict the state of wildlife in such a scenario. The conservation of rare and endangered wildlife like the tiger and rhino is not possible under just any type of forest management.

Their freedom in the land allocated to them should not be interfered with.

The Narayani River forms the northern border of the Chitwan National Park. The only place where fish are found in the Narayani River is in the national park area. They cannot flourish if too many people start entering the river and interfering with their life cycle. Ultimately, the fish will decrease in number and disappear. If hundreds of people were to mill around the deer while looking for fodder, then the deer would be forced to run for its life. In such a chaotic situation, many pregnant deer would miscarry while the younger ones might break their limbs and become handicapped for life.

Many animals are able to mate only in peaceful environs. These animals cannot possibly procreate if hordes of people carrying *dokos* to cut grass and collect firewood, fodder and fruits were to enter the park. If they cannot mate, then they cannot conceive either, as a result, they stop reproducing. There is that possibility of whole species of fauna becoming extinct in such a case. Hence, animals cannot be conserved in the same place where people come to collect fodder and grass for their livestock.

The Asian Paradise Flycatcher, which comes here all the way from Sri Lanka in spring, makes a small nest on small branches of short trees. Where would these birds live if the trees were to be stripped bare of their leaves? And for  what purpose would they continue to fly to Nepal all the way from Sri Lanka? There are many other species of birds which make their nests on the ground. When people cut the grass, they destroy the nests, too. When people divide the dry and fallen trees of the forest among themselves, where will the beautiful birds and snakes build their homes? Where will the termites live, and what will the birds and bears eat? How will we be able to see the whole ecosystem resting on a single log of wood? And if they cannot see this, then why would tourists visit our country?

It has been said that several ethnic and disadvantaged communities like the Bote, Majhi and Musahar earn their living fishing in the Narayani River. If it was that simple, then these communities would have also settled on the northern banks of the river, beyond Sikhrauli in Nawalparasi district, which marks the border of the park. However, they have not settled there, because though the same Narayani River flows there, there are no fish in that part of the river. That part of the Narayani is outside the national park, and there have been no conservation efforts there. As a result, the community of fishermen has congregated in the area between Sikhrauli and Triveni, both of which mark the borders of the park. However, they do not realise that it is harmful to poison the waters of the Narayani River. They are also ignorant of the fact that fish lay their eggs and raise their young between the months of April and August, which is when they should avoid fishing. They also ignore the advice to use handmade nets instead of nets that catch fishes of all sizes.

Ultimately, neither the livelihood of these people nor the biodiversity can be protected if we continue to act with such disregard for the ecosystem. We should put a stop to human activities that upset the routine of wild animals. Nobody has the right to stop the crocodile from basking for hours in the sunshine on the river banks or other animals from raising their young without any worry. Not every part of the country

can become a protected area. So in the land designated as a "protected area" for biodiversity and wildlife conservation, human activities should be limited.

WITHIN THE AREA of the Chitwan National Park, the rivers Narayani, Rapti and Reu, and the trees that fall into the rivers play an important role in the conservation of the ecosystem and biodiversity. While I was the assistant warden and while officiating as the chief warden, many teachers from the nearby schools came with requests for logs for their schools. Once, a delegation comprising the headmaster of Prabhat Higher Secondary School, located at Shukranagar village near the park, approached us.

"Our kids are getting wet as we don't have doors and windows," they said. "So give us the wood of the fallen trees in the park or, if not, the trees that have fallen into the rivers."

Though their request was perfectly reasonable, I could not give them the trees that had fallen into the rivers. Not because I did not have the right, but because the role that the trees played in the river ecosystem is very important. The trees that fall into the rivers have their roots in the water, and as a result, they reduce the flow of current in the river. Usually, whirlpools form in such areas, and the river becomes deeper. The fish lay eggs and rear their youngs more easily in such deep waters. When fishes become plentiful, it means plenty of food for the crocodiles.

Similarly, birds like the kingfisher, darter, egret, heron and stork, which depend on fish, also flourish in such areas. Kingfishers, in fact, wait on the branches of fallen trees, and dive into the water to pick up fish. It is not possible for kingfishers to do the same from the tall and upright trees on the banks. Bears come in search of termites in the fallen trees. Otters also wait on the same trees to catch fish, and tigers, in turn, come in search of these very otters. The same process can be observed on the fallen trees inside the jungle, too.

When I explained to the delegations how the fragile ecosystem rested on the rotting trees or logs, they nodded in agreement, but they again insisted that they needed wood for the doors and windows of the school. I then promised to get them wood from some other place, i.e., the buffer zone forests.

Sometimes, there have been suggestions that the national parks should be managed by the local community. Many people think that this is a good idea. However, the same concepts, systems and methods cannot be applied in managing the diverse forest resources of the country. Different concepts, policies, programmes, systems and methods are required for managing the forest resources as per the different geographical locations, importance of biodiversity, aims and needs of the local communities.

SAD DEATH OF A COLLEAGUE

I HAD GONE TO Kathmandu on official business. On Baisakh 1,[1] 2061 (April 13, 2004), I exchanged New Year greetings with my colleagues at Kasara by phone. *Mukhiya* Shriranga was a very close friend of mine, and we had exchanged best wishes. That very day I was returning to Chitwan from Kathmandu when upon reaching Bharatpur, Ranger Bishnu called me to say, "Shriranga has had a motorcycle accident."

I hurried to the clinic where he was admitted. He had suffered injuries on his head and was throwing up. I talked to him and asked him not to be anxious. He looked disheartened.

The computerized tomography scan showed blood clots in the brain. The doctors advised us to take him to Kathmandu. We decided to take him to the Norvic Hospital and consult a neurologist. He underwent an operation on April 16, 2004, and the following day, he passed away.

His dedication, diligence, skills, knowledge and dexterity in rhino conservation were unmatched. His contribution to the Anti-poaching Unit was unparalleled. Rhino conservation work suffered due to his death.

Actually, *mukhiya* Shriranga had suffered a head injury in his childhood and was taking medicines for it. On New Year's Day (2061 B.S.), his motorcycle had skidded at a turning near the Rapti bridge while going from Kasara to Jagatpur. The helmet got detached and his head struck the ground and suffered internal injuries. Since the woman riding pillion too was injured, he had tried to help her, but while doing so, he himself had fainted. He was first taken to the Ganesh Pharmacy at Patihani and then to Bharatpur. In Bharatpur, when I said, "Don't worry, nothing will happen to you," he looked at me for a moment. I still remember that scene vividly.

---

[1]   According to the Nepali calendar, the New Year begins on Baisakh 1 which falls in mid-April.

HORN IN A POT

IN MID-APRIL, gunshots had been heard a kilometre and a half away from the army headquarters at Kasara. However, nobody went to investigate the incident then. The patrol team found a dead rhino the next day with its horn missing. This was shameful. When rhinos were being killed so near the army headquarters, how could our unarmed posts save the rhinos? This showed the state of our security measures. In fact, I don't recall a single incident where the patrol team was able to find rhino poachers, chase or even come face to face with them.

Barring a few cases, our informers could not provide us with information about the poachers before they entered the rhino habitat. They only informed us after the poaching incidents and that too only at times. If 10 rhinos were killed, we could only get information about poachers and smugglers for one rhino from our informers. It was almost impossible to figure out exactly who was running the poaching business. We did not have enough means or resources to pay the informers sufficiently. We were dependent on the TAL programme, TRCP and ITNC. We could only recruit informers if we received funds from these organisations.

Also, cooperation between the different agencies was weak. Sharing of information among the District Forest Office, Armed Forest Guard Training Centre at Tikauli, the police, administration and other government and non-government organisations was not very efficient.

On April 17, a team of soldiers and park staff had gone for regular patrolling. A team of poachers, including Jit Bahadur Moktan, who had killed a rhino and stolen the horn just a month back, had arrived at Tamor Lake to hunt rhinos again. The team found them cooking at the site. Two of them escaped while our team attempted to arrest them. Only Jit Bahadur was arrested with his semi-automatic home-made pistol.

It was the first time that poachers were found and arrested within the park by our patrol team. They had hidden the horn of the rhino killed the previous month inside a large vessel, known as a *ghyampo* used for storing grains, in Khairang village of Makwanpur. But there was no way we could go to the village immediately. With armed soldiers accompanying us, the possibility of an encounter with the Maoist rebels was high.

After Jit Bahadur was found in the jungle, we guessed that others too might be hiding there. So a joint patrolling team was sent out the following day. Another team of poachers had shot and wounded a rhino in the jungles of the Churia hills. A few of them were sighted, but when they were surrounded and shot at, only Ram Bahadur Bam of Thori could be arrested. One home-made gun was confiscated from him. The rest managed to escape.

Ram Bahadur told us that Aitaram and Sukhe Bote from Gardi village (Madi) had accompanied him. We relayed the message to the informer from Madi, and a team from the Bankatta post arrested them on April 22, 2004. They had all been arrested previously for killing rhinos and then released from jail. Kajiman Tamang, too, had been in jail with them.

Our team, led by Ranger Bishnu and Captain Bishal Shah, had arrested them two months before when they had gone to meet Kajiman at Kathar after being released from jail. They were brought to Sauraha, and when they were taken to the elephant keeper's kitchen for their meal, one of them had escaped while going out on the pretext of attending to the call of nature. While our team had run to give him chase, the other one had managed to escape, too.

Notorious Poacher

Bir Bahadur Praja called Birman was a name mentioned by most of the poachers we arrested. It seemed as if he was the one who led the rhino smugglers, and all poaching could be controlled if we could arrest this one man. We had tried many times to arrest him, but all in vain.

Anil Ghising and Jhalendra Gurung, who had been arrested for rhino poaching and then killed two years before, had mentioned Birman's name during their interrogation in the army barracks. We had been on the lookout for him after Rajan Praja's arrest. Our informers told us that after the raid on his and his in-laws' house at Birendranagar, he had run away to Thori, Parsa district near the Nepal-India border. Previously, he was used to throwing parties in Onegroup village (Birendranagar), feasting on deer meat, getting drunk and harassing the villagers. He led a luxurious life from the money he earned by poaching and even encouraged other youths to poach with him. "Come with me if you want to earn money. Why do you work hard for nothing, why do you want to go abroad?" he told them.

I sent an informer to Thori to identify exactly where Birman was staying. When this informer returned, I sent out another team of two members to ascertain it. After they returned, our Anti-poaching Unit left on April 28. I reached Madi at 11 in the morning with two friends, Game Scout Buddhinath Lamicchane and Bhimraj Sedhai, and from there, we proceeded to the Bagai post with two informers. I got in touch with the second lieutenant there and informed him of my reason for going to Thori. "If I find that man there, I will return in the evening and will need your help," I told him.

We reached Thori, which I had assumed to be a sprawling market, noisy with people and vehicles all around. But it turned out to be just the opposite. It was quite empty. There were just a few shops and a couple of buses at the bus stop. We parked at one end of the bus stop and walked to the Indian part of Thori.

We had a talk at the edge of a jungle across the border. After returning to the Nepali side, we sent informers to the village where Birman lived to find out what he was doing. We then stopped at a tea shop for some refreshment.

"The man we want is here," the informers said. Now we would have to return to the Bagai post for the soldiers.

When we were returning to Bagai, our vehicle got stuck on the bank of a stream, and a tyre got punctured. It was late evening. I had never changed a tyre in my life, and I did not even have a driver with me that day. But I had seen other people changing tyres and so started to remove the tyre with the help of the two staff members. When we replaced the tyre, we found that it was deflated.

I had left the jeep at the Thori market, thinking it to be as safe as Narayangadh or Tandi. However, some hooligans had hammered a nail into one of the tyres and deflated the spare one.

We were in quite a fix. There was no place nearby where we could repair the tyres. Seeing our predicament, the villagers gathered around and told me that I would have to go to the Indian side to repair the tyres. I decided to send two of the villagers to the Indian side along with my staff. When I promised them money, they left, rolling the tyre between them. They told me that it would take about an hour to reach there. We calculated that it would be around 10 at night by the time we got the tyre repaired. "This is hashish smuggling route, it's very dangerous," the villagers said.

Bhimraj left for the house of Min Prasad Gurung, chairman of the Thori Buffer Zone User Committee. After a while, a motorcycle approached us with its headlights on. It was Min Prasad, and he had with him a hand pump to inflate the tyres. We pumped up the spare tyre and got it ready. Min Prasad then left to cook food in his home, and we left for the Indian side to look for our staff. We started waiting for them at a shop near the road. It was 10 by the time they returned with the repaired tyre. Then we went to Min Prasad's house, where we were served dinner. After dinner, I talked to Min Prasad about the probability of nabbing Birman that night without the help of the army. However, there were risks as the area lay near the border, and so we returned to Bagai.

It was midnight by the time we reached the Bagai post. I gave a detailed description of our situation and asked for help. It was 1 at night by the time an army team got ready. The jeep was small, and there were 16 people in the team, including 11 soldiers, two staff members, two informers and me. And there was the army communication set. The jeep could actually accommodate just three people in the front, including the driver, and six people in the back. As there was no room inside, five soldiers climbed on to the hood, and I had to ask Buddhi and Bhimraj to sleep at the post. But they were keen on going in the operation. Generally most of the staff are very excited to participate in the anti-poaching operations although high risks, challenges, dangers and threats to life are involved. There was always that danger of coming face to face with the Maoist rebels or being ambushed.

The road was only fit for driving larger vehicles, and we were quite uncomfortable. Our small jeep was buffeted by the huge ditches on the road, and when it veered towards the edge, we felt as if it was going to overturn.

It was half past two in the morning when we reached Thori. We asked our local informer, who happened to be our own informer's contact, to show us Birman's house, the shelter. We raided the house, but he was not there. We asked the people of the house, "Where do the people from Chitwan stay?" They pointed to a house nearby. A woman was sleeping outside.

"Where is your husband?" we asked her.

"He has gone out... he is suffering from diarrhoea," she replied.

"Where does Birman live?"

"There," she pointed to a thatched house nearby.

I hurried to that house. There was a couple sleeping in the open on the ground floor. I knew that Birman went by a different name here, so I called him by that name.

"I am not that person," he said.

"All right, if you are not him, then you are Birman."

"I am not Birman either."

His wife too woke up when I started questioning him. I had seen her before in Birendranagar and recognised her immediately. She too recognised me.

"Isn't this your husband?" I asked her.

"Yes," she replied.

Back on May 30, 2003, we had made a search of Birman's house in Onegroup, Birendranagar and gone through the photographs. And that was why I was able to recognise Birman Praja. We had finally captured the poacher that we had been on the lookout for. We also arrested Prem Bahadur Lama who had been protecting Birman by giving him shelter in his house. We searched Prem's house but found nothing. The man, whose wife had said he had diarrhoea, had managed to run away while we were raiding the adjacent house.

We now had to arrest some other poachers in Ichhanagar village at Thori on the basis of the statement given by Ram Bahadur Bal of the village, who had been arrested a month ago in April. They had gone to poach rhinos with Ram Bahadur but had managed to escape from the jungle. During our search of Ichhanagar, we came across a thatched hut where an old man and a middle-aged woman lived. It was Ram Bahadur's house. His wife was not aware of his arrest. The criminals who had managed to escape had already fled to India. We raided a few houses but found no one. It was morning by the time we were through with our operation.

There was no way everyone could fit in the small jeep anymore, now that Birman, his wife and house owner had been added to the group. I ferried everyone in turns and got them to the Amuwa post at Thori. The army had deserted the post because of the Maoist rebels. Birman told us that he had hidden guns in the jungle about two hours away from that place. We decided to go and look for the guns right away so that we wouldn't have to come back such a long distance. We walked upwards along the bank of the stream with Birman. After nearly an hour of

walking, inside a hole in a tree we found a gun, iron rod bullets and matches wrapped in plastic. When we found the gun, we forgot all our fatigue, sadness, hunger and sleep. The lieutenant, too, was elated that the mission had been successful.

When we returned to the Amuwa post, it was already broad daylight, and it was around half past 11. We had neither washed nor had any breakfast. A local bus was getting ready to leave for Madi. We decided that some of us should go on the bus while others, including Birman, would travel in the jeep. I was exhausted from hunger, sleep and fatigue all combined. As soon as our jeep set out for Bagai, heavy rains started pouring. It was difficult to even see the road in the heavy rains. Besides, the Toyota land cruiser jeep was old, and slippery red mud covered the roads. Also, the jeep's wiper had stopped functioning, and I could see virtually nothing. I had to pull the windshield down and drive with my head outside in order to see the road, and as a result, I was soaked to the skin.

At that moment, I thought of God. Birman and his gang worshipped Goddess Manakamana before setting out to poach. I even wondered whether we were facing such difficulties because we had arrested such a notorious poacher. "No," I decided. "All living things, including the souls of the rhinos, came from the greatest God, Krishna. Maybe it is raining because the gods are celebrating the arrest of a notorious poacher who had killed dozens of rhinos."

It was 1 in the afternoon when we finally reached the Bagai post. The rains hadn't stopped, and our meal was cooking. Everyone was worried in Kasara because there had been no radio contact all night with the army headquarters. I took a brief nap tired as I was. It was 4 when we finished eating, and we left for Kasara.

The small Madi stream was flooded by the heavy rains. The jeep, though old, was quite strong and did not give trouble although we were expecting it to break down any moment. Near the Reu River, however, it got stuck along with the other vehicles. We then walked to the Bankatta post, asked for another jeep from Kasara and got there only in the evening.

Poachers sound menacing only until they are nabbed, as in this case, too. We used to wonder what Birman would be like, but after arresting him, he turned out to be a flea. He admitted to having killed 14 rhinos. He named everyone who had gone poaching with him. He didn't hide anything from us. Either he was regretting what he had done or trying to win us over with his frankness. His penalty should have been reduced, considering his frankness, but the chief warden sentenced him to a full jail term of 15 years with a fine of $1,377.

A colleague who was guarding the prisoners told me one day that Birman wanted to meet me.

"I don't know how to say this, sir, but there is a powerful leader involved. I don't know if you people can arrest him," Birman said.

"Don't be scared, tell me everything, and we will arrest him if we have proof," I replied.

I was expecting some big names, but all he said was, "Madhav Giri, Chairman of the Kalika Community Forest, and Kedar Giri, his brother, are the ones who initially taught me how to poach rhinos."

Ranger Madhav and I left for Birendranagar in east Chitwan

on May 3. We sent an informer to see if they were there. We were told that Kedar was at a house construction site and Madhav in the community forest office. We went up to Kedar and said, "We are from the District Forest Office, please take us to your brother."

When we reached the community forest office, I said, "There is a programme at the District Forest Office, and we have come to get the chairman." Thus, Madhav too climbed into our jeep.

"I will get off here," said Kedar when we neared his house.

"Have a Coke with us at the bazaar," we told him. Again at the bazaar, Kedar insisted on getting off. Finally, we told him why we were there, and both of them were stunned to learn that they had just been arrested.

BIHARI IN A NET

OUR INFORMER FROM Kawasoti informed us that tiger skins and rhino horns were being sold at Triveni, the south-western part of the park close to the Indo-Nepal border. "I have found out everything, we should approach them as customers," he told me.

I reached Triveni with him on August 11. First of all, we got in touch with the army barracks there and sought their help should the need arise. Then we booked rooms at the Triveni Sangam Hotel, and on the same day set off for Balmikinagar, Tanki bazaar in India.

On the right side of Tanki bazaar, we came across a house of a man of Nepali origin. The house was made of mud and had a roof of thatch. A tall, dark boy in his late teens arrived with a sack on a cycle and entered the house. Inside, in a room, he opened the sack and showed us two skins that might have been of two or three-year-old tigers. They were well preserved with preservatives and were quite soft. This was the first time in my life I was posing as a buyer of a tiger skin.

"I will get you ten more skins if you buy these," said the boy.

These guys are going to finish all the tigers, I thought to myself. "From where?" I asked him.

"From a village near the Bareli market (in India)."

If an ordinary broker could procure so many skins, one could well imagine just how severe tiger poaching is.

The boy pointed at the broker and said, "I only got this stuff because he had been asking for it for several days. It is someone else's, and I have already paid for it, so pay me immediately."

He seemed worried that we might not be paying him right away. My aim was to take him into confidence, and I immediately gave him Indian Rs. 10,000 ($220), or Nepalese Rs. 16,000.

"I will get you more stuff," he told me.

"Keep the money, and the stuff, too, I will take them all together later," I told him.

The main broker had also mentioned about the horns, and I asked him to bring those too the next time we were meeting. We returned to Kasara, promising to return in two days.

Two days later, we again went to Triveni. I would have to show them some money, and hence, I had borrowed $826 from the owner of Sangam Shirting Suiting in Narayangadh. We had a game scout with us too this time. As in the previous case, we talked to the barracks and then left for the Indian side of Tanki bazaar.

Indian brokers there told us that we would have to go 90 kilometre inland in India to get the horn. Our informer left on a motorcycle with one of them to confirm that the horn existed. I spent the whole day with a few burly Biharis and a couple of Nepalese in a tea shop at Tanki. For lunch, we, however, came to the Nepal side.

At 4 in the afternoon, it started raining, but still there was no sign of the man who had left at 8 in the morning. I had also given some money to the informer. I was worried that someone might have looted the money and abandoned him somewhere. As evening fell, I climbed onto a rickshaw and started for Nepal in the rain. The informer arrived minutes after me, and so did the Nepali and Bihari brokers who were with me during the day.

I had asked the soldiers to stand ready in civil dress at the border. They were there and started moving around when they saw me. I had not made any signs to them, but they seemed to be preparing to come and talk to me. I did not want the brokers to notice that I was a friend of the soldiers. So I told the brokers, "Soldiers in civil dress are milling around, we should leave." They agreed and demanded some money. I gave them $14. Our informer in the meantime was talking to someone else on the other side. "Let us leave," I said. The informer asked the other man to come to the Triveni Sangam Hotel the following day.

It was decided that the tiger skins that we had paid for in advance would be brought over the next day. At around 11 the following morning, the Bihari boy arrived with both skins in a bag. I was supposed to pay him the rest after deducting the $220. It would not be appropriate to have him in the hotel for long since the horn dealer would also be arriving soon. So I gave the money to the informer and instructed him to go with the boy, pay him on the way, and once he was on his way, point him out to the army.

I was waiting for the horn broker at the hotel. Suddenly the informer arrived huffing and puffing. "The boy escaped, I asked the army to pursue him, but they refused."

What actually happened was that the informer had taken the boy along, promising to give him the money. When they were in front of the barracks, he had asked the sentry to arrest the boy. When the sentry did not pay any heed, he himself had caught the boy by his arms, but the boy escaped. The sentry was not wrong in ignoring the request because he could not arrest someone without an order from his superior. Besides, it was during the period of the Maoist insurgency. If the informer had only paid the boy and then called the army as instructed, then the boy would have walked past the barracks and been arrested. But he was able to escape as our informer was unwilling to give him the money.

"Let's put this behind us. Now we will talk to the horn broker and arrest him," I said.

The horn broker arrived in a while. The informer talked to him, and he left on a motorcycle. We drove behind him in the jeep.

"What is the plan?" I asked the informer.

"We are supposed to go and look at the stuff. He has quoted $9,642 for the horn, and I have assured him we will pay him there and leave." But we had with us neither the money nor any firearms. There was no way we could arrest him. Under the circumstances, I formulated a different plan of operation and instructed the informer accordingly.

The horn broker had seen only the two of us, but there was another staff Pauwari Yadav with us in the jeep. Near the *Sisau* forest, I told him to get off the vehicle without being seen by the broker and instructed him to have soldiers in civil dress come to the hotel. "Arrest him when I signal."

From Triveni, we proceeded to Rupauliya village. The horn broker parked near Rupauliya School, and I parked there, too. "Stay here," he said in Hindi.

As instructed, our informer bargained with him. "We want to check if the horn is real. If it is genuine, then we will pay you some advance. And then we will go to the hotel and fetch the remaining money."

"OK," said he and left on the motorcycle.

After about 10 minutes, he came from the direction of the school with a bag in his hand. After approaching us, he asked us to come to the bushes. From a plastic bag, he took out an object wrapped in carbon paper. I took it in my hand and inspected it. The originality of a horn can be ascertained by looking at the base. Other parts of the horn can be imitated but not the base because there is a net like structure. On seeing the net like structure at the base, I knew that this was real stuff.

"Give me the advance, fast," he said. I looked around and saw two people peeping from behind a school wall. I assumed they were his men and paid him $689. He walked away with the horn as well as the money. We were watching him go, and when he had reached a little farther, he turned to us and shouted "Go now, you guys leave."

"Oh no, this Bihari has taken the horn as well as the money," I thought.

This was the first time that I had looked at a horn with a smuggler, and he wasn't being arrested. I was tense should he try to escape after all this drama.

After turning the jeep around, we waited on the way. He arrived after a long time and said, "Let us go."

Ahead of us, he was driving his Hero Honda motorcycle at breakneck speed. I drove rickety old Pajero jeep, the dirt road was full of ditches, but still I was trying my best to keep up with him. I was afraid that he might get to the hotel ahead of us and run away on seeing the army.

There was a small by-lane before reaching Triveni, and he quickly took the road. Our jeep would not fit in the lane. I was tense again. I turned the jeep towards the hotel instead. A tractor with a corpse was coming that way, which blocked my way for a while. My heart beat fast as I wondered where he might have gone. But luckily, I reached the hotel just when he was entering the hotel with his helmet in his hand. They say the sight of a corpse brings good luck, which turned out to be true.

We entered the hotel together, closed the door and pretended to chat for a while. Then we signalled to our staff and soldiers present there. According to the plan, we all were to be arrested on suspicion that we were Maoists. We did not want anyone to learn of the horn broker's arrest, at least not those people who had possession of the horn at the moment.

When we reached the barracks, the captain and several other soldiers were standing outside. When the captain had heard that the tiger skin broker had escaped, he had ordered the borders to be sealed and had ordered a thorough search at several places, including Ranibari village close to the Indian border. He was quite angry with us. "You guys don't inform us of what you are doing and work at random," he ranted.

I gave him full details of the incident and told him that a horn broker had been arrested. He was quite pleased with the news.

Now we had to reach the man who actually had the horn. The man that we had arrested was Rajbanshi Kaji from Daruwabari village in India. He told us that he had left the horn with someone in Rupauliya village (in Nepal). We had to leave immediately before that man learned of Rajbanshi's arrest. Also, the man might run away if he saw too many people approaching him. Just the two of us had gone to check the horn. So we decided that only three of us would go on a bike. A soldier drove the bike, while an armed *jamdar* sat behind with Rajbanshi sandwiched in between. They would make the arrest once Rajbanshi pointed out the person, and would shoot if he tried to flee. More people would follow them in jeeps for backup.

Our jeep with the team of soldiers followed them. When we reached Rupauliya village, they had already arrested a man, Jayanarayan Kumal, who owned a pharmacy there.

"Where is the horn?" we asked.

He had given the horn to someone else for safekeeping.

He took us to the house and asked a woman there, "Where is that stuff?"

She took us inside and unlocked a wooden cabinet. She took out the horn that Rajbanshi showed us near the school and gave it to us. We should have arrested her too for keeping the horn, but we did not as she was a woman.

"Where is the money we gave you?" we asked Jayanarayan.

"This guy took it away," he replied.

"Which guy?"

"Gangaram Chaudhari."

"Where is he?"

"Must have gone home."

But Gangaram wasn't in his house. We learnt that he had been drinking only a while ago, but nobody knew where he had gone after that. It was not safe to stay in that place for long. Since night was falling, and the soldiers were getting tense, we left. I regretted not being able to arrest Gangaram with the $689, but we confiscated a motorcycle that was equal in value.

The next day we left for Kasara after our meal. Since we were near Bihar of India, we did not deem it safe to go on our own. We reserved a bus, and a group of soldiers accompanied us till Bardaghat, Nawalparasi. A mine blast proof vehicle escorted us to Bharatpur, Chitwan. From Bharatpur, the informer, I and the criminals drove to Kasara in our jeep. The staff arrived behind our jeep on the confiscated motorcycle. This was the first time that I had arrested a criminal red handed with a horn.

That horn belonged to a rhino that was killed at Gaida Khasa in the western part of the national park. Rajbanshi's team used to gang up with the Nepalese, come near the Temple Tiger Lodge and Gaida Khasa area from India and kill rhinos. After the arrest of Rajbanshi, rhino killing stopped in that area. Narsingh Chaudhari from Banda Khola village of Nawalparasi district, who was also in his team, was later arrested, but Kedar Musahar from India has till now eluded arrest.

In this way, we had arrested two people along with one horn, two tiger skins and a motorcycle with the help of the Durgabhanjan Company of the Nepal Army at Triveni, Nawalparasi. The commander-in-chief of the army later sent me a letter of appreciation for accomplishing the task.

According to Rajbanshi Kaji, Narsingh Chaudhari of Makar, Nawalparasi was also a rhino poacher. He worked with Kedar Musahar and killed rhinos in the park by entering the forests from Triveni. Our informer tipped us off that he was coming to Bardaghat on August 26.

"Three men are walking on the road," said our informer. "Among them, the tall, plump and dark man is Narsingh Chaudhari."

We arrested him on the road and put him in the vehicle.

We were going uphill on the road to Daunne towards Chitwan, when Narsingh Chaudhari tried to jump out from the window. Though our staff were stationed on both windows of the vehicle, he had already gotten his head out. He was so strong that it was tough even for four people to get him back in the vehicle. We then tied his hands with a rope. Had he tried this stunt earlier, we would not have been able to arrest him at all. But since I had given him no time to think and had shoved him into the vehicle, he gave no trouble. He did hesitate to get into the jeep, but I had held the tip of my mobile to his waist and threatened to shoot him if he tried to run away. He looked scared at that moment. But once in the jeep, he probably understood that we did not have guns, and so he tried to escape.

Upon interrogation at Kasara, he admitted to killing more than six rhinos with a team of Indians in the western part of the park - Gaida Khasa and Temple Tiger Lodge area.

One evening, the custody cell was opened for mealtime. All of a sudden there was a power cut. Immediately, there were shouts of, "Escaped! Escaped!" On hearing the shouts, I immediately ran with an emergency light towards the place. While fleeing, Narsingh happened to bump into our kitchen staff Som Bahadur Darai, who was bringing matches and candles. Som Bahadur tried to jump onto him and catch him by the neck. In doing so, the two fell down in opposite directions. Other colleagues then dragged Narsingh Chaudhari back. In their anger, my colleagues started beating him up for trying to escape, but I stopped them. He might have died if a dozen people had beaten him up like that.

A Photo Helps

WE HAD TRIED many times to arrest a poacher called Shankar Praja, but we were unsuccessful. He was very clever and arrogant, too. Though he had a house in Padampur village, Chitwan, he was living with his second wife in Raksirang in Makwanpur. He would come to the park to look for bamboo shoots and asparagus, and fish in the Manahari stream.

Our informer told us that Shankar was in the village. Though I was alone, I talked to the army. At 9 in the evening on October 30, I headed northwards from Manahari with 22 soldiers from the Bhandara Base Camp and two informers. There were a lot of *bhailo* singers at Manahari as it was *Tihar* (Festival of Lights). We took another path so that they would not see us. This path, which we were walking for the first time, turned out to be very difficult. Since this was a stronghold of the Maoists, we dared not switch on our torchlights. After an hour of going uphill and down, we saw a line of torchlights beaming in our direction from another hill. We paused on seeing the lights. The army lieutenant insisted that we return. "We will be in greater danger if we return the way we've come, so it's better we move forward," I told him.

We reached Raksirang after walking for nearly two hours. As we neared the village, the barking of dogs got louder, and we had to take precaution while walking. We couldn't even see the people near us, as we were in the midst of a dense cornfield. As we neared the house of Shankar's in-laws, we surrounded a few houses and raided them. We could not find Shankar in the house indicated by the informer. We found a boy in another house, who professed his ignorance about Shankar's whereabouts. I began to panic. A few colleagues were interrogating a man in yet another house. A woman with a small baby sat in a corner of the room, while in another corner, a young man was trying to prove his innocence.

As there was only an oil lamp in the room, I had to shine the torchlight on his face to see who it was.

"What is your name?" I asked

He mentioned some other name.

"Aren't you Shankar Praja?" I asked again.

"No, I am Shankar Thapa, not Praja," said he.

"You liar," I shot back.

"No, sir, I am not Shankar Praja," he insisted, but I recognised him. My informer had shown me a photo of him in a studio at Manahari. "Let this be for remembrance should I die," Shanker had told the studio owner and his friends. He knew that he could get killed any day.

We arrested him as well as a couple of his helpers. It was half past midnight by the time we returned with him.

We were scared of an encounter with the Maoists on the way, but thankfully nothing of the sort happened. We were relieved once we got to the highway. Then we came to Sunachuri village, surrounded Surya Bahadur Tamang's house and asked him to open the door. When he refused, we forced our way inside and arrested him.

Earlier, Surya Bahadur had managed to escape while we arrested Til Bahadur. Surya had sold a horn of a rhino killed by his father-in-law, the notorious poacher Gorey Ghalan. It was raining, and we had gone to his house through the jungle soaked to the skin upon being informed that he was playing cards there. But he happened to be at a neighbour's house, and he had hid there when he saw us approach. We had arrested his wife, but she had escaped while we were attending to another man. Later, our informers told us that Surya had gathered his people and divided the money from the sale of the horn.

After arresting Surya Bahadur, we proceeded to another place to arrest two more people for poisoning a herd of deer a week ago. By this time, there were 30 people in our Mitsubishi jeep, counting the five additions. It was very cramped. I was very tired, and sometimes the vehicle lurched when I drove. It was half past four in the morning when we arrived at the Bhandara Security Base Camp. I decided to take the culprits to Kasara and had a few soldiers accompany me.

COLONEL'S ECCENTRICITY

AFTER THE ARREST of a man with a horn at Triveni, many people volunteered to give us information. On December 13, we received news that a horn was being sold. I was asked to come to Bardaghat to investigate. I was at that time officiating as the chief warden as the chief warden was in Kathmandu. I left for Bardaghat early in the morning with a couple of staff members.

There, our informer pointed out the brokers. I waited for them at a bus stand on the East-West Highway near the crossroad on the way to Triveni. Our staff Laptan Tharu and Sukaram Darai stood nearby. After a while, the horn brokers passed us on their way to the jungle. There were two of them. Deciding that this was the right moment, I held them both by their shirt collars from behind. Laptan and Sukaram also approached and held them. We then started for Bharatpur.

"Where's the horn?" we asked when we were some distance way.

"It is with a man at the bazaar," they told me. We returned to Bardaghat and looked for the man, but he was not there. We then decided to search them instead. In the pant pocket of Devilal Aidi was the horn. It was small, weighing only about 200 grams. This was the second time that I was confiscating a horn.

We reached Kasara, happy to have arrested a criminal along with a horn. A soldier from the barracks arrived in the midst and said, "Major Ganga Khadka from the barracks wants to see you."

Upon reaching the barracks, the major told me, "The colonel is very angry with you. He has ordered me to take you into custody and put you in the quarter guard."

I was shocked and did not know what to say. After a while I asked him, "Why? What have I done to deserve this?"

"He is angry that you took your office vehicle and left without taking his permission."

I was astonished. Our office was not accountable to the army. As an officer I was not answerable to Colonel Ajit Thapa, but those were the days of the king's rule, and he assumed that all officers should obey the army. On many occasions, he had repeated to me an incident in the Bardia National Park, where he had an assistant forest officer put in custody for 25 days because he did not obey the colonel. He was probably trying to warn me that the same could happen to me.

Since I had not made any mistakes, I did not contact the colonel. When we came face to face later, he did not mention the subject. But he apparently complained about me to the chief warden and Major Ganga.

AT BARDAGHAT, along with Devilal from Mugu, we had also arrested Krishna Prasad Pudasaini. Upon interrogation, they told us that they had procured the horn from Rajendra Bhattarai and Shyam Kumar Shrestha. Then with help from Krishna Prasad, we arrested both Rajendra and Shyam Kumar. Shyam Kumar, in turn, told us that he had gotten the horn from Makansingh B.K., who was a private clerk at the Land Revenue Office.

When we found that Makansingh was involved in buying and selling land, we visited his house on the pretext of buying land. But he had gone away to his daughter's place. We followed him there and cajoled him into coming to Kasara with us, asking him to show us the land. After a few days, he confessed from where he got the horn. He named Ramsharan Lamsal from Jagatpur village, and we turned up at his home as chicken buyers.

Ramsharan, in turn, revealed that Santaram Bote from Ghailaghari at Jagatpur had given him the horn. Santaram, however, had already fled when he heard of Makansingh's arrest. According to Ramsharan, Santaram had told him that he had taken the horn of a rhino he had found dead.

"COME AND ARREST brokers dealing in tiger bones," said our informers from Triveni, and three of us reached there on December 29. But the bones did not arrive that day. So we left Game Scout Ambar Bahadur Shikari there.

The next day, December 30, an Indian man called Bhola Shah walked straight into the hotel with the bones in a sack. We arrested him right away and brought him to Kasara.

DISCLOSURE OF BRIBERY

RELATIVES OF Til Bahadur Gurung made every effort to get him freed from jail. In fact, they had started to visit my in-laws' house, since they too lived in Chainpur village. Til Bahadur even sent a letter to my mother-in-law, addressing her as sister. She showed me the letter, in which he had pleaded with her to secure his release. "The decision is not in my hands, only the chief can decide this," I told her.

After that, his family told my father-in-law and mother-in-law that they had paid *subba* Uttam Prasad Kharel $2,755 for the release of Til Bahadur, but he was still in jail. My in-laws also told me that Til Bahadur's nephew Purna Bahadur Gurung was willing to reveal everything. I thought I should see him.

I had been hearing that *subba* Uttam Prasad accepted money from rhino poachers and smugglers with assurances to solve their cases. But I had found no evidence so far. The informers had told me that a senior game scout, who had gone to deliver a summons to an accused, had met his relatives and demanded money at the insistence of Uttam Prasad to see the case.

Once Gupte Bhujel's son came to Kasara and had complained to Major Ganga Khadka that Uttam Prasad had demanded $689 just to look into the case. When Major Ganga asked me about this, I was shocked, and on reaching office, I asked for *subba* Uttam Prasad. The *subba* told me that, on the contrary, he had informed Gupte's son that a fine of upto $689 could be slapped by the park on his father. I believed the *subba* at that time.

But later, I found that this was far from the truth. The *subba* had indeed asked for a bribe. Later it was also found that he took similar bribes from nearly every criminal. He had accepted $2,755 from Chet Prasad Kharel in two installments, before and after the case was solved. I only learnt about this when Yamunath Acharya, chairperson of the Buffer Zone User Committee, was released from jail. He had been accused of giving a motorcycle to the Maoist rebels, and in jail he had learnt who bribed whom and for what purpose.

The verdict of Chief Warden Shivaraj Bhatta in favour of Tanzing Nima, Nagendra Shrestha, Chet Prasad Kharel and Chandra Bahadur Poudel only encouraged *subba* Uttam. Tanzing's case was terminated when his relatives submitted a general application stating he had died in a private nursing home in India. Nagendra Shrestha was released, assumed to have paid almost $9,642 in bribes to Uttam Prasad and others. Similarly, accepting money from Chet Prasad and Chandra Bahadur and releasing them with a fine of just $1,377 each was akin to a pardon for them.

I met Purna Bahadur, nephew of Til Bahadur, a few days later. "I gave $2,755 to Uttam Kharel to have Til Bahadur released on bail," he said to me plainly. He had paid the money through Som Bahadur Darai. When I conveyed the whole thing to the chief warden, Shivaraj, he asked me to submit a complaint in writing. On March 2, 2005, Purna Bahadur submitted a complaint against Uttam.

Shivaraj was leaving for Kathmandu the next day. At Hakim Chowk of Bharatpur, I submitted a file to him containing the letter. He stamped the application and told me, "Don't have too high hopes."

I was dumbstruck. He continued, "People who study law know all sorts of loopholes. Besides, they have friends at every rung of the system." I was disappointed.

Since the chief warden had appointed me as the investigation officer in this case, I called Purna Bahadur to endorse the application. When I enquired with the mediator, Som Bahadur Darai, he informed me that out of the $2,755, he had given only $551 to Uttam and kept the rest for himself. Though he and Purna Bahadur had come to the office together to make the payment at Uttam's behest, Som Bahadur had given only $551 to him in an envelope in the adjacent room when Purna Bahadur was not there, with the agreement to pay the rest after the job was done. Purna Bahadur, however, assumed that Uttam had received the full amount.

I then asked for a written explanation from Uttam, and in the privacy of my office told him the whole story. He was completely dazed. He gave me no explanation. Instead he sent a 10-page explanation to the chief warden, accusing me of all sorts of wrong-doings. He also called Purna Bahadur secretly to a hotel in Narayangadh and threatened him into taking back his complaint or risk facing difficulties with the case. He banned Som Bahadur from coming to Kasara.

In his letter to Shivaraj, he accused me of accepting bribes for failing to arrest Ramchandra and Raj Kumar Praja; misappropriating money from the Anti-poaching Unit with fake bills; buying land in Pokhara, Kathmandu, Chitwan and other areas with the money so acquired; buying land for relatives; and hoarding money in the banks. When the chief warden read this, he decided that it was better to dismiss the case.

"On the one hand, the park's staff members are earning a bad reputation because this man accepts bribes, and on the other, smugglers are being encouraged by what they can accomplish with money. If we penalise this man, then the people too will know we do not allow criminals to go scot free, smugglers will lose their morale and future staff members will not dare show such appalling behaviour," I told the chief warden. Also, I reassured him that all accusations against me were false.

"Let's talk it over with Purna Bahadur," he then said. The chief warden, Purna Bahadur, Uttam and I were at the chief's office. Uttam was adamant that he did not know this person, Purna Bahadur.

"I have met you so many times, didn't I come to your office with Som?" said Purna again and again, but still he insisted that he did not know Purna. Seeing that they were on the brink of a brawl, we sent Purna Bahadur out and started talking to Uttam only.

"I will not spare you either," he threatened me. "What harm can you possibly inflict on me?" he retorted. Afterwards, in the second week of April, I submitted his file along with my report to the office. It was sent to the Ministry of Law and Justice since Uttam was deputed by the ministry. However, no action was taken against him on the ground that the procedure of the complaint was incomplete.

In the meantime, Uttam filed cases against me at the Commission for the Investigation of Abuse of Authority (CIAA), Royal Commission, Ministry of Forests, Department of Forests, Nepal Army, DNPWC, Department of Forest Research and Survey, National Investigation Department, National Vigilance Centre, District Forest Office of Nawalparasi, Regional Administration Office of Hetauda, Office of the Appellate Court Lawyers, Hetauda, National Human Rights Commission and the District Administration Office in Chitwan. Many of them did not have the authority to penalise me or even to investigate the complaints, which Uttam seemed to be unaware of, despite being a student of law.

I started receiving summons as well as investigation teams from the offices. To each of them, I gave my statement. I even challenged them to find one single piece of land that I had bought after starting my job in 1991. Should they find, I am ready to face the toughest penalties, I told them. Also, they could penalise me if they found more than $69 in my bank account. An officer from the CIAA too came to investigate my case. After listening to me, he labelled it a case of prejudice, and there were no more enquiries after that.

When Uttam Prasad's complaints reached the Ministry of Forests, a weekly newspaper in Kathmandu published a news story about me. In the meantime, my name had been nominated for the Abraham Conservation Award. But then Joint Secretary Damodar Prasad Parajuli objected on the grounds that quite a few cases had been filed against me.

"You might not get this award, the ministry is apparently objecting to it," said the chief warden to me.

"I am not working for awards. If the situation arises, I don't mind losing an award or even my job," I told him. He said nothing.

Though the Ministry of Law and Justice did not penalise Uttam, it did summon him to Kathmandu when news of his misdeeds became public. He was reluctant to go since he had accepted money from many poachers, brokers and smugglers, having given assurances that their cases would be solved. Some staff members told me that when there was no way out, he returned the money to the criminals.

In any case, a disease from the park was eradicated through his transfer, although it is unfortunate that he was not penalised for his crime. After the re-establishment of democracy in 2006, however, all transfers made during the royal regime were rendered void, and he returned to Chitwan. But before long he was transferred again.

POACHERS TO ARREST SMUGGLERS

ACCORDING TO KEDAR GIRI - whom Birman Praja had named Dil Bahadur B.K. was a notorious poacher from Chhatiwan village of Parsa district. As he had been a sharp shooter since he was a young boy, he was called "Shikari Kami" or "hunter man". Army officers and rich landlords took him along when they went hunting. He made his living shooting animals. He had two wives.

At around 11 one mid-February morning, we had set out together with Birman towards Hetauda to catch Shikari Kami. "There is a big shot in Hetauda, I don't know if you will be able to arrest him," Birman said on the way. I wanted to see where this big shot lived. As directed by Birman, we turned east towards Seema Lodge when we reached the Timber Corporation of Nepal (TCN) road in Hetauda. After walking for about 30 metres, we reached the house indicated.

Gyamjo had brought Birman to this house in a car back in 2001-2002. When the car entered the compound, Gyamjo had left Birman outside. Inside the house was a fair, plump man with the facial features of a Thakuri. He wore high power glasses. After Gyamjo greeted him, the man had instructed his sons to take Birman to a garden where lichee trees were growing. There Birman was asked to use an automatic weapon - the first time he was handling one.

"He is OK," the man had said after Birman had fired a shot. Upon returning to Narayangadh, Gyamjo had given the gun to Birman to shoot rhinos. But Birman, who was used to home-made guns, found the automatic gun complicated and returned it to Gyamjo in a few days. Birman told us that he had never killed anything with that gun.

This incident tells us that the rhino horn smugglers were then trying to introduce automatic weapons to poach rhinos but could not do so as shooters were more comfortable with home-made guns. Poachers earlier used poison and ditches to kill rhinos. But the process often took months, as rhinos seldom fell into the ditches. Also while waiting for the rhinos, they could be spotted by the park patrolling team. The patrolling teams would also fill up the ditches if they saw one. As a result, spears came into use around 1996-1998.

Occasionally, the park elephant keepers were found using elephants to push rhinos into the ditches and to surround them and then spear them. Mandal Mahato and Bhadai Mahato were jailed for using elephants to kill rhinos near the Amrite post. In 1998-99, tow chains to kill rhinos were introduced. The villagers also killed rhinos by electrocuting them. In 2004-2005, Bhagirath Chaudhari's group smuggled in a gun called Marco Polo from India. This gun was home-made but used bullets from a Self Loading Rifle (SLR).

After having identified the house of the big shot in Hetauda, we went to Parsa Wildlife Reserve, and along with two staff members from there, started for Baguwan village through Jitpur of Bara. On the way, there was a stream. Just 10 days ago, seven policemen had been killed in an ambush by the Maoists near this very stream. I was driving that day. We proceeded despite the fear that the rebels might mistake us for the army and blow us up.

When we reached the forest office at Baguwan, the staff were quite pleased to see us. Shikari Kami's house was right in front of their range post at Chhatiwan. But going there immediately involved risks. The area was a stronghold of the Maoists, and by arresting anyone in there, one was playing with death. The local staff advised us not to go, and we returned.

ON APRIL 15, I deputed *mukhiya* Ramchandra Shrestha and informer Mahavir Chaudhari (informer's name is used with his consent) to arrest Shikari Kami. After making all arrangements, Mahavir spent the night in the jungle near Shikari's house. The captain - the team commander - gathered everyone around and said he was looking for Maoists and asked everyone to show their citizenship cards. Shikari Kami was arrested when they saw his citizenship paper that read Dil Bahadur B.K. If they had instead asked who Shikari Kami was, he might have escaped.

Shikari Kami told us about whom he was working for and his clients. He had been in this business for a long time, and many people had betrayed him in the process. Lahure had run away with a horn when they were in Pokhara to sell it to a Manange.

After returning to Kasara, I called my friend at the TCN road to find out who owned the house that we had seen. It belonged to a man called Laxman K.C. - one who wore the high power spectacles. He ran a contracting business as a front, but, in fact, he turned out to be even more powerful than Gyamjo.

Previously, I had received information that a *Bhote* woman from Kathmandu would come to Hetauda to buy horns. Deepak Singh was a famous smuggler who lived in Hetauda and dealt in horns and similar items. But it was only then that it dawned on me that Deepak and Laxman were partners and worked together.

FRIEND BURIED ALIVE

IN 1997-98, SOME poachers had killed one of their own team members while poaching in the old Padampur forest area of the national park. A loaded gun had gone off when the poacher, who was chasing a rhino, fell into a ditch. The bullet had ricocheted and injured Hathana Darai. While they were carrying him back, one of the poachers realised that Hathana could get them all arrested, and so it was better to kill him. All the poachers agreed to the plan, and they buried him alive in the ditch.

When they all returned to the village, Hathana's wife saw that her husband was missing and asked them where he was. They gave her some money and said, "He has gone to India and asked us to say he will be back soon." She believed them, but when he did not turn up for a long time and she did not receive any news either, she started looking for him. After coming to know how he had been killed, she filed a complaint with the police, but no one has been arrested till date.

In the meantime, Jumle Kanchha from Dumre Khadi of Korak in Chitwan was sentenced to 15 years in jail in absentia for poaching rhinos. One day, a volunteer informer from Bhandara tipped us off that he was going around with two strangers and was regularly seen going towards the Pyaridhap post area close to the rhino habitat. At this, I concluded that Jumle was active again and planning to poach.

At around 8:30 in the morning of May 2, we received information that Rumba Sainlo aka Jumle Kanchha was shopping at Bhandara. Since my wife was about to deliver, I had rented rooms near the hospital in Bharatpur. I told my wife to have her breakfast and left immediately in my vehicle. I called and asked some of my staff to come to Tandi from the Sauraha sector office. Only Game Scout Laptan Tharu and a *hattisare* arrived. Since it would take some time to call the army and

Rumba Sainlo might finish his shopping and leave, I decided not to call them.

Along with the staff from Tandi, we raced to Bhandara at high speed, parked on one side and met our informer. He pointed out Rumba Sainlo to me. He was looking for a rope in a shop to the north of the road. I asked my friends to follow me and walked towards him. When we were right behind him, I said politely, "Jumle Kanchha brother?" He turned to look at me. I grabbed him by the collar of his T-shirt and said, "OK, come with me."

I took the rope that was in his hand. I asked my staff to hold him on both sides and put him in the jeep. We paid for the rope and tied his hands up so that he couldn't escape.

We took him straight to Kasara. We decided to interrogate him immediately, unlike the other people we used to arrest.

"I am not Jumle Kanchha, my name is Hasta Bahadur Rumba. If you don't believe me, go and enquire at Bhandara. My citizenship paper bears my name Hasta Bahadur," he said.

We tried to force him to accept his crime. His show of strength at this time surprised me. If he had displayed the same strength before, we would not have been able to arrest him. Among us, Laptan Tharu was the strongest, but Jumle Kanchha wrestled with all of us, including Laptan, to the ground. Always when I arrested people without the help of the army, I would stick the tip of my mobile to their waist and say, "Beware, I will shoot if you run."

I had done the same to him, and that was why he came with us so easily in the jeep. He might have assumed we were from the police or the army. If he had known we were unarmed, he could have crushed us all and escaped.

When he kept insisting for days that he was not Jumle Kanchha, I took a few clips of him with a movie camera and also a few photos with a still camera. I took them to Bhandara where

I had asked Hathana Darai's wife to come. I showed her the photographs and movie clips and asked her, "Who is this man?"

"This is Jumle Kanchha," she replied.

"Is this the man who took away your husband?" I asked her.

"Yes, my husband went with this guy and hasn't returned yet," she replied.

I returned to Kasara. It was the first week of May, and the sun was scorching hot. I hit him with a thin bamboo stick on the head, and it was starting to bleed. "I will die, don't hit me," he said.

"Tell me the truth, or else you will suffer," I told him before leaving for Bharatpur. After a while, he asked the staff to call me as he "wanted to confess everything." That evening he admitted to having killed rhinos to the staff.

When I reached Kasara the next day, he confessed he was Jumle Kanchha. "But I lied in the hope that I might get away and survive," he said. He admitted to killing Hathana a few years ago. He also confessed that on January 3, 2004, he had killed a rhino on the bank of the Rapti near the Khagendramalli post. "I was the one who killed the rhino at Dhruba," he said later. I was quite shocked to hear all this.

I vividly remember the Dhruba incident. Rhino counting for the year 2005 (March-April) had officially closed on April 13 at the Sukhibhar post. There was a huge gathering of representatives from the DNPWC and donor organisations, officials, soldiers, park staff, rhino counting management team, rhino specialists and other officials. After a round of speeches, there was a musical performance. Everyone started dancing to the beat of the folk songs. A gunshot was heard by the staff of the Dhruba post. The post is 4-5 km east of Sukhibhar, and Kasara is 3 km further east. At around 7:30 in the evening, though dozens of vehicles were driving through the Dhruba post to the Kasara quarters, no one had heard anything. When the post staff were informed, they went in an army jeep around the forest road once and did not notice anything.

The next day was the Nepali New Year, and as pleasantries were being exchanged, we received news that a rhino had been found dead in the Stinking Solvent area near the Dhruba post. I headed for the post in a vehicle. Some women who were illegally picking leaves in the park had seen the rhino and informed our staff about it. A post-mortem team led by veterinary surgeon Dr. Kamal Prasad Gaire had already arrived when I reached there. As its body was cut up to look for the bullet, we saw a foetus of about 13 or 14 months. My eyes welled up with tears at the sight. The bullet had passed right above the baby and struck the rhino's heart. Since it was an iron rod bullet, we were sure that the gun was home-made.

I had tried many times to find that poacher. I set informers after him but got no results. I did not give up my search though. Today Jumle Kanchha's arrest had ended that quest. Sher Bahadur Tamang had taken him to Dhruba, arranged for his stay at Suman Tamang's house at Naya Basti village, near the national park, and got him to kill the rhino.

The rhino had run away after being shot. They had fled that day due to the heavy traffic and headlights, and had come back for the horn the following day. They had later sold the horn to a Tamang man from Dallu, Kathmandu. The Tamang passed it on to Karma Lama, who gave it to Yakche's wife.

THREE GENERATIONS OF RHINO POACHERS

ACCORDING TO JUMLE KANCHHA, Sher Bahadur Tamang was a key member of the poaching team. Shikari Kami, Riphal Rai and Prem Bahadur B.K. - who was arrested before Jumle Kanchha - had also said the same thing. Since he was a dangerous poacher, it was crucial to arrest him at any cost. We went to look for him in his home village Korak, and found that he had moved to Ratanpur of Bara district. I set informer Mahavir Chaudhari on him to find out where he was living.

Sher Bahadur's father and grandfather were also notorious poachers in their days. His grandfather used to kill rhinos and give them to notorious smuggler Gunaraj Pathak (1950s - 1970s). Sher Bahadur's father, Indra Bahadur, continued in the profession and made it a family tradition. When I learnt these facts, I ordered my staff to arrest both father and son.

Ratanpur was near a jungle 6-7 km away from the Parsa Wildlife Reserve Office, Adhavar. Our team landed there on the morning of June 9 and arrested both father and son. The team came to learn that Sher Bahadur's sister was a Maoist cadre, so they arrested her, too. If I had been there, I would not have allowed her arrest. Our job is to track poachers and smugglers. Secondly, it is best not to earn the enmity of the Maoists. I had made this clear to my staff, but that day they were unable to convince the army and the police.

When Maoists got to know that one of their cadres had been arrested, they called one of our staff members who was a resident of Bara. Since he was a local, he was able to contact the Maoists through other locals and helpers and explain what had transpired. The Maoists did not hurt him, but he was made to pay a fine. Due to our efforts, the army also did not penalise the woman they had arrested, and instead handed her to the court. Had we not taken those steps, anything might have happened to our staff. At any rate, we paid the fine and made peace with the Maoists.

Jumle Kanchha had stated that he had given the horn to Harka Bahadur Khulal. On August 11, we received information from an informer: Harka Bahadur has been seen at Lothar.

We immediately left for Lothar in a vehicle and ordered food at an eatery. The informer also arrived and told us that Harka Bahadur had just entered a *momo* shop at the other end of Lothar. I got there and asked two of my colleagues to stand on either side of the *momo* shop. I entered with a colleague and asked for *momos*.

He was short, with graying hair. He was wearing a T-shirt and shorts. His *momo* and soup had just arrived. There were two of them at the table. "How are you Khulal?" I asked.

"I am OK," he said as he turned to me.

"Come out," I said to him as I caught him by the hand, and with the help of my colleagues got him inside the jeep. His friend, the hotel owner and other people in the *momo* shop were startled, but no one said anything.

$26,000 FOR A HORN

SINCE COLONEL AJIT THAPA wanted to meet an informer, I had introduced him to one. Since the colonel could use money to engage our informer in operations other than anti-poaching ones, I had strictly instructed him to refuse any such request.

That informer frequently called the colonel to say, "Just give me $69, and I can get a poacher arrested right in the jungle." When the colonel realised that running informers was not as easy as ordering soldiers, he complained to me that the informer was blackmailing him.

I had met the informer on June 7 at Kawasoti. "If you give me some money, I can get you a man along with a horn," he told me. I was slightly angry at him, but, on second thoughts, I realised that he might be speaking the truth. I had just received my salary of $124, and from that, I gave him the $96. Just a month back, a rhino had been killed and its horn taken from the Bhelauji area near the Baguwan post in the western part of the national park. I had received information that someone was hiding that horn in the village and that it weighed one kilo and 900 grams. Since the horn that this informer described matched, I had paid him.

I had asked Ranger Bishnu Thapaliya to continue with this

operation. After two days, on June 9, he received a call from the informer. He asked Colonel Ajit for help. Since the Kawasoti area was not under his jurisdiction, Colonel Ajit said he would refer him to the Aridaman Battalion at Kawasoti instead. But when Bishnu and his team reached there in a reserved vehicle, they found that the army had not been informed. He, therefore, proceeded with a team of his own staff.

The smuggler had set the price of the horn at $26,171. Of course, Bishnu did not have the money with him. So they bought 19 packs of playing cards, put two mounds of $413 on either side, and tied them all up with a rubber band. When their vehicle turned north from the East-West Highway, some of the staff members disembarked in the jungle near the village, and only Bishnu, the informer and the driver went towards the village. They reached the house of Lil Bahadur Jhyadi Magar of Belhani village and found only his wife at home. They asked her to call her husband. After a while, he arrived with another man. They talked business, and Bishnu showed him the money while the poacher showed him the horn. It was decided that he would take the horn to the vehicle and count the money there.

Bishnu drove them to the jungle and signalled to his staff. After a brief encounter, both were arrested. Upon learning of the arrest along with the horn, the colonel immediately sent an army team from the Amaltari barracks to Kawasoti, just to show that the army was part of the operation.

The arrested criminals told us that there were two more horns in a house in Baguwan village. Also, the man who gave them the horn was Rishiram Sarumagar from Nawalparasi, Dumkibas. We sent a staff to investigate, and he informed us that the man was at home. When we talked to the barracks, they refused help, and there was no way we could go unarmed. But one of our staff had waited for us and spent the night in a primary school alone near the village.

Thrilled by the arrest of a man along with a horn and a reward of $510, the informer called us again and said, "I have called another horn smuggler, come soon." I asked Ranger Bishnu to handle this too, since he already had good relations with the Kawasoti barracks. His team arrested Thakursingh Baraili from Bhairahawa and Narayan Prasad Tharu from Dumduwa, Rupandehi on June 10, 2005. On interrogation, they revealed that they had sold one horn to an Indian.

Thakursingh's motorcycle was also confiscated. His family was worried about his whereabouts. His father Pahalsingh looked around for him in the police stations and other security offices. After 10 days, he dropped in at our office with a leader from the Janamorcha Party (communist party). Pahalsingh himself was on the list of horn smugglers. Both father and son had discussed the horn deal before his son had left for Kawasoti. I detained Pahalsingh too for questioning after convincing the party leader.

KEEPING WATCH OF THE RESTAURANT

WE WERE UNABLE to arrest Karma Lama, the notorious smuggler pointed out by Prem Bahadur B.K., for two years. We knew his phone number, his address, even what he looked like. And we had Prem Bahadur to help us. Yet we could not, which was our weakness.

One day, Prem was at Kasara for further questioning. As usual, he again said, "It would be great if people like Karma Lama could be arrested, but they never get arrested." He was being sarcastic, meaning we do not, or cannot, arrest the big fish, and only concentrate on the small ones like him.

When he said this, a ranger sitting nearby uttered, "I know about Karma."

"Keep quiet, it's best you don't talk about him...he couldn't be found when I sent people to look for him," I told him.

The *mukhiya* and I had tried to find Karma's house after

arresting Prem, but we had failed. Hence, I was very happy to hear that a ranger knew about him. At the same time, I did not want the discussion to reach Karma somehow and so had asked him to be quiet.

The ranger seemed to have a lot of information about Karma. He knew about Karma's trade links, behaviour, expenses and sources of income. I immediately sent him to Kathmandu with some money to find out more about him. He returned from Kathmandu with fresh information.

On June 10, I was to be honoured with the Abraham Conservation Award which is managed by World Wildlife Fund (WWF) Nepal programme. I decided that this was the perfect time to start the operation. I left two days early for Kathmandu, taking the ranger along with me, and we stayed at a hotel in Lazimpat, arranged by the WWF. The next day I went out alone in search of the restaurant at Thamel situated on the ground floor of Karma's rented house.

It was around 3 in the afternoon, and there were just a few customers in the restaurant. I ordered a beer and took my time. Customers started trooping in. Mostly teenagers came and sat close by in a corner. They would talk in a low voice, with their mouths near to each others' ears. In no time, the restaurant was full, and people came and sat at my table, too.

I was watching the door of the restaurant. Two Mongoloid youths carrying helmets went upstairs. While they were climbing the stairs, dogs barked loudly. It was obvious that a small dog and a huge dog were together. Prem too had mentioned that there were two dogs that barked as you went near, and I was glad I had arrived at the right place.

I left my table and went to sit on a tall stool at the bar. An English song was playing. Though I do not smoke, I ordered a cigarette and a beer. There was a handsome young man at the bar. He had long hair, spoke Nepali but looked foreign.

I introduced myself to him.

He told me his name.

I asked him about his work.

"This restaurant," he told me.

From his conversation with friends, it seemed he had just arrived from France.

"What do you do in France?" I asked.

"I ran this restaurant before leaving for France. There I worked in a restaurant, too."

"I am here from Pokhara, looking for a place to open a travel agency," I said.

We talked for a while, until I was sure he was opening up. And then I asked, "Is there space to rent upstairs?"

"No," he replied.

"Why? Who lives there?"

"Someone from Manang."

"A lot of people are coming and going, what is going on upstairs?" I asked again.

"Maybe because his wife has just died," he replied.

"Oh really, how did she die?"

"They say it's suicide. Apparently because her son married someone from another caste. She used to drink, too."

"Oh really, then where is the husband?"

"I have not seen him, but I think he is upstairs."

By the time I found all this out, it was already evening, and the beer was having its effect, too. I decided to call it a day. I was sure of the operation's success.

ABRAHAM CONSERVATION AWARD

I WAS OCCUPIED with the Abraham Conservation Award on June 10. There was a get together in the morning at the Hotel Yak and Yeti. The award winners were introduced in the beginning. The reasons for awarding me were: significant contribution to anti-poaching operations, arresting poachers and smugglers, and confiscating horns, tiger skins, guns and bullets.

In the evening, the award distribution ceremony was held at the same hotel. The award winners were requested to bring a family member or a friend along, and I had brought my uncle Ram Thapa. Three individuals, including me, and seven organisations were being awarded. Biodiversity expert Tirtha Bahadur Shrestha was recognised with the lifetime achievement award.

The programme started with a song from popular singer Ani Choying Dolma. The DNPWC's Director-general Tirthaman Maskey then praised my work and my contribution to rhino conservation, and I was invited to accept the award. I was very happy to receive the award and made a resolve to work even harder in the future. The award was really an inspiration for me. There was a photo session after the prize giving ceremony. I took pictures with many people, with a garland around my neck and the letter of appreciation in my hand. All the guests present congratulated me and praised my work.

At dinner time, I was walking with a glass in hand when I found myself near Ani Choying. She congratulated me, and we took a picture together. I wanted to request her to join the anti-poaching movement. So many smugglers chant *Om Mani Padme Hoom* at Swayambhu and Bouddha while planning their next move to smuggle rhino horns and tiger skins. I wanted to request Ani to boycott them and apply social pressure on them, which is the duty of a real Buddhist.

I am not sure if she heard my voice from within.

NOT A TIGER, BUT A JACKAL

ON JUNE 11, our ranger and I were in the same restaurant, ordering cold drinks. We were observing the activities on the first floor. A couple of people descended, with Buddhist Scriptures on their head. We paid our money and left in a hurry, not knowing if Karma Lama had just walked out. We studied them from behind. The ranger signalled, meaning "this is the guy, we should catch him." But he did not match Prem's description of Karma. In my opinion, a smuggler wouldn't walk on the road with books on his head. So I was convinced that this wasn't him.

We returned to the restaurant. Today there was a different barman whom the ranger was familiar with. "We have to give something to Karma, I wonder if he is at home," I said to him.

"I don't know."

"We would have gone upstairs, but there seems to be a dog," I said and requested, "could you please check if Karma brother is at home?"

"OK," he obliged us. "Yes, he is home," he said upon returning.

"OK, then we will go in a while," we said, and we went out. I posted the ranger to check if anyone moved out from upstairs and I called the colonel. He informed the army headquarters in Kathmandu, and soon a captain arrived.

"A team is arriving, I will introduce you to them," he said. We waited for 15 minutes, and under a young captain's command, an army team arrived. I briefed him about the operation.

We were standing in front of the Kathmandu Guest House. I suggested that we park there and walk to our destination. In the restaurant, after some cold drinks, we moved upstairs. I and the captain led the team. The dogs started barking madly.

There was a small channel gate upstairs. I requested that the dogs be tied up.

"Why?" said the man who came to the door.

"I have come from Chame (the district headquarters of Manang) to pay my condolences to Karma brother."

He then ordered someone to tie up the dogs. Relieved, we climbed upstairs. A man who matched the description given by Prem B.K. was sitting on the terrace with another man, drinking *chhyang*, a kind of home-made beer. "*Namaskar* Karma brother, I am very sad to hear of your wife's death," I said as soon as I saw him.

"We have some business with you, please come downstairs," we then said to him. He followed us and took us to his living room. But we asked him to proceed to the restaurant.

He then asked, "Why are you here?"

"The Maoists said they have given you money for safekeeping. We are from the army and have come to enquire about it," said the captain.

"No, I have done no such thing," said he.

"If you are innocent, let's go downstairs with us and talk to our boss," we told him.

Just then the dogs started barking loudly, and the captain left hurriedly. Getting Karma downstairs all by myself was really a Herculean task.

Once down in the restaurant, I whispered to him, "Come quietly with us. There are soldiers in civil dress here, we have come to arrest you. Don't resist if you do not want to be humiliated in public."

"Where are we going?" he asked.

"To the army headquarters," I replied. "Talk to our boss there, and then you can return home."

He had no option but to walk quietly with us. His daughter was obstructing our way, demanding to know the reason.

"Don't worry, he will be back soon," we reassured her. We walked him to the vehicle parked near the Kathmandu Guest House while his daughter kept talking on the cordless phone. Our vehicle passed her on our way, and she dictated its number to someone over the phone. We were driving fast, when barely two minutes later, two motorcycles swerved in front of us and blocked our way. The riders looked like Mananges (from Manang district) in their mid-twenties.

They signalled from their bikes to stop the vehicle, but the captain refused. After a while, they tried to stop us again by parking their motorcycles and standing on the street. When the driver still refused to pay heed and kept on driving, they fell by the roadside. We heard them shouting, "Stop! Stop!" They followed us for a while but were no longer seen.

I knew that Karma was the uncle of Deepak Manange, a don of Kathmandu, and he had the blessings of Nepal's leaders and royalty. The barman in the restaurant had informed us that Karma's eldest son named *Mukhiya* was also a member of Deepak's gang.

Our vehicle headed for Singha Durbar the government secretariat, through Sundhara, Tripureshwor and then Thapathali. As we neared the Prime Minister's Office, the captain ordered that Karma be blindfolded. The vehicle reached the army barracks, then came out through the small gate to the north of the main gate at Ramshahpath. We then headed for the Chhauni barracks through Kalimati. There, after some cold drinks, we started interrogating Karma.

At first, he denied everything. Then I named Prem B.K. "He said he came to your house and that you had asked him to go to Chitwan again. Why do you keep lying?"

He was still not ready to admit his crimes. The ranger gave him a tight slap, and then he started speaking. He was very scared, and his face was twisted in a strange expression. He was probably thinking he was going to die, not because of us but because of his boss. Karma was not a big shot as we had assumed from Prem's accounts. His dress and looks also suggested that he was just an agent or errand-boy for someone, and he turned out to be just that.

"I just earn $110-138 for the brokering work, and I provide for myself and children through that. I am a small man, sir, I have nothing, not even a home. I live in a rented house. Please don't do anything to me, the boss is someone else, not me."

"Who is the boss, tell us?" I asked.

"He will kill me if he finds out I have revealed the name. He knows all the big people, generals, colonels and high-level police officers!"

But this is what we had been hearing from everyone we had arrested. We reassured him, "We will not tell him that you informed us, no one will know."

After a lot of convincing, he mentioned a name: Yakche. He further told us, "He has more than $5,509,642, his house at Sitapaila, in Kathmandu, alone costs $275,482. He has 2-3 houses in Kathmandu and has 3 vehicles, including a Pajero."

He went on in the Manange tone, "His wife too accepts the stuff. Sometimes I give it to him, sometimes to his wife. His wife is very clever, sir. She is a Sherpa woman from Dolakha. The husband is Tibetan, he is quite plump, fair and tall, aged around 40. The wife has a wheatish complexion, is a couple of years older than the husband, and they have two small children, sir."

The Karma that we imagined to be a tiger was now trembling with fear. This is what happens in the smuggling world. People are scared of those just above them. Karma was as scared of Yakche as Prem was of Karma. Nara Bahadur had been just as scared to mention Prem.

"Yakche has threatened not to spare me if I mentioned him, so I am scared, sir," he continued.

Karma was the brother of Gyamjo, leader of the smugglers. Gyamjo died in 2002 of a heart attack. His daughter lived in Mumbai, India at the time. Karma had then taken over the smuggling business after Gyamjo's death. Gyamjo would make poaching plans while staying at the Rhino Hotel at Pulchowk, Narayangadh. Harka Gurung, the owner of the hotel, was Gyamjo's drinking partner. It was Nagendra Shrestha who had introduced Prem B.K. to Gyamjo.

While we were interrogating Karma, the captain went to report to his boss. At around 9 in the evening, we left Karma with him and returned to the hotel, glad to have arrested Karma.

If the park staff had guns at their disposal, we could have taken Karma to Chitwan, but since we did not, we were forced to seek the help of the army. The next day I phoned Colonel Ajit and told him, "I will reserve a vehicle, or request one from the department, and bring Karma to Chitwan." But he asked us to come by plane instead.

"OK, then," I said, "the army will drop us at the airport, and I can bring him from there." He was against this plan, too, but I went ahead and bought two tickets. I went to the Chhauni barracks to get Karma, and from there we went to the Valley Division of the Army at Singha Durbar.

When the paperwork was complete, Karma was handed over to me, and we went to the airport accompanied by the army. As soon as we landed at Bharatpur airport, we met Lieutenant Ganesh Mahat. A rented vehicle was ready to take us to Kasara. There were motorcycles to escort us at times from Bharatpur to Kasara, as if a powerful don had been arrested. This was all drama on the part of the colonel to make it look as if we had accomplished something big. However, the security measures might have proved suicidal as the Maoists could have set up ambushes on the way in anticipation of an important visitor. Luckily, nothing of the sort happened. At Kasara, the colonel insisted on keeping Karma in custody himself. I was unable to resist his stubbornness, even though it is illegal for the army to detain wildlife smugglers. Custody in the park is the only legal custody.

I was fed up with the colonel's behaviour. That evening I went to the barracks to interrogate Karma. The colonel was there, too. Instead of congratulating me for the award, he started questioning, "How come only you got the award, and not us? Why didn't you let us know?"

"Why do you ask me, ask WWF who awarded me," I shot back at him.

He got annoyed and shouted, "Why shouldn't our company commander be awarded also? How could you accept the award alone and not let us know?"

I too got irritated and left that day without interrogating Karma.

Grand House

The next day when I talked to Karma, he revealed that in the past he had given horns to both Yakche and Tamling, but each of them got angry for dealing with the other. Yakche's house was located at Sitapaila, Kathmandu, and sometimes Karma went there and gave the horn to his wife Phinjo Sherpa. We then decided to go to Kathmandu to arrest Yakche. My wife's uncle lived in Sitapaila. They always complained that I never visited them. This time I decided to pay them a visit, and it would be a convenient location for me, too.

Once in Kathmandu, I set out in search of Yakche after leaving my briefcase in the house. Karma had given me the location: A small road to the west of the Ring Road leads to a *Gumba*, that is, a monastery. Going uphill, you come to a *Pipal* tree, near which is a house just before Comfort Housing. It has a huge black gate. The building is said to cost hundreds of thousands of dollars. Inside the compound is a statue of the Buddha with a fountain on its head."

I reached the said location, having asked for directions on the way. I entered a department store at Comfort Housing, bought a cake and peeped at the house as I ate. The house had a large area and a high wall. It was a Western-style house and was painted white. Though there was the said statue of the Buddha inside, there was no fountain. However, I decided that this must be the very house I was looking for.

I then started observing the house from a grocery shop to the north. As I was trying to get close to the shopkeeper by buying cigarettes and chewing gum, a vehicle with a blue number plate entered the house. I wanted to find out who was in the car, however, due to the high wall and gate, I could not.

After a short while, the vehicle exited the house. Its number started with 061-..., meaning it was a vehicle used by American diplomats.

Even when I waited at the grocery shop till nightfall, not a single person who matched Yakche's description was seen. So I returned to my uncle's place.

Early the next morning I got there. The shopkeeper even ordered tea for me as we introduced ourselves. I told him I was a trader. After a brief conversation, I asked him, "I wonder who owns this grand and attractive house? I wonder how much it cost to build and who lives in such a palace?"

"Apparently it cost $275,482 to build. This house belongs to one *Bhote*. The head of USAID has been living here since the past few months. I hear he has rented it for $1,653 a month."

I was shocked. I had come to look for Yakche, and here was just his house. I again asked the shopkeeper, "Do you know where the house owner lives?"

"No, why?"

"I have a few herbs, medicinal plants with me, and I had heard he buys them," I said to convince him.

I concluded it was useless staying there any longer. I went my way smoking and called Kasara from a public telephone in a photo studio near the Ring Road. I couldn't talk to the chief warden and left a message with Ranger Bishnu to call me. Then I called the colonel. "Karma seems to have lied to us. A man from USAID lives in the Sitapaila house. Please ask him again for the address of Yakche's house."

I hung up and went to Swayambhu. Karma had also mentioned that Yakche went to Swayambhu everyday, sometimes in a white Santro car and sometimes in a green Pajero. I asked for directions to the parking lot and looked for Santros and Pajeros. Unable to locate a vehicle that matched the descriptions, I climbed the Swayambhu hill. It was crowded with devotees.

I prayed as I walked, "Please God, help me catch Yakche soon."

I looked upon Kathmandu from atop the hill. The concrete jungle with its packed houses was an eyesore, and I returned to the parking lot once again in the hope of finding a white Santro or green Pajero. But there was none.

I told myself: "What a foolish man I am. I am looking for a man I have never seen, based simply on the colour of his car. Can I ever find him like this?"

I returned to Sitapaila for lunch. As we were finishing lunch, Bishnu called. As soon as I said hello, he laughed and said, "We have already arrested Yakche."

I was surprised. I could not understand how this could be so and asked, "Where? When? How?"

He then narrated the whole story.

Yakche was in the habit of visiting different places like Chitwan, Nawalparasi, Nepalgunj and Bardia to buy horns. This way, he was able to save on the commission paid to brokers like Karma. Our informer in Kawasoti had been telling us that he could help arrest an important smuggler, not knowing Yakche was that person. While I was coming to Kathmandu to look for Yakche, the informer had called me to say that a horn deal was being finalised in Kawasoti. I had, in turn, called up Bishnu to arrest the dealer.

At Kawasoti, Bishnu, in coordination with Lieutenant Pratap Basnet from the Aridaman Battalion, prepared for the operation. The informer, however, kept changing the location of the said deal, from the jungle to a temple. After running around for nearly five hours, finally the informer informed that the horn was being delivered in a restaurant at Thakali Chowk of Kawasoti. Our team hurried there, where they saw a man get off from a car that looked as if it had come from Kathmandu. He took out a plastic bag from the car and walked inside. They followed him in and arrested Yakche, Pemba Gurung and Sonam *Bhote* along with a horn, money, mobiles and a scale to weight the horn.

At Kasara, Colonel Ajit again took them into custody. Until that moment, nobody knew that Yakche, whom we were looking for, had been arrested. The colonel put Karma and Yakche in the same room, where Yakche had threatened Karma to keep quiet. Later they were put in separate rooms at Bishnu's insistence. During the reinterrogation of Karma, he revealed, "The man who shared my cell yesterday is Yakche."

Ranger Tikaram Poudel was appointed the investigation officer in the case. After completing the investigation and judicial procedure, we held a press conference where we announced that since Yakche had revealed everything to us, we would soon

be arresting all other smugglers. We thus used the media to create pressure on the poachers and smugglers throughout the country. And soon we started receiving information that some of the culprits had already fled to India.

AXE UNDER THE PILLOW

WE HAD RELEASED Ramchandra Praja aka Mudha Sainla way back in March-April 2003 on guarantee that he would be present when summoned as we could find no proof against him. It was after Til Bahadur Gurung's arrest that we came to know of Mudha Sainla's involvement in the poaching of rhinos and smuggling of horns. We tried to arrest Mudha Sainla again in light of the fresh evidence, only to learn that he had fled immediately upon learning of Til Bahadur's arrest. Magara Chaudhari, former head of ward No. 4 of Khairahani VDC, who had offered to sit guarantee for him, could not contact him either.

A new informer from Korak contacted us to say that he knew where Mudha Sainla was hiding. In 2003, the *mukhiya*, I and other park staff had taken that informer on a night operation. He had shown us a cave and said, "That is where Ramchandre sleeps," and left. We had surrounded the cave, but Ramchandra happened to be sleeping outside in the field. Upon spotting him, a member of our team, Senior Game Scout Sushil Jha had suddenly shouted, "There's the thief." The shout had jerked awake Ramchandra, and he had run, wrapped in a blanket, across the fields like superman. It was a dark night, and we were on a small cliff overlooking a small stream, and there was no way we could descend easily. For Ramchandra, it was a different matter as this was where he had grown up, and besides, he was a Chepang. We searched everywhere but couldn't find him. Angry at the loss, the *mukhiya* had set fire to a small hut beneath the two trees where he had been hiding during the day.

The same informer again contacted us on July 23, 2005. According to him, to arrest Ramchandra, we would have to reach Kalikhola of Korak, past Birendranagar, a stronghold of the Maoists. I talked to Colonel Ajit, and he told me to go to Sunachuri to learn about the area. Night had fallen by the time we reached Sunachuri. But the major (company commander) at Sunachuri knew nothing about the area either. Then the colonel set another task for us: work in coordination with the Armed Police Force (APF) of the Bhandara Base Camp.

We were driving from Sunachuri to Bhandara with a team of soldiers at around 10 p.m. The car's battery had not been fully charged, and the headlights were starting to dim. When we turned west from Bhandara, a truck coming towards us failed to dim its headlights, and I could see nothing. I was driving blindly when I suddenly saw a group of people standing on the road. I put on the emergency brake and swerved to the left. They happened to be policemen from the APF and were standing without any traffic signs a hundred metres away from their checking barricade. It was good fortune that we did not hit them. Had we done so, they would probably have fired at us, thinking they were under attack. Our soldiers too might have opened fire, resulting in a deadly encounter. But a policeman did come and hit me on the cheek. I averted the blow, and it landed only lightly on the face.

Our lieutenant scolded them. I too joined in. "We have come from Kasara. We could not see anything due to the lights. But why are you guys standing so far away from your checking barricade without any traffic signs?"

Actually, they had been standing on the road expecting our arrival. But we had assumed we would be meeting in the barracks.

I felt very bad. "Let's go back and abort the operation," I said as our omens were not good. When we were near Patihani, we had gotten into an unnecessary dispute with the bus staff. Then, while driving at high speed through the jungles of Tikauli, the car must have run over a rock python, as a hissing sound was heard. I silently asked for the python's forgiveness.

We cancelled the discussion programme in the APF barracks and drove ahead. After we were past the APF gate, a colleague mentioned that our informer must be waiting for us, so we should go.

I, too, concluded that we should go. Our car and two motorcycles then turned northwards on the dirt road beside the Pampa stream.

We did not find our informer in Birendranagar and so went to his home. It was already half past 11 at night. We started for Ramchandra Praja's house together with the informer. There were small huts along the way, and we could see people sleeping in their yards. We could even hear them snoring from afar.

In one of the houses, a man was sleeping, and a member of our team, Game Scout Buddinath Lamichhane, pointed out that it belonged to Ramchandra. The informer, however, led us away on suspicion that Ramchandra was somewhere else. Our staff insisted that we surround that particular house while the informer was firm that we should move ahead. There was even a war of words, so I said, "Let's go with the informer. He has got us this far, he will get us ahead, too."

I and Lieutenant Sagar Karki followed the informer, who took us to Ramchandra's cave. There was a small path along the cliffs, and the grass seemed freshly cut. We reached the cave, and we could clearly see that people had been walking that way. It was a small hut with a fence built out of twigs. There was also a bed made out of branches for a person to sleep on. We walked quietly like cats. There was even a mosquito net over the bed. I slowly lifted the net and peeked inside. The bed was made, but no one was there.

I walked back fast to catch up with the informer who had already left after showing us the cave. "Which is his house? I asked.

The informer took us to the very house pointed out earlier by our staff. Ramchandra had not noticed our movements yet. He was in deep sleep. I called the other staff over and surrounded the hut. A soldier and I climbed the ladder to look around. A man, a woman and a small child were sleeping. The man's profile was clear but not his face. I switched on the torchlight and covered it up with my hand to dim it. I recognised Ramchandra immediately as I had arrested him before. Near his pillow were a big axe and a sickle. I took both of them, and then I shone the torch on his face. He jerked awake and was startled to see me.

His wife too got up and started arranging her clothes. We let Ramchandra wear his clothes and took him along. His wife was weeping and insisted on coming along, too. We consoled her and went our way.

We had to walk along the narrow margins of the water canals amidst the rice and maize fields in the dark. Sometimes we would be walking on all fours while at other times, our friends would be crawling after having fallen.

Suddenly, one of our soldiers cried, "I have lost my pistol's magazine." We all started looking for it. We searched for about an hour but failed to locate it. The soldier and the lieutenant were worried as they would have to give an explanation the next day.

It was already 2 at night, and we had other operations to conduct. So two of our team members stayed behind with Ramchandra, and the remaining five of us left for Kalikhola village.

IT'S A WOMAN!

AFTER WALKING FOR about 20 minutes, we reached Kalikhola. We were near a small stream. Below us lay fields and above us the village. From our targeted house, we saw a man descend, shining a torchlight. We paused where we were. He had probably come out to pee, and he walked back up again. "That is Raj Kumar," said our informer.

Our informer suggested that we catch another horn smuggler named Lila first and then go for Raj Kumar. I, however, felt that we should arrest Raj Kumar first as he was more dangerous. But the informer was very stubborn, so I had to give in. I asked two members of the team to descend towards the fields while we climbed uphill. But before we were midway, a dog started barking loudly. The moon was shining brightly, and we could probably be seen from above. Lila's house was at the entrance of the village, and two kids were sleeping outside. Our staff climbed the stairs and ordered, "Get up!"

"Why should I?" said a woman. Until that moment, I had assumed that Lila was a man, but it turned out to be a woman. "What? Why?" she was shouting rudely. My friend too scolded her just as rudely, asking her to come down. Suddenly we heard a gunshot down in the fields.

"Oh no, we are dead now! We will face great trouble," I told myself.

The sound of the gunshot scared Lila, and she climbed down quickly. The staff also got her album and purse. The gunshot also woke up the sleeping kids. Dogs went to hide in the corners and stopped barking. When we were taking Lila with us, her kids started crying. "Don't worry, I will just take your mummy a short distance and have her return," I told them.

Once down, we learnt that before our friends could reach the house of Raj Kumar, he had managed to flee. So they had to open fire.

Thus, he was able to escape twice, and both times by evading being shot. We returned disappointed, and a little farther on, arrested a man called Ghatware Kainlo (Jit Bahadur Lama) from a house on the slopes. We then started for Birbal Praja's house. As we were taking Birbal, his wife started crying and followed us for quite some distance, insisting on coming along. We assured her that Birbal would be safe and returned to her.

However, our operation was not yet over. We had to arrest Chandra Bahadur Praja who lived in another village on our way back.

Previously, when we had arrested Ram Kumar Praja in 2003, Chandra Bahadur had been sleeping on a *tauwa*. While we were looking for him in his house, he had found time to slip into the banana fields from the *tauwa*.

This time, too, the house that we had assumed to be Chandra's turned out to be his brother Kajiman's. Kajiman showed us Chandra's house, and that was how we arrested him.

Sweet Music before an Operation

According to Chandra Bahadur, the owner of the Langhali Hotel at Kurintar, near the entry to the Manakamana cable car station, had given him a gun to shoot rhinos. The man would invite people from Kathmandu and sell them the horns given by Chandra Bahadur and his friends Padam Bahadur Praja. On the basis of this information, we left for Kurintar on August 1, 2005.

We could not find the Langhali Hotel at the said location. I asked a passerby, "Where has this hotel shifted? We used to lunch at this place before."

"It has shifted there, right on the side of the road," said the man. We went to the hotel, where we saw the middle-aged proprietress. We ordered beer and asked her to fry some dried meat. As we were drinking, two teenage *Gandharvas* with their musical instrument, the *Sarangi*, arrived and began singing a folk song *banko kaphal banko charilai* (the wild box myrtle of the jungle for the jungle birds).

After we had eaten, the woman called her husband to work out our bill. A short, bald man of around 50, with a Mongoloid face, arrived. He looked like an ex-army man and his appearance matched the description given by Chandra Bahadur during interrogation. We paid our money and then said, "Come over, we have some business with you."

When we neared our vehicle, we told him, "We are from the army barracks in Bharatpur; our company commander (major) wants to talk to you about the Maoist party, come with us."

"OK," he said and changed his clothes. He told his wife he was going to Narayangadh and got into the vehicle with us. However, when he found out on the way that we were taking him to Kasara for enquiries, he was shocked. But since we could not find evidence against him, and he did not admit anything during the interrogation, we had to release him on general bail.

TIKARAM MARDANIYA had been arrested and then released on general bail in 2000-2001 in a case involving the sale of a fake horn. His name was on our list of suspects at large. A ranger in the western sector once looked at the list and commented that he knew the person well. "We have tea in the same shop, but the office never told me that this man was on the list," he said. I ordered him to coordinate with the army to arrest the man. On August 2, 2005, he arrested the man after coordinating with the barracks at Koluwa. Upon interrogation, he confessed to being on general bail in a case involving the sale of a fake rhino horn. Later, he was released after having paid a bribe of $28 to *subba* Uttam Prasad Kharel.

I, too, talked to Tikaram when he was brought to Kasara.

"I always came to the park office when asked to," he said. "Whenever I showed the slip of the summons at the park's checking post, the army would slap me, accusing me of killing rhinos. I wasted a lot of money on those trips to the park office.

"Darshanraj Ghimire who was also supposed to appear in the park office like me stopped going. I asked him how he could manage to do so. He told me that he had paid $138 to *subba* Uttam, and he offered to introduce me to the *subba*. At first, the *subba* demanded $138 from me, too. But then I pleaded that I was a poor man and could only afford to pay $28. 'OK, give me,' the *subba* had said. I took the money out of my pant pockets and he took it swiftly from my hand and put it in his pocket. He then told me he would delete my name from the list, and I also stopped coming, but again I am in trouble."

He had been arrested along with a horn and jailed by the District Forest Office of Nawalparasi. Later he had worked as an informer. The people he had pointed out had, in turn, named him in revenge, and he had been arrested again for selling a fake horn. "I am innocent," he said. "I grow vegetables on some leased land. I depend on this vegetable farming for a livelihood. I have two wives and 10 children."

LADDU IN BOTH HANDS

IN JUNE-JULY OF 2005, the Biodiversity Sector Programme for the Siwalik and Terai (BISEP-ST) had arranged a tour of Meghalaya in India. Since I was coordinating the BISEP-ST programme in the park, the Ministry of Forests had nominated me as a representative of the DNPWC.

"I don't want to go, you can send some other official," I had told the then Director-general Tirthaman Maskey. However, senior forestry officials Harihar Sigdel and Ramananda Shah insisted that they would only take with them the person nominated by the ministry. I did not want to go, but I received a message that said anyone who refused after being nominated by the ministry would face departmental action. So I was on my way to Bhadrapur, Jhapa, to travel to India the next day.

Though I had come half-heartedly, I was very glad that day to receive $620 as travel allowance. I was in debt, and the money was a great help in paying back the loan.

From Baghdogra, we flew to Guwahati (Assam), and from there we went by bus to Meghalaya. The geography of that area is similar to the hilly areas of Nepal. The plants and trees, weather, lifestyle, all seemed to resemble Nepal. While I was in the bus, I thought of the treatment meted out to the Nepalese living there in 1987.

The local Khasi people had treated the Nepali people inhumanely and had chased them from the land. Nepalis who had been living there for generations had to flee, leaving behind all their wealth, houses, land, livestock and jobs. So many were widowed, so many raped and so many mutilated. The *Panchayat* government of Nepal had put no pressure on the Indian government to assuage the pain of the Nepalese there. It showed no interest in the sufferings of the non-resident Nepalese.

The political parties, however, spoke against it even though they were banned. I, too, had taken part in a protest rally that started from Lamo Chautara (resting place) in lower Hemja. I was around 17 at that time. When our rally, consisting of around 25 people, reached Milanchowk, a group of *Mandales* (youths supporting the *Panchayat* political system and the king) had attacked us with sticks, stones, bottles, swords and knives.

In the course of our visit, we visited the Namkhyalam Wildlife Sanctuary, famous for its gibbons. Gibbons were widely poached for their meat, and when several attempts to control it failed, the rangers and officers had initiated the 'poacher use as anti-poacher' programme. According to the programme, arrested poachers are not sued in court or penalised. Instead they are recruited as informers for the sanctuary or made to teach the villagers that it is wrong to poach gibbons. This programme brought gibbon poaching to a halt in just a few years.

This programme touched my heart. I silently thanked the programme run with assistance of the Netherlands government and made a resolve to apply this technique in Nepal.

POACHER AGAINST POACHER

AFTER I RETURNED from Meghalaya, an informer came to meet me. He told me that a person on our list was willing to name some poachers and smugglers if we promised not to arrest him. For some months, I declined the offer on the grounds that it is against the law, and someone might file a case against me. But when the informer again insisted that I at least meet the man, I agreed.

The man seemed pretty scared and kept repeating that he was innocent. I asked him to get some poachers arrested for me. He sought a week's time. I agreed and asked our informer to keep an eye on him. Within a week, he was back with information about the poachers.

On that day, August 8, 2005, I was in Kasara. It was already 8 in the evening. So I called Sauraha and talked to Ranger Madhav. A few days back, a rhino had been killed near the Bhawanipur post of old Padampur. He, too, was excited and, in coordination with the army, they left immediately and arrested Lal Bahadur Kumal, Somlal Chaudhari and Raj Kumar Kumal. There were others to be arrested, too, but the team did not know them.

Upon interrogation the next day, the three revealed that they had hidden the gun used in poaching the rhino in the Chure hill inside the park, and given the horn to Manalal and Nara Bahadur Gurung of Chainpur. Two guns were unearthed from the hiding place with the help of Somlal. A team that included the army went to Siddhipur of Chainpur to arrest the criminals who had bought the horn from the poachers. Manalal was able to escape, but Nara Bahadur was arrested.

Raj Kumar was illiterate and quite simple. He had gotten into the poaching business because of his father. His father Rana Bahadur was in jail for killing rhinos, and whenever Raj Kumar went to meet him, he would weep and ask his son to get him out. His father's friend Rambihari convinced Raj Kumar that only poaching rhinos would get him the money to get his father out of jail. Raj Kumar, thus, turned to poaching and started making money.

One day he took his uncle, pastor Sanubabu Rokka, to the office of *subba* Uttam Prasad Kharel and paid him $826 right there and then. Uttam took the money, but Raj Kumar's father still got a seven-year sentence. Raj Kumar assumed that since he had paid such big money, his father's jail term had been shortened to seven years. He was such a simpleton that he would take his wife along when he went out to sell horns. And when he was arrested, he happily declared, "I have earned enough for them, they can live on that."

Nara Bahadur, though, was clever. In the village, everyone was surprised by his earnings, high spending and big house. They would wonder how he was making so much. He had four wives. Sometimes when they quarrelled, they even threatened to get him arrested.

Thus, I was happy to have arrested four poachers and confiscated two guns in one day with the 'poacher use as anti-poacher' technique.

There were new people ready to help us. When I was out of station, I was informed that poachers were about to enter the park via Kumroj village.

Our team, including Ranger Pramod Yadav, arrested Krishna Bahadur Syangtan of Haadikhola, Makwanpur, Ram Bahadur Kumal of Jutpani, Chitwan, Surya Kumal of Padampur, Sanchasingh Moktan of Basmadi, Makwanpur and Gyalbo Tamang of Jutpani. Krishna Bahadur had managed to throw the bullets away in a field, and they were made to retrieve them the next day. This was perhaps the first time that our informers had informed us of poachers before they were able to enter the park, and we caught them on the way.

We had not been able to arrest many people in Nawalparasi. We were unable to find out who was killing the rhinos at the Gaida Khasa and Temple Tiger Lodge areas. Krishna Bahadur Syangtan stated that Ram Bahadur Kumal also poached rhinos with them. He was the brother-in-law of Raj Kumar Kumal who had been arrested in a case of rhino poaching last August. I was glad to hear this because if I arrested this guy, then we would know more about the people who operated from the western areas.

I relayed his address and description to a staff member at the Amaltari post, who located his house. The same day, Ram Bahadur Kumal was arrested at Koluwa with the help of the local people. However, we did not gain as much information as we had expected from him. I instead started pitying him when I found out about his extreme poverty and his wife's ill health.

On the basis of the information, we had that Shiva Chaudhari used to poach rhinos with Raj Kumar Kumal, we arrested him from a poultry farm at Mangalpur, Chitwan. Upon questioning, he revealed that Raj Kumar Kumal took his youngest brother along to poach. They hid the gun in a Bote's house on the way to Kumroj. They buried it in the room near the fire place and took it out when needed. We seized the gun.

IN HETAUDA LOOKING FOR SMUGGLERS

JUMLE KANCHHA HAD once mentioned that he had given a horn to Suire Kanchha's son-in-law. I went to Lothar with a volunteer informer and walked around, pretending to be a goat buyer. I asked people where I could get goats and looked for goats in every house. In this way, I reached Suire Kanchha's house. His wife was sorting rice grains. The smell of home-made liquor was quite strong. There were a few goats in the yard.

"Sister, don't you have goats to sell?" I asked.

"Right now, no, *babu*," she answered.

"Where is brother (her husband)?" I asked.

"I don't know *babu*, he said he was going to the market in the morning."

"Maybe he will sell me the goats at a good price," I said. "Please make me some tea, I am hungry."

"Make him some black tea," she ordered her daughter-in-law.

I broached my real topic. "How is your second daughter? Where do she and her husband live?"

"At Bastipur."

"Is it her house or is she living on rent?"

"On rent, *babu*, how can she build a house?"

Jumle Kanchha had told me that Suire's son-in-law dealt in medicinal plants. On the basis of that information, I asked her again, "He must be earning well from his business."

"I don't know, *babu*."

"Where is your son-in-law now? Doesn't he come to see you?"

"He stays at Bastipur, *babu*. It has been long since he came this way. Maybe he will visit us on *Janai Purnima*?"

"Do Tamangs also wear a *janai* these days?"

"No *babu*, but we do celebrate the *Purnima*."

That was all I needed to know. I paid for the tea and left, telling her I would be back for her goats once she had kids to sell.

I then went to Bastipur to find out about a trader in medicinal plants. I found out where Suire Kanchha's son-in-law was living. He was sleeping, covered with a red blanket. I couldn't see his face though. His daughter, aged five or six, and wife sat nearby. But I was alone that day and couldn't arrest him. I also found out that he had recently opened "My Dear Restaurant" in Hetauda, in partnership with some people.

On August 27, 2005, we reached Hetauda, parked near the traffic post and went southwards from there. There were banners on the road advertising the new restaurant. Game Scout Yam Bahadur Khanal and I entered the restaurant, while other team members waited outside. Once inside, we ordered cold drinks and started smoking. A young woman came to light cigarettes for us, sat at our table and began asking us what we wanted. We immediately understood that there was something fishy going on here. The customers moved in and out, while English music played loudly.

"Can we sit inside?" I asked her.

"Yes," she said.

We went inside. There was a row of small cabins in a hall. The decoration was not very appealing, and not many customers were around.

She brought us pegs of Royal Stag whiskey, and we started drinking. Though it was daytime, the lights were on as it was very dark inside. The young lady was still with us. When we asked her to drink with us, she was coy. "I drink only beer," she said.

"OK then, get the beer, we will pay later," I said to take her into confidence.

I was an old victim of the behaviour of such women who worked in restaurants. When I was officiating as the chief warden of the Sagarmatha (Mt. Everest) National Park, I had a friend Kaji Sherpa, who holds the world record in the Guinness book of climbing Mt. Everest in the shortest time. During the third week of January 2003, I had returned to Kathmandu and met Kaji at Thamel. We drank together at the Korean Villa restaurant. After a while, he proposed that we go to a *dohori* restaurant. Until that day, I had never been to a *dohori*, disco or dance restaurant. His proposal aroused my curiosity, and we went to the Dobhan Dohori Saanjh restaurant in Thamel. There were many customers. On stage were male singers dressed in *daura suruwal* and women in *phariya* and *chaubandi*. Kaji turned out to be an old customer of that place. A young lady in chaubandi greeted us and seated us at a table.

In a *dohori* restaurant, you request Nepali folk songs which are then sung by the singers. And people take to singing folk songs vociferously after getting high, and I was a man from Kaski district, known for Nepali folk songs. In drunken revelry, I sang a Nepali folk song *Kali Pare Dai* with singer Sheela Ale Magar. It turned out well, and everyone enjoyed it.

In the meantime, another Sherpa friend from Solukhumbu arrived and took us to another restaurant. There too I sang two songs in my drunken state. When we got out from there, our friend said, "Let's go to a disco." We stumbled into a disco at Durbar Marg. The disco hall was completely different from what I had imagined. Customers were dancing in varied movements to the loud music. On a sofa at a dark corner, several youths were lost in embraces. They must have paired up before coming in, I concluded. I had not brought anyone with me, so I thought I would just sit for a while and then leave. I was sitting on the sofa, watching them, when a girl approached me and sat next to me.

"What will you have? Whiskey?" she asked.

I was delirious at having found more than what I had expected. "Yes," I told her and gave her some money.

"I will have a juice," she said. I was happy to oblige. After all, that was what I wanted.

"What a fun place this is," I reflected as I drank.

After I had finished my peg, she held my hand, and said, "Come, let's dance."

I stood up instantly. We went to the stage and started dancing like the other couples, holding hands. I was amazed at this dream world. After dancing for a while, she had whiskey with me, and then we danced some more.

After a while, Kaji and another friend came looking for me and said, "Let's go now." I, however, had no desire to leave the place. But my friends were insistent, and I sadly bid the girl goodbye, promising to meet her again. The Sherpa friend took me to his room. I was completely drunk and did not know when or how we reached the room.

After that first experience, I started frequenting the *dohoris* and discos. I wasted a lot of money there. At one point, there wasn't a girl I hadn't bought a juice or whiskey for. Some days, I would be completely broke and stagger home with no money even to pay for the taxi. Today I am ashamed of myself when I think of the money and time I spent on these things.

But the skills I gained while talking to the girls have come handy today. I started the conversation with the girl in the Hetauda restaurant. "Is this restaurant new?"

"Yes?"

"How old is it, exactly?"

"Just a week."

"But these decorations seem pretty old. How popular is this?"

"It's OK, but plenty of troublemakers visit the place, too."

"Aren't the managers local?" I asked.

"One of them is my brother-in-law," she replied.

"Oh really, are there many of them?"

"There are a couple of partners."

"Who are the others?"

"One of them comes from Bastipur, but I don't know much about him."

I knew that we had come to the right place. Again I asked, "Who is the one standing outside? Your brother-in-law?"

"Yes."

"Won't he be displeased to see his sister-in-law with other guys?"

"No."

"Where is the one from Bastipur?"

"I don't know."

"When will he come back?"

"I don't know, why do you ask?" she seemed suspicious.

"Nothing serious. We were just worried that he might not like you chatting with us, even though your brother-in-law is cool."

She smiled coyly, "Oh, I was just wondering if you guys were spies."

"Why, do we look like spies?"

"He looks like a soldier or a policeman."

"Oh, really?"

"His hairstyle says so."

"Do spies look like us?"

"So many people come and trouble us."

"We are neither spies nor troublemakers, we have come to have some fun," I said.

"Oh, come on," she said and shyly lowered her head.

"If you are suspicious, then we will leave," I told her.

"Oh, no, that's not what I meant, please stay."

As we talked to her, the man who matched the informer's description arrived in front of the restaurant. Suire Kanchha's son-in-law Kanchhalal Waiba was thin, tall, with an olive complexion and hair combed to the right. We paid our bill and got out. I gave the young lady $2 in tips. She was very pleased, and said, "Keep coming," as we left.

Outside, our team was waiting for us. We, however, were tipsy in broad daylight. Suire Kanchha's son-in-law and a friend were chatting in front of a *paan* shop a little farther on. There were just the four of us. If we tried to arrest him in the middle of Hetauda bazaar, local hooligans might just create a racket and help him escape. It was not our area, and besides, the restaurant owners might have their own gang of rowdy boys scattered in the area. Hence, we had to arrest him in a lonely place.

That opportunity arrived soon. There was a drizzle. He crossed the road and turned east to buy some groceries at a roadside shop. I asked my team to take position. As he crossed the road to return, he ducked under the railings to step onto the side path. I held his arm and said, "Waiba, come with us for a while."

"Why?" said he.

"We have some business," I said.

"I will just drop this stuff," he said.

"My boy will do it for you," I replied and gave his shopping bag to Game Scout Basanta Lamichhane. Since a lot of people were walking on the road, no one paid us much attention. We got him into the vehicle and headed west. At first, he assumed that the police was going to question him about his newly opened restaurant. When we informed him of our real mission, he was shocked. And thus, without any weapons, just the four of us had captured a criminal in an unfamiliar place and brought him to Kasara.

POACHER FLEES

WE RECEIVED INFORMATION that Bhagirath Chaudhari called Bhagara, Madana Chaudhari and Kopuwa Chaudhari of Dibyanagar, Chitwan, had brought guns from India to go poaching. Concurrently, a couple of rhinos got killed in the park's island area (Dibyanagar).

An informer pointed out the rhino poachers to us. He also informed us where the guns were and who had what role to play in the poaching. We then made plans to arrest them. On April 5, 2005, we left for Dibyanagar, along with an army team under Junior Army Officer Hari Prasad Kafle of the Gajapur post. First we surrounded Bhagirath Chaudhari's house. No one responded when we asked them to open the door, so I broke the door open with two kicks. We arrested Bhagirath who was hiding behind a granary.

"Where is the gun?" I asked him.

"What gun? What are you talking about?" he asked me instead.

When he continued to refute everything, I gave him a hard slap, but he still would not speak out.

Our informer told us that the gun was hidden in the granary, but our search yielded nothing. We then took Bhagirath along to Kopuwa's house and arrested him as he slept. We then arrested Madana.

It was already midnight when we returned to the Gajapur post. We left the army team there and headed for Kasara. At around half past one, as we neared Chihan Danda of Jagatpur village, we discovered that we had a flat tyre. And we had no spare tyre. Since we had no option, we got the three captives out of the vehicle, blindfolded them and had them walk with the support of our staff. After a while, we reached the house of my relative at Jagatpur. There was a tractor outside his home and I asked if we could borrow it. But the tractor did not have headlights. We got the captives onto the tractor with their eyes still blindfolded. Our driver Man Bahadur Tamang drove the tractor while Basanta Lamichhane and I sat in front with the torchlights on. At Ghailaghari, about 2 km before reaching Kasara, we suddenly heard shouts of, "Escaped! Escaped!" I looked back to see a person jumping from the tractor. We ran behind Bhagirath, but he was running with such speed that he was soon lost in the darkness.

The next morning, our team went to look for Bhagirath in his house, but, of course, he was not to be found. We then released Madana and Kopuwa too on general bail. This was a ploy to make Bhagirath think that he was not in danger. And according to our plan, he was seen in the village a few months after. We were planning to arrest him during the rice transplantation season, but that could not happen.

On June 29, 2005, another rhino was killed in the island area. We found a bullet from a SLR in its body. Later we learnt through the villagers that on that day, three people had crossed the Narayani River on banana trunks and walked towards the park. About an hour later, gunshots had been heard. We learnt that those who crossed the Narayani were Bhagirath Chaudhari, Laxman Chaudhari and Maniram Chaudhari. If we arrested just one of them, the other two might run away. Hence, we planned to arrest all of them together. In the meantime, though, Hari Prasad of the Gajapur post had spotted Bhagirath during a patrol and arrested him on September 7.

The next day, during interrogation, he insisted that he did not kill the rhino. On September 8, I tried to drill some sense into him. "You ran away that day, you shouldn't have. We released Madana and Kopuwa on general bail. We would have released you, too." And then I cajoled him, "If you tell us the truth now, I will release you on general bail."

He then started crying.

"Why are you crying?" I asked.

"I have just found a girl from the Madi Valley. Now if her family knows about my arrest, we will not be able to marry."

"We will release you on general bail, and if her parents come and enquire, we will say we had held you for enquiries only. But you better tell us the truth," I said.

According to Bhagirath, he had given the horn to Pushpa Bhandari and Gupta Bhujel. This time, he admitted to killing the rhino together with Laxman Chaudhari and Maniram Chaudhari. He further told us that another friend of his Laxman Bhujel had taught them how to shoot and had bought the gun in India with the help of a man from Madi. Kopuwa, Laxman Chaudhari and he had contributed money to buy the gun. Kopuwa's brother Raj Kumar, who was in the Nepal Army, had provided the bullets. They had hidden the horn in a *tauwa* and the gun in a cattle shed.

Since coming to Chitwan, I had kept hearing that Pushpa, Gupta and Indra Gurung were the main rhino poachers and horn smugglers.

"If you don't arrest the leaders, how can the poaching stop?" informers and well wishers often asked.

Previously, when Pushpa and Gupta had been arrested for rhino poaching, the then army Major of the Devidutta Battalion Preetam Rana had given them a clean chit and released them. Indra was a defendant in the same case. I hadn't been able to garner evidence or proof to convict them. But now that Bhagirath had named them, I was ready to go after them.

That day I had to go to the Langtang National Park. Hence, I called the chief warden, Ranger Bishnu and the colonel together and told them, "I have found proof against Pushpa and Gupta. They will be appearing in the park office asked to on September 12. Don't let Bhagirath pass any news on to the village until then. When they come to the park office, we will arrest them there and then immediately send a team to arrest Maniram and Laxman."

OF TIGER SKINS AND BONES IN LANGTANG

ON THE WAY TO Langtang, I decided to arrest Ravi Pakhrin who had been pointed out by Kanchhalal Waiba. So while leaving for Kathmandu, an informer who could identify Ravi accompanied me. I intended to kill two birds with one stone.

Our office vehicle broke down before reaching Muglin, so we got onto a Kathmandu-bound public bus. Ravi was to be found in the vegetable market at Kalimati in Kathmandu. The following day, we screened hundreds of people for hours in the morning but were unable to find him. I was exhausted.

The informer and I went there again in the evening. There was no sight of him. I had to reach the Langtang National Park at Dhunche, Rasuwa, the next day. "Keep looking for the guy," I told the informer and left.

I was going to Nuwakot and Rasuwa district for the first time, and senior clerk Bhim Bahadur K.C. of the Bardia National Park was also with me. The road was full of hairpin bends and difficult to navigate. About an hour's drive from Bidur Municipality, one particular spot was quite terrifying. The Trishuli River was flowing way below. The dirt road was narrow and had become slippery due to water gushing from the mountain. At that point, the vehicle refused to move forward. The driver Rajendra Giri then applied four wheels and put on the brake and accelerator at the same time. For a moment, I was terrified. We were able to reach the park only in the evening.

Large quantities of tiger skins and bones, leopard skins had been confiscated there. The DNPWC had sent me there to investigate into the matter as these confiscated goods were said to have been sent by T. Chhiring aka Chhawang wanted by the Indian police. The case had not been filed properly. I tried to correct the procedure so that the court did not find reasons to dump the case or release the suspects for not following the procedures properly. The interrogation began, and, as expected, some new suspects were named. The new information revealed a relationship between Pemba Lama aka Yakche and Nutupu Lama a notorious smuggler in the smuggling of wildlife parts.

Chhawang was a man of the notorious Indian smuggler Sansar Chand. Sansar is said to have killed about 200 tigers in India and was arrested in April-May 2005. It was he who had told CBI that Chhawang of Kathmandu was an important member of his gang. Hence, the CBI had forwarded the details of Chhawang to the Nepal Police through Interpol.

Chhawang's stuff had been confiscated by the army's patrol team at Syafrubesi, Rasuwa, inside the Langtang National Park. His personal assistant Balaram Shrestha, who was arrested, confided that Chhawang was headed towards Dolpa through Nepalgunj to buy the herb *Yarsagumba*.

Upon accomplishing my job, I returned to Kathmandu. On our way, the vehicle's axle snapped, and a wheel went rolling on the road. However, we escaped unhurt, only because the road was straight and plane, otherwise we might have lost our lives.

The next day, September 14, was again duty time at the Kalimati vegetable market. The informer had found out where Ravi lived. We had been keeping an eye on his apartment, about 50 to 60 metres away from the market, since 4 in the morning. He came out at around 5 in the morning, climbed the fence and walked straight into the market. But due to the crowds of people and the darkness, I could not tail him. He was wearing a white half jacket. I looked for anyone wearing such a jacket but could not find him. I kept looking for him, and after a long time, caught sight of him. He was returning with vegetables.

I called my office at Kasara and asked the chief warden to contact the army for me. He gave me the telephone number of a lieutenant colonel of the Kathmandu barracks. When I called him, he promised to send a team immediately. We waited a while, but the team failed to arrive. Since the operation was aborted in the morning, we called again in the evening and waited near his apartment. But still the team did not arrive. We returned disappointed.

The next morning, I asked for help from the chief warden of the Shivapuri-Nagarjun National Park, Kathmandu. We were keeping an eye on Ravi's apartment, lest he should leave. When the team from Shivapuri arrived, we proceeded with our operation. I left the team a little far from his room and I went in alone. I pushed open the door of Ravi's room. He was sleeping, covered in a blanket.

"Can I get a room here?" I asked.

"I don't know," said a woman who pushed the door back from inside.

Then I called my team over and entered the room. I woke Ravi up and said, "Let us go, I have some business with you." I had already taken his mobile in my hand.

His wife began asking, "Why? What is this?"

"You come with me, and you will know," I told her.

His kids were watching. We put both of them into our vehicle and took them to the DNPWC Office in Kathmandu.

Now we had to look for Nima Waiba. Kanchhalal had told us that he raised wild boars and sold their meat at Lazimpat. But we could not find him anywhere.

The next day, I reserved a microbus and returned to Kasara with Ravi and his wife, Game Scout Binod Sapkota and Krishna Ram Magar from the DNPWC. In the evening, we interrogated Ravi, who told us many things. He would take horns from Saman Bahadur B.K. aka Mistri of Tandi, and notorious horn smuggler Tamling's son Nima would come to pick them up.

I was surprised to learn that Tamling had sent his son to Kathmandu to take care of the horn business, since he himself had fled to Delhi because he was a suspect in the smuggling business. Men lose their integrity and wisdom when greed for money envelops them. What else could explain the fact that Tamling got his own son involved in the smuggling business, knowing fully well that he could get jailed or even killed, in case he tried to escape during an encounter.

Ravi also revealed that he and Gokul Panta had sold a horn to Yakche. I was very glad that now I had enough evidence to file another case against Yakche, and could also go after another gang in Narayangadh.

SUICIDE TO SAVE A SMUGGLER

ON SEPTEMBER 17, we headed for Tandi to arrest Saman Bahadur. While trying to arrest Raj Kumar Kumal, our informer had told us that Saman Bahadur was the one who repaired Raj Kumar's gun. But since Raj Kumar lied about it every time we asked, the evidence was not strong enough. This time I was sure of myself and left on a motorbike, the informer in tow. He lived near the house of Gunaraj Pathak, a notorious horn trader of his time. I stayed outside while my informer went inside to investigate. Saman Bahadur was at home. So I called for a vehicle and park staff from Sauraha.

When they arrived, I asked one of the elephant keepers to carry a piece of spring iron of a truck.

"Is anyone home?" I asked.

He appeared on the veranda and replied, "Why do you ask?"

The man matched the description given by our informer as well as Ravi.

"I want to make a *khukuri* from this piece of spring iron," said I. He came down. As I chatted with him, I signalled to my friend to call the rest of the team. We continued talking until our team arrived. I then told him to come with us. He did not resist and came quietly. His wife followed us to the parked vehicle. He had already gotten into the vehicle, when his wife screwed up her face and mumbled, "Don't know where they are taking you." We took him to Kasara.

During the interrogation in the evening, he repeated that he had done nothing. The District Forest Office had also arrested him a fortnight ago, but he was released after he refuted all accusations. "I am innocent, sir," he repeated.

When he refused to admit anything, I posed a direct question, "Didn't you give a horn to Ravi Pakhrin?"

"Bring the guy to me," he replied.

When Ravi was brought forth, he was dumbfounded.

"I took three horns from him," said Ravi and mentioned the dates and value of the transactions, too. In the end, he admitted that he had made available those horns.

And then we asked him who had given him those horns, and how many horns he himself had sold. "Hari B.K. of Dumarwana village, Bara, is one of the rhino poachers," he replied. He admitted to having sold a total of nine horns. "Hari gave the horns to a retired pilot named Ramesh from Bara district.

I was very pleased to have gotten such a valuable piece of information from Saman Bahadur. I was glad that now we could tell the people who smuggles horns and how they do it. "Don't let this information leak, and don't let it reach Ramesh," I told all the staff present.

He was returned to his cell, and we went to our rooms. One of our staff members informed me that he refused to have dinner that night. He was fasting because the next day was *Bishwokarma Puja*.

"OK then," I said. There were five or six criminals in the cell along with him.

At about 4 in the morning, there was a knock on my door. It was Game Scout Pahuwari Yadav. He sounded very distressed.

"What is it?" I asked when I woke up.

"Sir, the man we brought yesterday has hanged himself," he said.

I was greatly disturbed. I put on my clothes and headed for the prisoners' cell. There was an attached toilet in the custody room. Inside, the man was hanging from an iron bar in the toilet's

ventilation. I went closer and noticed that he was already dead.

"How did this happen?" I asked the other prisoners in the cell.

"After you brought him to the cell yesterday, he turned to the other side and slept," said Kanchhalal. "I got up to pee in the morning and found him hanging. I was scared and woke my friends, and then called sir (Pahuwari)."

At that time, the chief warden was in Sauraha. The chief warden talked to the Chief District Officer (CDO) and the Superintendent of Police (SP), and a police team arrived. After completing the necessary procedures, the corpse was taken to Bharatpur for the post-mortem. I called Jit Bahadur Lama of Birendra Auto Workshop at Tandi and asked him to inform Saman Bahadur's family. When they arrived, we gave the family members some money to conduct the funeral rites.

I was very sad that a person who could provide solid evidence was now dead. I regretted how easily our hard earned piece of evidence against the heads of the smuggling rings had slipped from our hands. It was our weakness not to be able to save the life of a person in our custody. The incident gave our detractors an opportunity to point their fingers at us. As I pondered over the incident, I concluded that it was a mistake on our part to interrogate him alone. We should have had Ravi Pakhrin with us at all times. Saman Bahadur was probably scared that Ravi had revealed more than what he intended to tell us. With the evidences stacked up against him, he must have concluded that he had no way out and decided to take the drastic measure.

Saman Bahadur had been involved in rhino poaching for a very long time. He had been jailed previously in a poaching case. His father too was in the same business. They used to give horns to Gunaraj, the notorious smuggler. It was from his father that he learned the trade. Saman Bahadur, who made guns himself to shoot rhinos, coincidentally died on the day of *Bishwokarma Puja*, when Hindus worship the deity of the mechanics.

After his death, I decided not to go in search of Hari B.K., the man Saman Bahadur had named, and instead sent my staff. The staff found Hari riding a motorcycle near Simara of Bara. But he sped away on his motorcycle when they tried to catch him.

After a few days, he was seen in a restaurant in Simara. But he stopped at the restaurant for a few minutes only and sped away on his motorcycle again when he saw us. Thus, for the second time, he was able to avoid arrest.

TIGER SKIN HIDDEN IN A RICKSHAW

OUR INFORMER TIPPED us off that tiger skins were being sold near the Chitrasari bridge on the way to Sauraha. So we were there at 8 in the morning on September 30. We were at the western end of the bridge. Two men with Mongoloid faces appeared at the eastern side of the bridge. We asked the informer to keep watch of the person who was coming to deliver the skins. We were taking precautions should the smugglers be suspicious with too many people hovering around.

Shortly after, the seller appeared on the eastern side of the bridge and handed over a sack to the two young men. They got on a rickshaw and started coming towards us. The informer told us to get ready to catch them. But the rickshaw failed to arrive even after a long time. So I went to check, but there was no sign of the rickshaw. I then got on my motorcycle with Game Scout Yam Bahadur Khanal riding pillion.

We left for Devauli village, a probable route of their escape. We asked the rest of the team to follow in their vehicles. I was driving fast. When I asked the people on the road if they had seen a rickshaw pass, they all said no. When we arrived near Tandi, we finally spotted a rickshaw. We were relieved that we had finally found it, but nobody was on it. As we moved on, we spotted two rickshaws. In one of them, the young men were riding. As I neared, I asked Yam Bahadur to get off the bike while I kept driving. I too jumped off the bike and left it on the road as I ran towards them.

Yam Bahadur had caught them both before I got to them. They were startled.

"Where is the stuff?" I asked them, but they refused to answer.

I then asked the rickshaw puller, "Where have these guys put the sack?"

"Under that rug," he replied. I pulled the rickshaw carpet to find a sack. Inside it was a tiger skin. People from around started gathering, wanting to know what was happening. We borrowed a piece of rope from a nearby house to tie the hands of Surendra Gurung of Sirdi and Bir Bahadur Gurung of Simjung villages in Gorkha district. They had been involved in smuggling tiger skins for a long time. We also confiscated $565 from them. However, the man who gave them the skin could not be found.

Kanchhalal Waiba, Ravi Pakhrin and Surendra Gurung all concluded that Bhim Bahadur Syangtan of Bastipur, Makwanpur dealt in horns and tiger skins. For a while after Kanchhalal was arrested, Bhim was not seen in the village, but as time passed, he was more frequently spotted by our informer.

Early in the morning of October 24, we went to Bastipur to arrest him. The informer and one other man went to check if he was at home. The informers returned to tell us that he had gone to the market and was sitting in a shop nearby. But he could not be found there.

Soon, another informer informed us that Bhim Bahadur was chatting with someone on the suspension bridge over the Rapti River. After the man he was chatting with left, I held him from behind by his shirt collar. "Aren't you Bhim Bahadur?" I asked.

"Yes" he replied.

"We have come to take you, come quietly with us," I told him. He did not resist. A little farther on, he tried to talk to a Tamang boy in the Tamang language, but I did not allow him to. I was scared that he might gather the local boys and create a situation. But nothing of the sort happened. We put him in the car and drove off.

WE LEARNT THAT Gopal Praja, brother of Rajan Praja, was coming to Tandi from Padampur on November 18, 2005. Along with an informer who could identify him, I waited at Bakular of Tandi from early morning. At around 11, he got off a tempo. While he was paying his fare, I arrested him.

I asked him how he was. "I am innocent, if you don't believe me, call my wife, my mother," he began saying.

"Why should they prove you false?" I asked him and brought him to Kasara. Like Gopal, several poachers of Padampur, Siddhi, Korak and Shaktikhor had killed many rhinos.

TROUBLE WITH LIEUTENANT COLONEL

INDRA BAHADUR GURUNG, a leader of the rhino poaching team in the island area, was convicted in a case but was set free. The irony was that he was the vice-chairman of the Kalabanjar Buffer Zone User Committee. And he was meeting *subba*

Uttam Prasad on the sly regarding his case. But Bhagirath Chaudhari had stated that Indra Bahadur and his gang members had sold a horn to Yakche in Gokul Panta's house. Indra Bahadur was thus entangled in a new case.

I thought for quite a long time about the best place to nab him. We could arrest him in his home or village, or while he was on his way to the Bhrikuti Paper Mills to sell grass, or while he was going to Narayangadh. But it would be easiest to arrest him when he came to the Gajapur army post, which he was in the habit of frequenting. I discussed this issue with Ranger Bishnu Thapaliya and had a letter written to the battalion headquarters. "Since Indra Bahadur is a defendant in a rhino case," the letter read, "would the Gajapur post please help by arresting and delivering him to us?" Since I was the officiating chief warden then, I myself had signed the letter.

When Lieutenant Colonel Ajit saw the letter, he went wild. "Who is he to order me?" said he. Though I probably should have talked to him before writing the letter, I meant well. Besides, the letter was not written to an individual, but to an office. He telephoned the Chief Warden, Shivaraj Bhatta, demanding to know how someone could possibly dare to order the Royal Nepal Army. I was shocked when the chief warden called me from Kathmandu.

"I have the office copy of the letter, let us discuss this when you are back," I told him.

After the colonel created unnecessary trouble, I decided to arrest Indra Bahadur without the help of the army. In the meantime, Tirtha Bahadur Shrestha, a biodiversity expert was on a field visit to re-evaluate the park's five-year management plan and prepare a new one. I got to know that he had an interaction programme scheduled with the Kalabanjar Buffer Zone User Committee on November 30. The chairman of the committee had gone to India, so I assumed the vice-chairman would be present. I decided to arrest Indra Bahadur there.

However, on that very day I had to go to Bharatpur. Immediately upon returning from my trip, I hurried to the interaction spot, only to see Tirtha Bahadur Shrestha returning from the programme. But we still hurried towards the office of the user committee. Upon enquiry, a man told us that Indra Bahadur had gone to a teashop. A lot of people were having tea there, and Indra asked us to join him.

After the tea, I called Indra Bahadur aside and told him, "We have come to take you. The chief warden wants to talk to you."

"I understand," he replied. "I will come later."

"Now," I told him. Don't try to run away, we will take you anyhow."

He was hesitating. "I have to go home to take some clothes," he said.

"Fine, let's go together in the vehicle, and then we can go to Kasara later," I said. We then pretended to drive towards his home, but changed track and headed for Kasara.

Indra Bahadur confirmed the statements given by Puspa, Gupta and Ravi Pakhrin, and admitted that he had given the horn to Gokul, who, in turn, had given it to Yakche. He also admitted to receiving $289. We questioned him mildly without exerting too much pressure, so he was still hiding a lot of information.

Though we had arrested him without any help from outside, we still reported the incident to the DNPWC that the arrest had been made through the combined efforts of the Purano Gorakh Battalion and the Anti-poaching Unit team.

At that point, the colonel again created trouble, wanting to know why the army was mentioned when they weren't involved in the operation. Previously, when we didn't include the name of the battalion while arresting culprits without the help of the army, he would complain. But in this case what had actually happened was that Indra Bahadur had passed on the news of his arrest to a Gurung general through family members. When the general talked to Ajit about it, he made the operation a prestige issue and decided to free Indra Bahadur. He was looking for me to get Indra Bahadur's release, but I was in Bharatpur attending a two-day workshop organised by BISEP-ST.

The chief warden was still not back from Kathmandu when I returned from the workshop. "The chief warden talked to me over the phone and asked that you resolve the issue with the colonel," Ranger Bishnu told me.

I took Bishnu along with me to the meeting with the colonel. In an arrogant tone, he told me, "How dare you challenge the army?"

I politely told him my side of the story. He, however, got only more irritated and asked me, "Why did you arrest Indre?"

"Because he is a defendant in a case that was filed after the army arrested his poaching partner," I explained. Bhagirath had been arrested by the Gajapur post. I had taken the file of the case along, and Major Ganga had perused it.

"Release Indre, and then I will order the major to arrest him," the colonel said.

"I cannot release a defendant after arresting him, this is no child's play," I said. "The villagers will think he bribed us. The media will start writing about us. Our enemies will get a chance to blame us, I cannot do that."

He then called Chief Warden Shivaraj Bhatta on his mobile. "Sir, you must convince this fellow," he said.

I told the chief warden I couldn't release Indra Bahadur for the reasons mentioned above. "But you are the boss, and if you want to release him, then I will take a few days' leave. You can ask someone else to be the officiating chief."

"It's a sticky situation," said the chief warden in a low voice and stopped speaking.

"Give it to me," said the colonel and snatched the receiver from my hands. "Now there is no way I can hold dialogue with you guys," said he.

We prepared to leave. "*Namaskar*, sir," we said to him.

"Get lost," he replied. Major Ganga tried to console us when we were out of the office.

THE CDO'S PLAN

I HAD ARRESTED and jailed Yakche. But Narendraraj Poudel, the CDO of Chitwan, had close family relations with the notorious horn smuggler. *Subba* Uttam Prasad had officially complained about me to the CDO's office, too. In an attempt to corner me, Poudel had a fake document prepared that stated Yakche was ill. He then had me talk to Narayan Dahal, a journalist friend of Yakche. When he couldn't get Yakche released even then, he requested for the prisoner's transfer. Our office did not grant the request, but he forced Yakche's transfer to the Central Jail in Kathmandu. He himself went to Kathmandu to talk to the director-general of the Jail Management Department.

I was already demoralised by this incident, when the CDO summoned me again to tell me, "A prisoner serving a sentence in the district jail in a rhino case has apparently contracted Hepatitis B. Other prisoners are threatening to rebel as they might contract the disease. So I have talked to the Central Jail, where his accommodation will be ready in a few days. Until then you must keep this man at Kasara."

"There are just two rooms at Kasara for the detainees. So they too might contract Hepatitis B," I told him. But he refused to listen and instead brought the man to Kasara with the help of the police and jail officials.

We emptied one room and had the patient, Mangale Praja aka Taakule, stay in there. The staff would place the food for him from afar, scared that they might contract the disease.

"It's just a matter of two weeks, please cooperate," I requested them. However, even after 15 days, the CDO did not bother to take him away and always made excuses when I broached the subject.

At that point, I thought of releasing Mangale on bail. However, the chief warden cautioned me that it might be a ploy on the part of the CDO. "If we release Mangale, then he will ask us to release Yakche who is sick as well. If we release one person, then others too will create excuses to be released on bail, and it will become a disease in itself. So we can't release him."

After nearly six months in our custody, Mangale died.

THE WRONG CALL

I WAS IN KATHMANDU on official business when Yakche's mobile that we had confiscated rang on January 31, 2006. The area code showed Bara district. We mostly received calls from smugglers on this phone. One day a man from Rukum said, "I have 13 kilos of *Yarsagumba*." Smugglers usually looked for Yakche's wife Phinjo.

I received the phone.

"Hello, *Sahuji*?"

"Yes, what is it?"

"*Sahuji*, I am Kumar."

I sprang to attention. This man must be Raj Kumar Lama, I assumed. Mandal Mahato, an elephant keeper who had been arrested, had named him and said that he worked at Simara airport. I asked, "Is this Raj Kumar?"

"Yes," he replied.

"Raj Kumar, *Sahuji* has gone to India on business. Please tell me if you have anything to say."

"I have business with *Sahuji*."

"What is it?"

"I have something to sell."

"What is it? Is it a horn?"

"Yes."

"I need to talk to *Sahuji*, I will contact him today, please call me tomorrow," I said.

He called again the next day.

"I will come with a vehicle tomorrow," I said. "But what is the price? How much money should I bring?"

"$10,331"

"OK, but I will fix the price only after looking at the horn tomorrow."

I arrived in Kasara the same day and talked with the colonel. It would not be wise to go after him without weapons as he was a local don of sorts. We planned to go with an army team, but things didn't work out that day. He called me again.

"I have arrived in Chitwan," I lied. "I am staying here tonight as there seems to be a transport strike here. I will get there at 11 in the morning tomorrow."

February 2 was Wetlands Day. We were releasing Gharial crocodiles in the Rapti River, and there was another programme at the Bis-Hajari Lake. I had to go and sign letters of appreciation. It was already 2 in the afternoon by the time we finished doing so and reached Simara with Lieutenant Sagar Karki's team. Raj Kumar had asked me to call him from Simara Chowk.

"I will come with a friend," I had told him. We asked two of the soldiers and Game Scout Yam Bahadur Khanal to stay inside the District Forest Office, and we started walking towards Simara Chowk. I had given one of my phones to Yam Bahadur and asked him to come when I called. I also pointed out where Raj Kumar's house was located as an informer had shown me the house on my last visit to Simara.

On the way I asked the lieutenant, "You do have a pistol, don't you?"

"Yes," he replied.

Raj Kumar called as we were about to reach Simara Chowk.

"We are at Simara Chowk, where do we go next?" I asked him.

"I am coming on a bike 'Na 2 Pa 2278'. Stay right where you are."

We waited at Simara Chowk. In a short while, a man on a motorcycle came from the north. "*Namaste dai*," I greeted him first, making him feel important. We shook hands.

"I will go ahead," said he, "follow me and stop when I stop my bike."

I had assumed we were going to his home, but he went to the next home past the crossroad to the airport. We reached a house. A couple of women were watching TV in the living room.

"Where is Raja?" he asked the women. "Didn't I tell you to vacate the room?"

A fair man in his sixties entered the room and asked the women to leave. Once in the living room, we made small talk and then got down to business.

"I have to see it," I declared.

Raj Kumar asked the old man, "Please get it."

"Also call the man who has it," I requested. I was hoping to arrest both of them together.

"No brother, we can't, we are just brokers who make a few pennies out of every deal," said he.

"Alright then," I conceded.

The old man left, and Raj Kumar told us, "I have given five or six of them to Phinjo *didi* already. She hides them in her body and takes them. She is a very clever, very fearless woman."

According to what he said, Yakche's wife Phinjo herself came to get the horns. She would come in a loose *bakhkhu* (*Bhote* dress) and would hide the horns in it. My informer too had told me several times that a woman in a *Bhote* dress came by plane to Simara for the horns.

"I myself took one in a plane," continued Raj Kumar. "Since I am a staff myself, I wasn't checked. Then I took one on a motorcycle to Kathmandu, but I was very scared then." Thus he confessed to having sold nearly 10 horns to them, meaning Yakche and his wife Phinjo.

In a while the old man arrived with a plastic bag and put it in my hands. I looked at the horn inside the bag, smelled it and gave it to the lieutenant. He did the same.

"Is it OK?" I asked the lieutenant.

"Yes," he replied.

"How much?" I asked Raj Kumar.

"I was hoping for $10,331, but I will settle for $8,953."

"What's the weight?"

"One kilo."

"Please reconsider the price," I said.

"We ourselves just get a few pennies for working as brokers, no more."

The lieutenant and I swapped confidences in whispers. Then I told him, "We have arrested the man you called from Kathmandu. We have come from the Chitwan National Park to arrest you. Come quietly with us, otherwise it will turn bad for you."

They were shocked. I called Yam Bahadur on the phone and told him to come past the location I mentioned and to drive past the chowk. "You will see a motorcycle with plate No. 2278, come right in," I told him.

Raj Kumar tried to get up from the sofa, saying he wanted to go get his jacket.

"Don't get up," I threatened as I pushed him back onto the sofa. "We have weapons, we will shoot if you try to leave," I told him. The lieutenant pointed his pistol at them. The old man had been quiet all this time, and now both sat down at the sight of the gun.

I put the horn in my bag. In the bag were my diary, mobile charger, camera, letter authorising the arrest and office letter heads.

But our friends did not arrive even in five minutes. I did not think it wise to stay there for long. "They still haven't arrived, they are probably lost. I think I should go and pick them up. Can you cover them?" I said.

"Yes," he replied. I had the bag over my shoulders. But then again, I thought to myself, "If the police sees me walking around the airport with a red bag, they might get unduly suspicious (thinking I am a Maoist) and create unnecessary trouble for me. So I asked the lieutenant, "Can I leave the bag here?"

"Yes," he replied. I put the bag down on the sofa and hurried outside.

I walked fast towards the crossroad near the airport. However, there was no sight of the vehicle. I was very tense, as this was Raj Kumar's area, and if the locals found out, they might just go on a riot. As I turned west from the chowk, I saw the vehicle approaching. I got into it fast, and we drove towards the house. However, only the lieutenant was there.

"What happened?" I asked.

"They escaped," he replied. I was very depressed at having to lose the criminals we had just nabbed.

"Where is the bag?" I asked again.

"They took that, too," he said. I grew very worried.

"I have imprisoned one of them in there," said he. But when we opened the door, he wasn't to be found either. He had escaped from the back door.

We ran to the back of the house. Just behind the house, we saw the old man running. When he saw us, he got nervous and fell down. We arrested him, and our colleagues took him to the vehicle. On a hunch, we ran to the right, looking for the other man. We asked the women who were weeding the wheat field,

"Did you see a man run by?"

"Yes, he went this way," they pointed north. We ran that way but found no trace of the man even after running half a kilometre. Again we came across two women who were working in a wheat field. When we asked, they pointed towards the north by hand. After running about 300 more metres, we saw the man with a red half jacket walking ahead. Apparently he was tired from running and had taken off his jacket, unaware of our presence just behind him. We swooped down on him and took him to the vehicle even as people nearby looked on in surprise.

BAG OF TENSIONS

THOUGH WE HAD managed to arrest both the men, we hadn't found the bag. When I asked, Raj Kumar replied that a man waiting outside had run away with it. But the lieutenant insisted that Raj Kumar was the one who had taken it.

By this time a lot of people had gathered around. Raj Kumar was asking the people he knew to call the inspector. "I will go get you the inspector myself," said the lieutenant and left. We put both the culprits in our vehicle and did not allow other people to draw near. His sons and relatives were aggressive and trying to come near. "Don't come near," we threatened them, and our soldiers became just as aggressive. They then backed off.

In 15 minutes, a police team arrived with a sub-inspector. We were relieved. The lieutenant, however, arrived 15 minutes later on foot with the inspector. I tried to pull Raj Kumar out of the vehicle as I asked him to show me the bag.

"Don't force him now, we will help you look for your bag," said the inspector. I immediately understood why Raj Kumar had been looking for him.

The inspector's uniform bore the name tag L. Giri. As we were leaving with Raj Kumar, the lieutenant asked him his full name. It was Laxman Giri.

On the way back, we found out that the old man, called Yudhisthir Jung Rana, was married to Raj Kumar Lama's sister.

I again turned to Raj Kumar, "The situation might turn against your sister, too. Tell me, where is the bag?"

"Some guy took it," he repeated.

"Which guy?"

"He is a Tharu from Chitwan, Padampur. He lives in the Tharu area in Bara."

"What is his name?"

"I don't know, I think he said Bishnu Chaudhari."

I then concluded that he would not reveal anything more there, we would have to interrogate Raj Kumar in Kasara to really learn about the missing bag. At that time, I was more worried about some top police or army official calling us to get the man released than about the bag. Hence, we did not inform anyone about the operation, and proceeded straight to Hakim Chowk, Chitwan. We took snacks there and then headed for Kasara.

WHAT HAPPENED AFTER I left the room? Both Raj Kumar and Yudhishthir would try to get up from time to time, and the lieutenant would order them to sit down. Even as the lieutenant was pointing the gun at them, Yudhishthir made an attempt to take hold of the pistol. Grabbing the opportunity, Raj Kumar fled, taking the bag with him. Yudhishthir in his statement said that the lieutenant had bargained with him to "let go of my hand, and I promise nothing will happen to you." He released the lieutenant but got kicked and pushed into another room, and the door was shut on him. Yudhisthir, however, escaped from the back door. What with Yudhisthir holding onto the lieutenant's hand and the subsequent struggle to free himself, the magazine of the lieutenant's pistol had fallen to one side.

Later, our colleagues found it and gave it back to him.

"I didn't shoot at them as I thought it would create more problems," the lieutenant told us.

We again questioned Yudhisthir and Raj Kumar at Kasara, but they kept lying to us. "I lied to you about giving the horns to Phinjo, I only said that so that you would pay me more," Raj Kumar confided. "Mandal Mahato had given me one horn, which I sold in Kathmandu. The rest is all lies," he said. About the bag too, he kept repeating the previous lie.

Army officers questioned him at the barracks the next day, but they also could get no information about the bag. I was more worried about my diary than the horn now, as my diary contained a lot of information about smugglers, and it would set us back by miles if it fell into the hands of wrong people. When there was nothing else I could do, I submitted a report to the office explaining everything.

We then got busy in our own business. Ten days later, I was at the eye hospital in Bharatpur with my wife and son Kalpa Jung, when I received a call from Kasara. "Good news, sir," said a colleague. "Your bag has been found. It was found in a *tauwa*, and all your stuff is there."

When we returned from the hospital, a reporter identifying herself as Chandani called me from Kalika FM. "Apparently, a horn was found in your bag, can you explain it?" she demanded. I did not want to make the details of the operation public, as smugglers might gain information and plan accordingly. So I told her that since the case was under investigation, I could not tell her anything.

"The news we are doing isn't very positive about you, it might harm you," she told me, but I did not take her seriously.

A little while later, we were having tea at the Crystal Restaurant at Hakim Chowk when we heard the main news on the Kalika FM. It said: "Horn found in the bag of Assistant Warden

Kamal Jung Kunwar at Simara of Bara district." I still did not take the matter seriously. The news kept blaring: "Ghimire noticed an abandoned red bag in his *tauwa* and informed the police. On opening it, the police found Kamal Jung Kunwar's diary, camera, horn, charger, letter pad and letters authorising the arrest." Krishna Khaniya, owner of the restaurant, asked me jokingly what the matter was, and I described the incident to him in short.

I reached Kasara in the evening, and finally found out what had happened. The man called Ghimire had gone to his *tauwa* early in the morning and noticed an abandoned bag. It would have been tempting to take the bag home and see if there were precious things in it, but these were Maoist times, so he was scared and had called the police. Inspector Laxman Giri had arrived on the scene. We had informed him when we arrested Raj Kumar that a bag containing a horn had been lost. When the horn and the diary with my name clearly written on it were found, the people began saying that I was trying to frame Raj Kumar. Though the inspector knew the truth, he was staging a drama to get back at me for arresting Raj Kumar. He even talked of holding a press conference to accuse me. Commander (Major) of the Army Company at the Parsa Wildlife Reserve protection unit learnt about it and stopped the press conference from taking place.

The bag was delivered to the Parsa Wildlife Reserve Office. I went to take it the next day. The major called me, and I told him what had happened. He was shocked. "You guys work so hard, and yet so much backlash against you? This is a country cursed by a *sati*. No good will ever come to any honest person."

That day and several days after that, lots of well wishers called me to express their sympathies while others had gone to my relative Hari Bahadur Karki in the Madi Valley to jeer at him: "See what your relative has done!"

I was sick of repeating the incident to everyone. The one report aired by Kalika FM kept hounding me for long. I found out later that the park staff had told journalist Chandani the truth that very day. But the FM insisted on broadcasting its own version. Later Kalika FM tried to correct the newscast, but the damage had been done.

Had anyone wanted to frame Raj Kumar, he would have left the illegal stuff at his home, not in someone else's *tauwa*. If I did have the intention, then I wouldn't have put my identification in the bag along with the illegal stuff, knowing only too well that I would be landing myself in a sticky situation. I was surprised how people could believe such hard-to-believe news without even subjecting it to a cursory examination.

I was shocked by the way the police and journalists, who actually knew the truth, were trying to mislead the public. It was very painful for me to find that my own colleagues at the office had discussed this matter among themselves, wondering what I was up to. I was very glad that the lieutenant was with me that day, otherwise Colonel Ajit would have found even more reasons to go after me with full force.

RHINO CARCASS

SOMETIME AGO, poachers had shot at and wounded a rhino in broad daylight and fled. The spot was west of the Tiger Tops Hotel and south of the Baghmara post, nearly 200 metres away. As we followed their footsteps, we found that they had turned to Andraulighat of the Rapti River at Meghauli village. The next day, while the army was returning from its patrol and nearing the Khoriya Muhan post, a gunshot was heard about 10 minutes' walking distance towards Devi *Tal* to the south. The army immediately set out but couldn't catch the poachers even after chasing them till the Deurali hill of Tiger Tops. We could deduce from this that the poachers were very familiar with the location, and they were entering it from Meghauli.

After the death of Jhalendra Gurung and Anil Ghising in a case related to rhino poaching a few years back, many poachers from Meghauli had fled to India. We were suddenly tipped off that these people had been spotted in the village in the last couple of months. On the basis of this information, we had gone to Meghauli with a team in around November-December of 2005.

One day, a school at Jitpur was staging a cultural programme. The informer felt that we should arrest both Surya Bahadur Kumal (Patake Krishna) and Bir Bahadur Kumal there. But he didn't tell us when the programme would start. When we reached there, the programme had already ended.

The next day we received information that the two were at home. It would be more convenient for us to coordinate with the Baghmara post for this operation. Since poachers were getting active in Baghmara, the army had a post there, and a ranger from Amaltari was also posted there. I went to Baghmara and talked to the ranger and lieutenant, and returned to Kasara after preparing for the operation.

But the operation could not take place that day. The senior game scout, who had gone to the neighbouring village, returned late. And the lieutenant also said, "I have a feeling danger is lurking, so I do not want to go."

Poaching had kind of stopped in that area for a while, so we did not feel the necessity to go on an operation.

IN THE THIRD WEEK of January 2006, we found a dead rhino one kilometre east of the Tiger Tops Tented Camp. This was dangerous as the rhino had been dead for approximately two weeks, and the horn had been taken. It was indeed worrying for us that a rhino should be killed in an area thickly populated by rhinos, hitherto unknown to poachers. Hence, I called informers from Padampur and posted them at Madi and the Indian border.

In the meantime, we received news from Meghauli that Patake Krishna and Bir Bahadur were at home. I asked Ranger Shivanarayan Shah at the Bhimle post to coordinate with the army and carry out the operation. Accordingly, they arrested Patake Krishna on February 12. They did not go after Bir Bahadur.

Patake Krishna had been in the Nepal Army for five years. He admitted to killing a rhino near the tented camp with four others. The poacher was Hari Bahadur B.K. I was amazed to learn that a man from Bara district would come all the way to Meghauli to poach. But then, he was just a cog in the smuggling machinery. People like Pilot Ramesh, Jhalendra Gurung, Anil Ghising, Gyamjo, Karma Lama, Yakche, Tamling, Gokul Panta, Indra Bahadur Gurung and Saman Bahadur were the ones who ran the real show.

FIGHT WITH POACHERS

OUR INFORMER HAD told me that a man called Sanu Tamang of Jutpani was also a poacher. Patake Krishna, too, confirmed this in his statement. "Sanu of Jutpani is the one who brings in the poachers," said he. Sanu became more cautious after Patake Krishna was arrested. One day in February-March 2006, we received information from an informer who had only recently joined us that Sanu was at home, so we went after him. I parked my vehicle at the eastern side of Jutpani and walked alone towards his home. Near his home in a tea shop that happened to belong to his brother, I decided to have some tea.

As I was having tea, Sanu's wife and child came towards the shop. The child was quite endearing, and I gave him a biscuit.

I asked what his name was. Happy with the biscuit, he lisped his name to me.

Seizing the opportunity, I asked the woman, "Is this your child?"

"No," she said, looking uncomfortable.

She seemed to be suspicious of me. I was sure that this was Sanu's wife, as she matched the description given by Patake Krishna. She was slim, fair, wore glasses and had small rings on her ears.

Sanu, however, was nowhere to be seen. A little while later, the informer again informed me that he wasn't at home.

The next day, we received information that he came home in the evening and left early in the morning at 4. We decided to arrest him at the shop in the evening. Although there were only the two of us, Game Scout Nageshwor and I decided to give it a try. However, Sanu did not come home that day.

Again on March 5, we were alerted: Sanu Tamang is at home. I went on a motorcycle to check. I was sitting in a shop near a school beside his home when I was told he had arrived on a bike. I relayed the information to our team.

In a short while, we heard that Sanu and his wife were heading west on a cycle. I didn't know him. Since he had left on a cycle, I felt that this was the best time to get to know him. Seeing me overtake him and speed away, my colleagues had their vehicle hurtling after me. Sanu probably got suspicious, and we lost sight of him as he disappeared somewhere in between the houses on the way. We again returned to Jutpani. Those were Maoist times, and people stared at our big group with a vehicle in tow.

We were drinking tea, when the informer told us that Sanu was coming towards the market on a cycle. We were alert but saw no Sanu. When the informer arrived, he chided us for not arresting Sanu.

"Sanu is repairing his cycle, and Game Scout Pahuwari Yadav is standing nearby," he said pointing to one direction, but I saw no one. I looked all over the place when a crowd of people to the west caught my eye. I ran towards the place and found Pahuwari and Sanu engaged in a brawl. Pahuwari was trying to catch him, while Sanu was trying to run away.

"Catch him, don't let him go," I shouted at Pahuwari. Upon seeing me, Pahuwari held Sanu with renewed strength, and Sanu fell down.

"Why, what happened?" the people in the crowd were asking.

"Nothing, please leave all of you," I replied.

Pahuwari and I forcibly dragged him to our vehicle. Our colleagues arrived, too. We put his cycle on the vehicle's hood. "What are you doing?" his wife was shouting as she came towards us. But we sped away to Bharatpur.

I had planned to arrest Sanu quietly and get him to call Hari Bahadur B.K. The crowd had collected because Pahuwari had tried to arrest him all alone. These things happen while conducting operations. Since the family of Hari Bahadur's second wife lived at Jutpani, we were afraid he would come to know of what had happened. Just to make sure that Sanu's wife didn't warn Hari Bahadur, we got Sanu to instruct her accordingly by phone from Narayangadh.

Upon interrogation at Kasara, Sanu admitted to killing a rhino with Hari Bahadur and selling the horn to Gyalbo Gurung in Kathmandu. "I can give you Hari Bahadur and Gyalbo's address," he said. Lieutenant Sagar Karki and our team left for Kathmandu with Sanu on March 10.

We had information that Hari Bahadur had a grille workshop at Gongabu in Kathmandu. We went there, but it was closed. We then went to Gyalbo's abode at Hattigauda. He too was not to be found, only his motorcycle was standing there. Maybe someone had informed them of our departure from Kasara.

We looked for them the next day too but couldn't find them. We nearly arrested someone else in Gongabu, thinking it was Hari Bahadur. Since we were unable to find anyone, we returned to Chitwan late in the afternoon. A bus had met with an accident near Khaireni of Jalbire in Dhading. And at that place, our vehicle's battery ran out, so we needed to haul it along. After requesting several drivers, a truck driver finally agreed to tow it. With difficulty, we arrived in Chitwan at around 10 at night. This trip to Kathmandu wasn't very fruitful either. When Lieutenant Sagar and I are in the same team, there's always bad luck.

COMING QUIETLY, UNKNOWINGLY

BIR BAHADUR KUMAL, who should have been arrested with Patake Krishna but somehow was overlooked, was now seen with his second wife in Gunjanagar village. We went to the Gajapur post and asked them to confirm the information and arrest him. But they could not find him. Instead they found another man bearing the same name.

Early in the morning of March 25, we received a phone call: Bir Bahadur was seen at Sisawar of Dibyanagar village. Since the driver was late, Yam Bahadur Khanal and I left in a vehicle for the Bhagedi post. Senior Game Scout Sheshchandra Chaudhari joined us there, and we left for the house where Bir Bahadur was staying. We parked a little farther on and walked straight towards the house. He was drinking. We had with us a photograph of him from the Tiger Tops Lodge where he had been an employee previously. I recognised him immediately. When we tried to take him away, his sister-in-law tried to stop us, but we pushed her aside.

Bir Bahadur named many rhino poachers from Meghauli. We sent some staff and informers to find out if these people were at home. "All of them are at home," the staff said.

We sought the help of the barracks to carry out the operation and left the Bhimle post at night. We crossed the Rapti and started walking along the bank. At one place, there was a rhino just five metres away from us, but Game Scout Mahendra Thapa kept walking straight towards the animal. I pulled him back and shouted, "Go away." The rhino came towards us instead and only ran away when we all shouted at it.

When we reached our destination, we raided six or seven houses but found no one in any of them. Finally, we reached Lalu Kumal's house. I woke a man who was sleeping in a small house and asked him, "Are you Lalu Kumal?"

"Yes," he replied.

"Then get up, come with us."

He followed us quietly.

After walking for a while, Mahendra said, "Sir, this is not Lalu Kumal."

"How do you know?"

"Lalu Kumal is dark, and this man is fair. He is short, and I was wondering how he managed to become so tall."

"Where are you from?" I asked the man.

"Syangja district."

"Why are you here then?"

"To look for *musuro*."

"Then why did you say you are Lalu Kumal?"

"I was sleepy, and I didn't understand what you said."

We left the man there and ran back to Lalu Kumal's home. Lalu Kumal's wife and children were watching us from the courtyard.

"Where is Lalu?" we enquired.

"He is sleeping upstairs."

We went upstairs and woke him up. His wife and daughter also followed us, insisting on accompanying Lalu. They walked with us for quite a distance. We ran one operation after another the whole night and returned to the *ghat* near the Baghmara post. From there we drove to Kasara.

RHINO POACHING HAD more recently increased in eastern Chitwan. On March 27, 2006 as we waited for someone near Sauraha Chowk at Tandi, we joked amongst ourselves that we would arrest the person indicated by our informer on that day. Just then we saw a man on a cycle going from Bakulahar, Tandi to Sauraha Chowk. An informer recruited under the poacher use as anti-poacher plan pointed at the man and exclaimed, "That's Sukai on the cycle. He also is a poacher."

We instantly followed him in our vehicle. I parked our vehicle a little ahead of his cycle and arrested him as he was still riding. Other staff arrived, too, and we took him to Kasara. Our aim was to arrest at least one person a day. One of our colleagues joked that we had fulfilled the day's quota.

We questioned him. At first, he refused to admit anything. "They made me drink, and I don't know where they took me. They killed the rhino and gave me $138, too," he said.

On April 5, I went home. The following day, the people's movement of the seven political parties began. Since the movement went on for a long time, I couldn't return to Kasara immediately. In the meantime, Rajendra Prasad Chaudhari aka Sukai admitted to helping kill nine rhinos and earning $2,479 in return. When the colonel got wind of this, he transported him and Patake Krishna to the army barracks. But army barracks are not authorised to hold people in custody.

DEAD RHINO ON A WEBSITE

AN INCIDENT DATING back to September-October 2004 keeps haunting me. It was the day after *Dashain*, when I received information from the Machan Resort that said: "At 4 in the afternoon, gun shots were heard. On investigation, a dead rhino with a missing horn was found." Since the incident took place more than two hours ago, and it would take us nearly three hours to get to Sunachuri from Kasara, Ranger Bishnu and I decided to go only the next day.

We left for Sunachuri early the following morning. When Bishnu informed the barracks, he was assured of an army team from the Khagendramalli post at the site. Since our vehicle could not cross the Rapti, the Machan Resort had arranged for another vehicle for us. We got off and then went on elephant back. A guest from the resort was also with us on the elephant. Since I was worried about the rhino's death, I did not talk to him.

It took us about half an hour to reach the spot. It was a male rhino, around five years old. Its horn and tail were missing. There was a small pond nearby, and the rhino had been shot from a *kutmero* tree to

the north as it was wading in the water. The rhino had staggered around in pain and come west. From the broken branches, it was clear from which tree the poachers had kept watch of the rhino.

A post-mortem was conducted and the bullet taken out of its body. It was a sphere bullet, meaning a home-made gun had been used. We looked around. A poacher had left behind a blue Magic slipper while running away. There were clear footprints going west. They had even left behind a small piece of cloth used for carrying ammunition.

We took pictures of the spot. Still soldiers from the Khagendramalli army post had not arrived. We returned to the resort, where friends sympathised with us over the death of the rhino. The guest, who had been on the elephant with me, introduced himself. He was from the *Kantipur* newspaper. "Oh, so he is a journalist," I told myself. I learnt that on the previous day, a Swedish journalist had taken a picture of the dead rhino.

News of the death, along with pictures of the bleeding rhino, appeared on the Internet. There was a huge uproar over the news and the minister for forests reprimanded the Director-general of the DNPWC, Tirthaman Maskey: "I hear that there is no warden in Chitwan. And also nobody went to confirm the rhino's death." Maskey, in turn, telephoned me, and I explained everything to him.

"I know why the minister has such a viewpoint. The minister scolded me for no reason," said he. What had actually happened was that Colonel Ajit was not aware that I had attended office after *Dashain* and had gone to the site where the rhino was found dead. The colonel had complained to an advisor to the king, and he, in turn, had chastised the minister.

Later, the minister demanded a report of the incident. We sent a report to the DNPWC that included a photocopy of the affidavit. Upon seeing the report, the minister complained, "Kamal Jung Kunwar has sent me a predated affidavit." Bishnu was angry and sent him another report that included photographs of the site, on which the date was clearly visible. The minister made no further comments after that.

That incident left me with a sense of purpose. I was determined to arrest the man by any means. So I made a lot of promises and provided lots of incentives to an informer. I gave him quite a huge sum in pocket money. He asked for more money as he "had to pay his son's school fees and also pay back loans taken for the *Dashain* festival." I gave him the extra money, too. But despite the informer's efforts, we couldn't arrest the man.

In the fourth week of March, we received information that the poacher, Chandra Bahadur Magar, was seen at his home. I told my informer, "Let's arrest him during the day." Actually we had been planning to arrest Padaru and his brother Jhagaru Mahato of Padampur on March 29, 2006 when we received a phone call.

"Chandra Bahadur is at home," it said. We immediately left for Sunachuri. We couldn't find the informer at home, and his wife told us he had gone to Piple village in Chitwan.

"Do you know Chandra Bahadur Magar?" I asked her.

"Yes."

"Where does he live?"

"There is a petrol pump at Dhubichaur, Piple. His house is the one to the left just behind it. It's a thatched house facing north."

We asked at a shop near the petrol pump, "Do you know Chandra Bahadur Magar?"

The shopkeeper said no.

The shopkeeper then asked some of the school children who had dropped in at the shop if they knew Chandra Bahadur's house.

"That is the one," a student pointed out.

"Do you know him?"

"Yes, I do."

"Where is he?"

"See the people standing in front of the house? He is the one wearing the hat and a red vest."

"Why do you want to know?" he asked later.

"We have come from his village to meet him," I replied.

I asked my colleagues to come through a different route. Ranger Ritesh Bhushan Basnet was joining an anti-poaching operation for the first time. Game Scout Nageshwor Chaudhari and I started for Chandra Bahadur's house right away.

Chandra Bahadur was talking to his neighbours near his house. I made an excuse to talk to him. "We have come to talk about the Rapti Embankment Maintenance Project. Do you know where the chairman lives?"

"I don't know about the embankment committee, but a member of the buffer zone user committee lives there," he pointed to a house.

"OK, that will do. Can you come with us and show us the house?" I asked

As we neared his house, he wanted to go inside to change his clothes. I was afraid he might run away or return with weapons. "We have come for you, come with us," I said as I held him by the collar of his shirt. He was stronger than me and tried to twist my hand. I knew that when a man being held by the collar tries to escape, one should hold him by his pants. So I held him by the waist of his pants. As I had held him very tightly, I found out later that the last joint of my ring finger had got twisted.

Nageshwor held him by his arms. Ritesh Bhushan, who saw us dragging him, came running to help. Chandra Bahadur was still trying his best to escape as he was calling to the other villagers. His wife was tugging at the other end. Out of irritation, Ranger Ritesh nearly punched him.

We pulled him to the road. We had to walk beside a canal, and it was not easy for so many people to walk together on the narrow borders of the field. He then rested his back against the wall of the irrigation canal and refused to budge from there.

I took off my belt and fastened it to his waist. We then pulled him from the front towards the vehicle with great difficulty. He was asking the people who had gathered around to get him released.

As we were pushing him into the vehicle, his wife kept insisting that she come, too. "I will bring my two kids also," she said. We took everyone to Sauraha. There, we gave the kids food. The poor kids didn't know where they were and ate it with relish.

We left them at Sauraha and went to Bharatpur to arrest Padaru Mahato. We were told that he had gone to a construction site and would return only in the evening in a reserved minibus. We were given the minibus number. We would have to stop the bus and check. We had a man with us who could identify him. As we reached the middle of the Tikauli jungle, my mobile phone rang. It was Ranger Pramod Yadav on the phone. "Chandra Bahadur has just revealed that he has hidden two guns in the park. One of his poaching gang members is still in his home. He might run away if he learns of Chandra Bahadur's arrest, so Chandra Bahadur thinks we must leave right away."

We cancelled our plans to arrest Padaru and returned with our vehicle to Sauraha.

From Sauraha, we along with Chandra Bahadur and a few other friends left for Manahari. This time we had handcuffs with us. The other poacher happened to be his nephew. His house as well as the people inside could be seen from the highway. We waited and watched to see if anyone matching the description given by Chandra Bahadur was around. We saw no one.

Since it was late already, and the Maoists could be keeping a watch on us, we decided to leave. I called Chief Warden Tikaram Adhikari from the Machan Resort at Sunachuri and told him, "Chandra Bahadur has promised to show us his guns tomorrow, and we need to raid and arrest two others. We should go on a combined mission with the army."

He agreed and asked me to coordinate with the colonel.

When I called Colonel Ajit, he asked me where I was.

"I am at the Sunachuri post, talking from the Machan Resort," I said.

"I don't like the resort. Why are you calling from there?" he asked.

"There are no other phones around. It is late already, I cannot go anywhere else to call."

"I am suspicious about Machan Resort. I am telling you, I don't like it."

"We need to carry out this operation tonight, and we must have the army's help for it," I said politely.

"OK, I will tell the Khagendramalli post, go to them," he said.

It was not possible to go to the Khagendramalli post and return the same morning. I also told him, "It would be easier to search for the guns if we had the army with us. I can go to Manahari by myself with friends."

On March 30, 2006 we went to Manahari early in the morning. We asked for help from the Area Forest Office at Manahari, Makwanpur district, but they were afraid to help us. Chandra's nephew and his gang were skilled gun makers. They had made several guns and even given some to the Maoists. "They are dangerous," said our friends and backed off.

We continued the previous day's watch. We learnt that only his brother was at home, and he too had gone to Pratappur village across the Rapti River. "The younger brother too is a poacher," said Chandra. Now we would have to arrest both the brothers. The staff of the Parsa Wildlife Reserve lived in a rented house near their house. We met them while having tea at a nearby shop. But I winked at them not to talk to us so that it did not arouse suspicion among the people. We, however, didn't see the men we had come for even after waiting for a long time.

We returned to the park after having lunch at Manahari. Still there was no army team in sight. Then we went to the location where the guns were hidden as per Chandra Bahadur's statement. After driving for about 15 minutes west of the Sunachuri park post, we reached a rough track, about five minutes south of the fire-line. He pointed to a spot and said, "My nephew asked us to stay here, and he went that way to hide the guns. He returned after a few minutes and said he had hidden them in a hole of a tree. We then returned from this place."

We went in the direction he had pointed. There were several fallen trees in the area. We searched for holes in each of the trees using a stick to poke through them. Not even Chandra knew in which tree the guns had been hidden. In poaching gangs, the member who hides the gun usually doesn't show it to the other members.

After searching for a long time, Game Scout Nageshwor shouted in excitement, "I have found it, I have found it! Perhaps it was foretold that I should find it!"

From a hole at the bottom of a fallen tree, Nageshwor got out two home-made guns, an axe, some gunpowder, a few match boxes and iron bullets.

I took a few pictures. Everyone was pleased to find the guns. Poachers were about to use the guns to kill another rhino soon. Now, at least we were assured that these two guns wouldn't be used to kill more rhinos. However, I kept thinking to myself - we've deactivated two guns, but there must still be many more out there. It is more important to save the rhinos from the gun wielders than the guns. Even if there are no guns, they can find new ones, and some even make guns themselves.

We returned to the Sunachuri post. I met the resort manager on the way and told him that we had found the guns. "Any doubts or suspicions about your hotel are now cleared," I said. I also informed the chief warden over the phone and complained that the army did not come. "Colonel Ajit might ask how we found the guns without the army, please convince him," I said.

The colonel did exactly that. "Why and how were the guns obtained? Our team was on standby but wasn't taken along, why?" he questioned. The chief warden relayed the conversation to me in the evening. "Besides, former Chief Warden Shivaraj Bhatta told me that he had been up with having to coordinate between Colonel Ajit and Kamal," he added.

I, on my part, was no less fed up with the colonel's behaviour!

FOR A STRONGER CASE

OUR MISSION TO arrest Padaru had stopped after Pramod Yadav's phone call from Sauraha. But we were still at it. We learnt that he was living at his in-laws' place in Bairahani village. So I had asked a man in Bairahani to find out whether he was at home, as we planned to make the raid at 11 at night. Accordingly, when we reached Bairahani on April 1, we walked straight into the house.

The villagers hadn't slept yet. Upon seeing our group, some of them went into their houses while others who had come out to pee disappeared in the darkness. In the house we intended to raid, a lot of people had gathered to watch TV.

"Where is Padaru?" we asked them.

"He is not here," said they.

Apparently, there was no Padaru. We went to another house. A boy aged around 13 was sleeping.

"Where is Padaru?" we asked him.

"Over there," he said and led us. But after a while, we felt that the boy wouldn't be able to lead us to Padaru. So we returned to the house where the people were watching TV.

"Whose house is this?"

"It is mine," a man answered.

"Are you Padaru's relative?"

"I am his brother-in-law."

"Where is Padaru?"

"He said he was going to water the fields."

"Where is the water channel? Take us there ..."

They hesitated. But we took his brother-in-law and his wife along anyway. We reached his sister-in-law's house, south of the Pampa River near Bhandara. But he was not to be found there either.

From there we returned to Sauraha along with the two. Early the next day, we reached his home at Padampur. Again he was not there, and we went to Tandi. We had heard that his brother Jhagaru also involved in horn smuggling and drove a tempo. After a while we received information that Jhagaru was coming in his tempo!

Game Scout Yam Bahadur and I talked to Jhagaru about reserving a tempo. "We have to take some stuff from Krishna Mandir to Gitanagar village, some household stuff."

"OK," he said, and I sat in front and Yam Bahadur behind. My other colleagues followed us in their vehicle. We arrested him in front of the petrol pump at Tikauli and took him to Kasara. Upon interrogation in the evening, he confirmed what our informers had said.

He told us how he and his wife had hid the horn in a box of clothes and sold it to his daughter and son-in-law. Since the horn had already been sold, and we did not know where the rhino had been killed, we figured it was better to release him. That way, other criminals who had fled might return, assuming there was no danger. After arresting them, we could gather more evidence and make the case stronger. Accordingly, we released Jhagaru on general bail.

Secret Path

On April 29, 2006 I was in Kasara. From Narayangadh, we received a message: Gokul Panta has been seen.

I went there with two friends. The informer told me over the phone that he was at Shahid Chowk. We looked for him there but did not see Gokul Panta. We were disappointed and started to roam around his house at Pulchowk. Since I had seen him last *Asoj*, that is September-October 2005, I would recognise him.

In the meantime, Ranger Ritesh Bhushan Basnet's team, which had gone to Nawalparasi to bring timber smugglers who had been arrested the previous day, arrived. I asked Yam Bahadur to take the timber smugglers to the office while Ritesh Bhushan stayed with me. Ritesh was quite strong and looked like an army man. It could be dangerous with just two game scouts to arrest a local gangster of Narayangadh without weapons. But with Ritesh, a small scuffle wouldn't be a problem.

While we waited, Gokul Panta arrived on a motorcycle from the east.

I went close to him and asked, "Aren't you Gokul Panta?"

"Yes," he replied.

"Our chief warden wants to talk to you, come with us to the park," I told him.

He had a helmet in his hand. "Let me leave this at home," he said.

"We have come to take you, and we will take you by any means. Don't resist," I said.

He saw Ritesh standing directly in front and probably assumed that he was from the army.

There was another guy with him, who listened to our conversation without speaking. I put Gokul Panta into our waiting car, and he gave the helmet to the other guy. We went our way. On the looking glass, I saw the guy following us until the Bharatpur Cancer Hospital. We went south-west on the Anti -poaching Operation Unit (APU) road (used by the anti-poaching unit) from Geetanagar to Sundarbasti village.

Gokul then asked, "You say you are going to the national park, but why are we taking this route?"

"This is our secret path, don't worry," we assured him.

Upon questioning at Kasara, Gokul revealed that he took Gyamjo, who planned the rhino poaching operations, around town on his motorcycle. He had taken Gyamjo many times to Dibyanagar where he met with poachers, especially Indra, Pushpa, Gupta, Amber Bahadur Tamang and others. He would provide them with the money and weapons they needed, while they would kill rhinos and give him the horns. He gave Gokul about $75 per trip for taking him around, and Gyamjo would pay for their drinking parties in the evening at the Rhino Hotel. All poaching and smuggling plans were made at the hotel, where Gyamjo had a permanent room.

Gokul Panta also revealed that he had taken Gyamjo to Hetauda on his motorcycle, but did not reveal the contact's name. "He left me in the town and walked away but don't know where," he said.

Here, Gokul was lying to us. The houses he visited belonged to Laxman K.C. and Deepak Singh. If Gyamjo could take an ordinary poacher like Birman Praja to Laxman's house, then there was no reason why he couldn't take Gokul there, too. There was no doubt that Laxman and Deepak were the ones manoeuvring Gyamjo.

Gokul also told us that he and Yakche had bought a horn from a man called Chhiring in a hotel near Nepalgunj airport. Notorious smuggler Karma had also said the same thing to us before. Gokul had given Yakche the horn given by horn brokers Indra, Pushpa, Amber and Gupta Bahadur. Gokul also accepted horns of rhinos killed by Bhagirath Chaudhari.

According to Gokul, Yakche's wife had met him and asked him to use every means to free Yakche from jail. Gokul had appealed to his people in higher powers for help. But they had told him nothing could be done at the moment, a message he dutifully conveyed to Yakche's wife.

Partnership in Jail

THREE DAYS AFTER the re-establishment of democracy in 2006, I reached Kasara. There was a huge riot in the jail, said a ranger.

"We were planning to get a few more in for questioning, but the prisoners would not allow us. And they said nasty things about you and the chief warden," he said. "A Maoist leader as well as others also spoke against the government. They said that Kamal Jung Kunwar was turning a blind eye to smugglers and getting Maoists killed by the army instead. Now it is their turn to rot in jail."

I was wondering why the Maoists were suddenly attacking me. I hadn't done them any harm. I wanted to talk to them. Since lawyer Krishna Bhakta Pokhrel had cordial relations with a Maoist leader, I met him. According to his suggestion, I took a Maoist journalist along and went to the jail on May 3. There, the Maoist local leader Om Prakash Wagle labelled a lot of accusations against me.

I responded to each of his charges. "Raj Kumar Lama and Yudhisthir Jung Rana, whom you are supporting right now, are actually with Prabhuraja, the king's advisor." He was shocked to hear this.

After hearing me, he had one last complaint. "Til Bahadur Gurung of Chainpur is very sick, and still you guys refuse to release him."

"Well, the process for his release must be duly completed. The government hasn't released you people either even though we have democracy now." He shut up after that.

The Maoist cadre, Om Prakash, called me several times after that to seek Til Bahadur's release. I don't know why he was so keen to have him released. Til Bahadur had sold many tiger skins and rhino horns. He was an active member of the smuggling ring. Besides, it is up to the chief warden to decide what punishment should be awarded to the prisoners standing trial. It was the Maoists' lack of understanding to assume that I was the one doing everything.

Majority of the prisoners in Bharatpur jail were in for rhino cases. The Maoists tried to win them over by promising their release under a general pardon when they formed a government. Prisoners with a political background, like Indra Bahadur Gurung and Jayanarayan Kumal, had been telling the Maoists a lot of negative things about me. This got reflected in the attitude of the Maoists toward me. At that time, a large group was actively trying to demoralise me and oust me from Chitwan. Arrested rhino smugglers saw me - Kamal Jung Kunwar - as the sole reason behind their arrest, while those who had still to be arrested were always in fear of me.

PRICING A TIGER SKIN

WE WERE TRYING to arrest Sonam Chhiring as we had often heard that he was a smuggler of horns and skins. Meanwhile, the ward police office at Kalimati in Kathmandu arrested Bacchu Rai and Sonam at Kalanki on March 22, 2006. From there we brought them to Kasara. For several days during interrogation, they pretended not to know each other. However, the pretence could not last long.

Ritesh kept the mobile we had confiscated from Sonam. I had asked him not to receive any calls from unknown numbers on that phone. On April 30, we were going from Bharatpur to Tandi. As we neared Hakimchowk, the phone rang. "This number keeps calling frequently," said Ritesh.

I pulled over and received the phone.

When I said hello, the other end said, "I am Pashupati Shrestha from Kathmandu."

"How are you?" I asked.

"I am fine, I have been calling you so many times, and you never receive my phones," he said.

"I have been busy lately."

"I have an outer and an inner from a big one, do you want to buy?"

"OK, but I am out now. Where's the stuff?" I asked.

"I too have some business in Kathmandu. When I am done, I will call you from Hetauda (Makwanpur)."

"OK," I said and hung up. Maybe he did not notice my accent, for he made no comment.

I had to leave for Hemja as my uncle had passed away.

The man, Pashupati, had called on the phone again. "Let's fix it in a couple of days," Ritesh had told him. Again, he didn't recognise it was someone else's voice.

When I returned to Kasara, I asked Ritesh to tell him that I was away on business and that I would send my man to take the stuff. Since Pashupati knew Sonam, we couldn't pretend to be Sonam, and that is why I was trying a different tactic.

When he learnt that someone else was going to come, he was hesitant. "Are you sure he won't betray us?" he said.

"He is my man, and he has worked with me. You can trust him," Ritesh replied.

He agreed and fixed a meeting for the next day in Hetauda.

On May 9, we reached Hetauda. He called on the mobile.

"Where shall I come?" I asked.

"In the market in front of the traffic police office," he said.

"How do I recognise you?" I asked.

"I have grey hairs, look like an old man and I wear glasses,"

I, however, did not give my description. We had our vehicle at the parking lot of Seema Lodge. I had asked my colleagues to stay near and keep watch of me. In a while, Pashupati arrived. He was alone.

"Are you Pashupati?" I asked.

"Yes," he said, and we shook hands.

Over tea at a shop, he told me that he had a 10-foot-long tiger skin and asked me what I could pay per foot.

"What is your price?" I asked him.

"You name your price first. We should be satisfied too with the price. I've come all the way from Kathmandu just for a few pennies."

At the time, I had no idea what price a tiger skin commanded in the market. Hence, I tried to remember what the criminals arrested sometime ago had said. "I can give you around $110 per foot," I said.

"That's an old rate. I have sold a lot of these things. Sonam knows everything. I have been trading with him for a long time. It is not $110, it is $138 per foot."

He was bargaining like a seasoned trader. I, too, did not hesitate, as I would not be buying it anyway. Hence, I agreed to his price. I just wanted to convince him fast and arrest him with the skins. He was glad to have met a proper trader like me. Then he started bargaining for the bones.

"I have five kilos of dry bones. How much will you give?"

I again had to think about this. When we had confiscated tiger bones at Triveni, we had priced it at Indian Rs. 3,000 ($66). With the price in mind, I told him "$41."

"That was the price four years ago," he said.

"What's the current price then?"

"The price per kilo is $69, so the total price is $345. Along with the skin, the total price is $1,725... OK, I will give you a discount, I will charge you just $1,653."

We got up from the place. Once out, he bought some bananas. Since I was in mourning because of my uncle's death, I was not having anything except tea and fruits. I had not eaten anything in the morning, and I was very hungry by then. I felt relieved to have the bananas.

"Give me at least $14 in advance so that we can seal the deal," he requested.

I knew that he was a seasoned trader. "I will face a lot of trouble if you don't come tomorrow after all our deals," he was saying. "My hotel expenses and bus fares will have gone to waste."

Unfortunately, I did not have more than $3-4 with me. "My friend who has the money, is in the hotel," I told him. "Please wait here, I will get it."

He agreed, and I went to Seema Lodge, and got $7 each from Yam Bahadur Khanal and Ritesh. I gave him the $14, and we agreed to meet at 11 the next morning.

COMMANDO OF THE PARK

THE NEXT DAY May 10, 2006, we again went to Hetauda. I had told Pashupati that I would get a vehicle on hire from Narayangadh. Game Scout Gambarsingh Gurung and I went together, and Game Scout Mahendra Thapa was driving. It was a Toyata car of the office, not the hired one as I had told. Ritesh followed us in a different vehicle, unseen by Pashupati. The previous day he had informed us that we would have to go 11 km west to get the stuff. I had assumed it must be around Newarpani or Rajaiya village close to the East-West Highway. After meeting up, Pashupati asked for money to buy apples and mangoes. I gave him $14. He gave the money to a man on a motorcycle and sent him to buy the fruits. I made it a point to remember the motorcycle number.

"I will pack the stuff with the apples and mangoes, and give it to you as soon as we get there." Then he said he would go to a pharmacy since he would have to look for the other stuff, too.

I met Ritesh's team right then. "We will go with him, and you keep us in sight from behind," I told him.

When Pashupati returned, we went west in our vehicle.

On the way he told us, "Take this stuff first, and I will give you more to last for months." Once he touched his nose and said, "I have this, too."

He was hinting at the horns.

"Where is it?" I asked.

"Don't worry, I will get that too, talks are going on."

He grew excited as he told us how many tiger skins, elephant tusks and rhino horns he had. Listening to him, it looked as if he was running a business empire of wildlife products. I wondered if they had already managed to kill all the tigers, elephants and rhinos of Nepal.

We were driving, but I was keeping an eye on the vehicle behind. After a while, the other vehicle was no longer to be seen. I started getting agitated because there were only three of us, and there would surely be two or three other criminals, and we had no weapons! On the spot I drew up a new scheme: even if our team didn't arrive, we would ask them to put the illicit goods inside the car and persuade them to get into it, too. I would tell them we would pay them only in Hetauda. I would then stop when we saw our other vehicle and arrest them.

When we reached our destination, I saw the man who had taken the money to buy fruits in Hetauda standing on the side of the highway. But I asked Mahendra to drive past him. When he saw us, he signalled with the shirt he had in his hand. Inside the vehicle, Pashupati asked me for the money.

"Not without checking the stuff," I said.

"I've already checked it. Believe me, it's good, the stuff is already packed now."

"Put the stuff in my vehicle. I will take you to Hetauda and give you the money there."

"No, give it to me right now," Pashupati said.

I looked behind - there was no sign of our vehicle. There was only one option left. I asked Mahendra to drive on.

"Why? Why?" Pashupati asked repeatedly. Perhaps at that moment he suspected something was wrong. There was no way I could pay him then, as I had no money with me.

After driving for about a kilometre, I asked Mahendra to stop the car. He pulled over. I then pointed my finger at Pashupati and told him firmly, "We are commandos from the national park. We were acting out this whole drama simply to arrest a traitor like you. We have weapons with us, and our men are near your guy who is standing by the roadside. Do as I say quietly. You told us you have a lot of stuff. If you help us to get all of them, we will make you an informer and release you. Here, too, when your guy puts the stuff in the car, just ask him to come along to Hetauda, and say you will pay him on the way."

He was stunned. His mouth turned dry as he found himself in a hitherto unimagined situation. For a while, he just couldn't speak. Later, he put up a condition: "Release me once I bring those guys to you."

"No," I said. "I will only release you once we get the stuff and the people to Hetauda."

Then I asked Mahendra to turn the vehicle around. The guy on the motorcycle, who was signalling to us, was nowhere to be seen. We went to a nearby shop and asked if they had seen him. They pointed east. We were walking that way when a bespectacled man came in sight.

"The stuff is coming from across the Rapti River," the man said.

I looked towards the Rapti - a man with a sack was crossing it. This must be another gang member, I thought. I feared Pashupati might make some signs to the man, and I kept up with him. Following us was our vehicle.

We reached a turning near the police station at Newarpani. It was to the east of Rajaiya and was prone to landslides. We finally located the person who had signalled with his shirt from the roadside. He was furious. "Why did you drive on even as I signalled to you? We are late already." Mahendra also arrived in the car and parked on the roadside.

I threatened Pashupati not to make any signals. Just then, Ritesh's team arrived with the other vehicle. I signalled to them to drive on, and they went straight ahead. Had I stopped Ritesh, it would have aroused suspicion.

The motorcycle guy was now calling out to someone to move faster. I looked below, and the man had crossed the Rapti and was heaving the sack up the road.

"You are late, people are watching...," the motorcycle man scolded him. When he had delivered the sack to us, I asked him to put it in the car's dickey.

I then turned to the motorcycle guy and said, "Please sit in the vehicle."

"Where's the money?" he asked Pashupati.

"Come with us to Hetauda, I will give you the money there," I said.

"No, give me the money right now and fast," he insisted.

First of all, I had no money with me, and besides, he would leave as soon as he received it. And this was the man I wanted more than Pashupati now because he was either a poacher or knew enough poachers. There was to be no delay in arresting him.

DRAMATIC FIGHT

I CLUTCHED AT his arms and tried to force him into the vehicle. But he flung my hands away and stepped back. "Sit," I said and held him. Gambarsingh held him from the other side. But instead of getting into the vehicle, the man suddenly stepped onto the vehicle and flipped back. I did not want to let go of a man I'd already caught, and I held him by his neck before his feet landed on the ground. We both started rolling towards the cliff. I kept holding his neck tightly. We rolled nearly 15 metres, sometimes with me above him and sometimes with him above me. I had shaved my head as I was in mourning. Thank God my head did not hit a stone that day. After a while, a tree broke our fall. He used force, and we fell farther into a bush. Gambarsingh had been following us. We both started punching the man in his late twenties, but he was quite muscular and strong. But right then, Mahendra arrived, and the three of us held him tightly. I took off my belt and tied it around his waist. "Hold him, and I will climb up and get the other friends," I said.

I was afraid that Pashupati might have fled when all of us were in pursuit of this guy. But he happened to be quietly watching the scuffle from above. I hurriedly climbed up and asked Pashupati to sit in the car. We drove to the place where our other friends were. A little ahead, I saw Ritesh coming towards us on foot. The man who had brought the sack was walking ahead of me.

"I must pull over and arrest this guy, and if he runs, Ritesh will catch him from the other side," I said to myself.

As expected, the man ran as soon as I pulled over.

"Catch him, catch him," I shouted to Ranger Ritesh. When the man saw Ranger Ritesh in front, he ran straight down a cliff. The cliffs were so steep that a normal person wouldn't be able to even walk on them, but this man was running down. After a while, he rolled and struck a rock.

"Oh, no," I thought to myself, "that's bad news, he is probably dead, and we will have to take his corpse back." But unbelievably, the man got up immediately. Ranger Ritesh ran, too, and jumped from the cliff at the man just when he was getting up. Upon seeing Ranger Ritesh, the man made a dart for the Rapti River as if nothing had happened to him.

The Rapti had swollen, and its waters were murky. The man dove straight into its currents, and Ranger Ritesh followed suit. "Oh no, this man is going to drown in the Rapti," I thought again. Ranger Ritesh, too, was nowhere to be seen.

"Forget about him," I shouted at Ranger Ritesh, but he refused to listen. Ranger Ritesh had nearly caught up with the man, but the strong current swept him away. The current swept away the man, too, but since he was ahead, he swam on and escaped. At this point, Ranger Ritesh looked at me, and I motioned to him to return. Quite a few people had gathered to watch the scene that was truly dramatic, almost out of a movie.

There had been several encounters during the anti-poaching operations, but this incident was simply unforgettable. I was relieved that Ranger Ritesh was safe. If he had gone farther, the man's villagers might have surrounded or attacked him.

About this time, Basanta Lamichhane, Yam Bahadur Khanal and Pahuwari Yadav arrived. I told them to go get the motorcycle guy. The six of us hauled the guy up and put him in our vehicle, and we headed west. Ranger Ritesh had climbed up the cliff by then and got into the vehicle.

Just then, I saw the bespectacled man walking ahead of us. I braked and told my colleagues to arrest him. "Why?" he kept questioning, but we already had him inside the vehicle. At Rajaiya Chowk, we ran into our other vehicle and I had it proceed ahead of us.

The bespectacled man got active. "What is this? Why are you guys doing this?" he kept asking.

"Don't ask what we are doing, think what you have done!" I said.

"What have I done?" he shouted.

"You are the one who did everything," said the motorcycle guy. He shut up after that.

After driving nearly five kilometres, we divided the men and put them in two vehicles. We then asked for their names. Madhav Prasad Upreti was the name of the man with the glasses while the motorcycle guy was Chandra Bahadur Rai.

"That Chepang carried our sack only because we asked him to, he isn't really in the gang," said Chandra Bahadur. I was relieved to hear that since it would make no difference whether we had caught that man or not. But we had forgotten to bring Chandra Bahadur's motorcycle, distracted by the dramatic happenings.

Later, upon questioning at Kasara, we learnt that Chandra Bahadur and the Chepang had poisoned a tiger's kill with thiodan inside the Parsa Wildlife Reserve. When the tiger ate its kill - a bull - it died. The two had skinned the tiger together and asked Madhav to sell it. Madhav was living in Rajaiya to build a poultry farm, and Rai had helped him in the endeavour. Since Madhav knew Pashupati, he was called to help sell the products. It was decided that Pashupati would sell the skin and bones to us and they would receive $826 (50% of the total amount). The previous day, Pashupati had been to the village, seen the merchandise and returned to Hetauda that morning.

When we opened the sack in Kasara, there was a well-packed carton inside. On the top were apples and mangoes, well arranged. Below it, skilfully concealed, were the tiger skin and bones.

GOING THROUGH THE arrest statistics, we found that fewer poachers and smugglers were arrested in 2005 than in the previous years. That year we were lax, assuming that the number of smugglers had dwindled, since we had arrested many people in 2003 and 2004. It was the year *mukhiya* Shriranga Kandel had died an untimely death. Temporary army posts at Dumariya and Baghmara were removed. As a result, rhino poaching actually went up in 2005.

During this period, I was tense due to unnecessary pressures and problems. Since I had exposed how *subba* Uttam Prasad was indulging in corrupt practices, he was trying hard to get even. He had filed five cases against me in different offices.

Rhino poaching was not under control. The list of poachers and smugglers still on the run was quite long. Besides, I faced family problems. As I was fully absorbed in the task of conserving rhinos, I forgot my responsibilities to my family.

Sometimes I sought feedback from the chief warden. "Sir, do you have any problems with my behaviour? Have your relations with other individuals or offices been strained because of me?" I asked.

"No, you are fine," he said.

I fervently dreamt of a year when a single rhino would not be poached. But that seemed almost impossible under the circumstances.

Jailed for No Reason

PUSHPA, GUPTA AND Madana were supposed to appear at the park office on September 12, 2005, as asked to. On my orders, my colleagues arrested them when they arrived. After that, while pursuing Laxman and Maniram, Laxman was arrested but Maniram was able to escape. Laxman showed a gun that they had hidden. He said that a horn had been hidden in a *tauwa*, but no horn was found even after looking in three *tauwas*. Later we learnt that Maniram had taken the horn, and with Bhagirath's father, Shikharam Chaudhari, keeping watch, he had buried it at the foot of a *Sisau* tree near Shikharam's toilet and fled to India. Shikharam had, in turn, dug up the horn and hid it in another place.

In the meantime, we met Maniram's father-in-law at Tandi. "It will be better for Maniram if he surrenders himself," I tried convincing him. "One day he will surely be arrested and will have to face a lot more trouble." Later, his brother-in-law persuaded Maniram to give himself up. At first he refused to admit anything but later opened up.

We took him along to look for the horn at Shikharam's house in Sisawar village, Dibyanagar. We looked around at the spot he indicated but found nothing. We planned to arrest Shikharam, too, that day, but he wasn't around. He had made his escape when he saw us get off our vehicle and head straight for the *Sisau* tree. "If we pretend to ignore him, he will come, and then we can arrest him," I told myself. But he was clever.

Maniram had told us that Bhagirath's father and brother had seen him bury the horn. Hence, we assumed that they were the ones who had taken it.

The villagers knew of Maniram's surrender to the park office, and if there was anyone who was greatly troubled by this news, it was Shikharam. He had been making the rounds on his cycle to the buffer zone user committee's Chairman Ambar Bahadur Tamang and to other people. I was told that Shikharam was willing to surrender the horn to us, but the chairman would not allow him to.

On June 2, 2006, an informer told me that Shikharam was at home. The same afternoon we left from Narayangadh. But since a culvert near the Bhagedi post had collapsed, we couldn't proceed further.

On June 3, after taking care of other businesses in Narayangadh, we again left for Sisawar village in the afternoon. We learnt that Shikharam was working in the field. But if we went to meet him there, there was every possibility that he would see us from afar and run away, and take cover in the maize fields. We were hungry after a whole day's work and decided to stop at the Bhagedi post. By the time we cooked and ate, it was 6 in the evening. We then left for Sisawar but parked our vehicles quite far from the village.

Ranger Ritesh and Senior Game Scout Sheshchandra Chaudhari started out on foot. We stayed behind in the vehicle. We saw two people coming from the east with spades on their shoulders. I immediately recognised Shikharam. I asked him to sit in the vehicle and left after picking up Ritesh in the village.

That evening, we interrogated Shikharam and Maniram together. Shikharam admitted to seeing Maniram boil the horn, giving Maniram a sharp tool to dig and watching Maniram bury the horn. But he insisted that he did not know where the horn was now. So we handed him over to the office along with a report. On June 4, he was interrogated by Ritesh again. After that, I did not meet him anymore and also saw no reason to question him.

THREATS FROM JAIL

ON THE MORNING OF June 8, 2006, an informer we had despatched to Mahendranagar, of Kanchanpur district in the far west, called us. "Mandal Mahato, who ran away from the Devnagar post on June 27, 2000, is now in Bhuswa-bhurai village of India, across the border at Kanchanpur."

I discussed this with the chief warden. When he gave permission, I prepared to go to Kanchanpur with Game Scouts Bishnu Thapa and Mahendra Thapa, and driver Dillijung Tamang. Since I was going on a trip that could last several days, I left my wife and son at my in-laws' place. As we headed for Narayangadh, I got a call when I was near Sundarnagar village. It was from the jail.

I pulled over.

"I am Ramchandra Adhikari," said the voice on the other side.

He was a jailed Maoist cadre. He was one of those who had been vilifying me.

"Aren't you out of jail yet? I thought you guys had been released already," I said.

"I need to stay here for a few more days to teach you guys a lesson," he said tersely.

I was surprised by the tone.

"Where are you?" he asked.

"I am somewhere around the office," I lied.

"I hear that Bhagirath's father was beaten to an inch of death. Let me talk to him."

"I am unable to get you in touch with him right now."

He began making accusations against me. "We should talk face to face instead of speaking on the phone and clear our misunderstandings," I told him. The connection got cut.

Ramchandra had been arrested by the Purano Gorakh Battalion at Kasara. Later he was taken to the Bharatpur Police Office and was jailed for the murder of Inspector Bharat Bahadur Khadka from the National Investigation Department. During the insurgency, Bharat had confided to a close friend, "Ramchandra keeps calling me, maybe he is going to kill me someday." And indeed, one day he was called and shot right in front of his young son. The child was mentally deranged as a result.

In my opinion, Bharat was a simple officer. He was neither a symbol of feudalism nor its protector. I still don't understood what the Maoists gained by murdering him. The then head of the investigation department, Deviram Sharma, is now the unofficial advisor to the Chairman of the Maoist Party, Prachanda. He enjoys an honourable position in the Maoist party.

I was quite depressed after the phone conversation. How just was it for this man to go on threatening me over the phone to kill me based on malicious hearsay from my detractors? Anxiety gripped me as I drove on. Leaving my wife and son at my father-in-law's house in Chainpur, I returned to Narayangadh.

There was some vehicle repair to do, so we could only leave at 3 in the afternoon. On the way, I was reading the *Kantipur* daily dated June 8, 2006. On it was a quotation: Those who chain others might find the other end of the chain in their own hands. Already depressed by the phone conversation, this quotation jerked me awake. "I have arrested and jailed so many people, maybe circumstances will lead me to jail, too, one day," I thought. Silently I prayed, "Oh, God, please don't let this happen to me. I am a devotee of nature, I am its protector.

I have never arrested or jailed anyone for personal gain."

We reached western Chisapani, on the bank of the Karnali River, which lies in Kailali district, at around 11 at night. We had not eaten dinner till then. So we decided to look for a place to have a bite. We looked around for some food, but did not find any. Since it would take too long to cook, we decided to scout some more for a place to it. By the time we reached Atariya of the same district, all restaurants had closed down. We thought we might get something at Mahendranagar, Kanchanpur, but that city looked completely deserted. It was already half past 1 at night, and all hotels and lodges were closed. We dialled the numbers displayed on the signboards outside the hotels. Many did not even pick up the calls while others just said, "No rooms are available," and hung up.

After wandering around for a long time, a night guard helped us to find two rooms in Gandaki Lodge at the bus park. But the windowpanes were missing, and so the mosquitoes swarmed into the room like bees. We turned on the fan, but it was of no help. We had neither mosquito repellents nor nets to keep them out. Worst of all, we had no food. We just wanted to give some rest to our eyes now, and fell onto the dirty bed sheets and pillows without a thought.

LOOKING FOR SMUGGLERS IN INDIA

WE MET OUR INFORMER on June 9 at around 7 in the morning. We had breakfast with him and went towards Gadda Chauki, the Nepal-India border checkpoint. We had to get to Khatima in India. Since we were government officials, there wasn't much checking at the border after we had registered our vehicle number and destination. When I was at the Shuklaphanta Wildlife Reserve for three months in July-September 2000, I had been to Chadani and Dodhara villages of Nepal, across the Mahakali River but no further. We reached the forest office at Khatima at around 9 in the morning, passing Banbasa on the way. There, range officials asked us to proceed to the guest house.

At the guest house, we met the junior forest ranger who showed respectful behaviour. Just then, a forest official, who looked familiar, arrived in a vehicle. He turned out to be Range Officer Babulal from the Surai range post, someone I had acquainted myself with while working at the Shuklaphanta Wildlife Reserve. I was glad to meet him, as now our job would be easier. I do not know Hindi very well, and my English is just as weak.

The District Forest Officer also happened to be in the guest house. Babulal introduced me to him, and I introduced myself and my objective, and requested him for help. I would speak sometimes in Hindi and sometimes in broken English. Since he was about to leave for the city of Haldawani, he asked Babulal to do the needful. After he left, Babulal and I had a detailed discussion. I informed the two that Mandal Mahato was hiding in Bhuswa-bhurai village. The junior forest ranger already had information that a runaway from Nepal was hiding there. It seemed that there was an official of Nepali origin working at the Forest Department, who had good knowledge of the area. Babulal called him by phone. This official happened to know Mandal and said that he and his family had been hiding there for more than five years. Mandal's wife sold liquor, and he had even bought land in the area.

He then left for the village to find out what Mandal was doing. We went to the police office (in Hindi Kotwali) to talk to the police officer. There we met Inspector Pathak. I informed them of Mandal's crimes and also told them that he had escaped from custody.

"He is a member of Sansar Chand's gang," Babulal further added. The police became alert after that. They promised full cooperation. They agreed to hand him over once he was arrested.

It was almost midday by then. After lunch, we rested in the guest house. They had planned to find out what he did during the day and arrest him at night. But there was no news of him even by nightfall.

Having received no news even by the morning of June 10, we went to the range post. We met Babulal there and learnt that nothing had been done the previous day. A man arrested for murder had died in police custody, and as a result, the whole of Khatima bazaar was tense. So all the policemen were busy.

At around that time, we heard that Mandal had gone to Banbasa. "Avoid being seen," said Babulal. "He might know your vehicle and people. Stay in Mahendranagar (Nepal). I will call you once he is arrested."

We felt this was good advice and returned to Mahendranagar. We went to a hotel in Mahendranagar and ordered lunch. Along with the informer, all of us had a bottle of beer each. Given Mahendranagar's hot weather, we began to feel giddy after just one bottle. An informer called me from Chitwan to inform about the whereabouts of some criminals. I named a colleague and ordered him to coordinate and arrest them.

Just then my mobile rang. It was Babulal. He said in Hindi, "Your job is done." Suddenly I got another call, too. It was a female voice, and then the connection got cut off. My right eye started flickering. I wasn't sure if it was a good omen or a bad one. I waited for another call from Babulal, but it never came. Then we left for Khatima, India, planning to take the man home if he had been arrested.

As soon as we reached there, the junior forest ranger and forest guards congratulated us. "Your job is done," they said. I was glad. They asked me to go to the Surai range post and meet Babulal. Babulal, however, seemed a little troubled. He wouldn't talk openly, just said, "You may think your job is done."

I assumed there were some technical difficulties. After a while he opened up, "It would have been better if I could have handed him over to you as soon as I had arrested him. But you guys were away," said he.

Babulal had himself arrested Mandal from the Khatima market. "A few people saw us as we made the arrest." Babulal said. At first he refused to admit his name was Mandal Mahato. But after Babulal told him he had been arrested with the help of the Nepali intelligence, he had changed track and said, "Please don't give me up to the Nepali authorities, I will give you Indian Rs. 50,000 instead."

Upon interrogation, he had also revealed that two people were coming from Mahendranagar, Nepal, at 9 in the evening, and they were going to Pilibhit town in India to fetch tiger skins. He was, thus, involved in wildlife trophy smuggling in India, too.

"Please hand over Mandal to us, we will take him with us right away," we requested Babulal.

"Tomorrow, if his wife asks where he is, we won't know what to tell her. Human rights activists will create trouble. I have talked to a lawyer, tomorrow we will give him to you in the presence of the village head and his wife. We will take pictures so that the whole thing is risk free for us."

"I will call his wife from Mahendranagar, Nepal, and tell her that we arrested him from Mahendranagar, and then there will be no problem for you," I tried convincing him. But he refused since many people had already seen Mandal being arrested in Khatima.

ON THE MORNING OF June 11, we reached the Surai range post. Babulal hadn't woken up, as he had gone to bed only at 2 at night. He woke up an hour later and talked to us. "Upon interrogation, Mandal also told the inspector that he had a gun at home. We raided his house at night and found it." Since the case just seemed to stretch on and on, I became restless, wondering if there was a conspiracy brewing.

"What will happen now?" I asked.

He, too, was in a quandary. "I will talk to the inspector, and then we will let you know," he said.

"Please convince the police," I requested him.

From there we went to the Khatima Police Office at around 10 in the morning. We met the inspector, and I thanked him, and he congratulated me in return. But he was not ready to hand Mandal over to me. "We found a gun with him, we will have to present him in court, I cannot hand him over unofficially," he said. I just had a hunch that this was all drama because Mandal had offered Rs. 50,000 if the police didn't hand him over to Nepali officials.

I glanced at Babulal, who didn't speak. The inspector started calling up TV and newspaper reporters on his cell phone.

In a short while, there was a huge crowd of media persons. There was also a reporter from Nepal 1 Television. He wanted to take my interview, but I refused, since there was no point in creating a media stir when we didn't have the criminal with us. The inspector told the press how a wildlife smuggler had been arrested. I, the inspector, Range Officer Babulal and other staff, including the Indian police and forest staff, took pictures with a gun-toting Mandal.

"Let him interrogate the man," said the inspector pointing at me and went his way. Mandal Mahato greeted me with a sad face. I, too, was sad that I wasn't taking him along.

When we returned to the range post, Babulal said that

Mandal could be extradited if we had a written request from the Nepalese Home Ministry. I prepared documents to prevent his release, even on bail, until then. I gave those documents to a private lawyer brought by Babulal. It was 1 in the afternoon by the time we finished the procedure. Since there was nothing else we could do there, we returned to Mahendranagar. But I was still hopeful about taking him with us sooner than later.

In Mahendranagar, we were unable to have lunch anywhere, not even in Atariya, Kailali. It was 2:30 in the afternoon before we could eat something. By the time we reached Daunne of Nawalparasi and had dinner, it was 1 at night. We reached Narayangadh at around 2:30 at night on June 12. We dropped off Dillijung at his home in Bharatpur, and it was 3:30 in the morning by the time we reached Kasara.

BAD LUCK

ON JUNE 12, Ranger Sujan Maharjan woke me up in the morning at 7 and said, "Shikharam has been taken to hospital as he is very ill. Ranger Ritesh and his team apparently do not have money, and we need to send some for his treatment."

I was shaken, I expected the worst.

"What's the matter with him?"

"The doctor says it's a brain haemorrhage but can be cured."

I was a bit relieved. "OK, then talk to the chief warden for the money, I don't have any with me right now."

Sleepy as I was, I went to sleep again. Ritesh was back from the hospital by the time I woke up. "It's a brain haemorrhage, but the doctor says he will be fine," he said.

"Was he beaten?"

"No."

"Are there any wounds, bruises?"

"No, I looked for them myself. There's only a small scar on his back and a small wound on his leg."

I was relieved. I met the chief warden and talked to him. As head of the APU, I felt that I should visit the hospital. Shikharam was lying unconscious when I went there in the afternoon.

Dr. Kamal Dawadi was on duty. He informed me that Shikharam's condition was serious.

"We will be blamed if something happens to a man in our custody. So please tell me plainly, what is the matter?"

"The cause is natural. He would have suffered the brain haemorrhage even if he wasn't in your custody."

"Please inform his relatives of this," I said.

"OK," he said.

I called Kasara and informed the chief warden of the patient's condition. Since Shikharam was from the Kalabanjar Buffer Zone settlement, he asked me to call the chairman of the buffer zone user committee to inform his family members. But the chairman was in Kathmandu, so he asked me to inform Jeevan Chaudhari, the former VDC vice-chairman.

I could send a vehicle for Shikharam's relatives and get them here, I reasoned. But then again, if they already had information of the incident, they would be here by the time the vehicle reached them. I got in touch with a local guy from the area to locate Jeevan and have him call me. But there was no call even by evening, and I grew restless. And I could not get myself to return to Kasara. When night fell, I went to Sher Bahadur uncle's house located nearby.

On the morning of June 13, I woke up early and left for the hospital without bed tea. I looked at the patient, his condition was still serious. At around 6 in the morning, Jeevan Chaudhari called me.

"Shikharam is very ill, get his family members here immediately in a microbus," I told him. By the time they arrived at half past seven, he was dead. Records later showed that he had died at half past six. I took the family along to see Shikharam.

I told Jeevan what the doctor had said about the case. Afraid that people might go on a riot, I left for Chainpur, where I picked up my family before heading for Kasara.

At 7, I had met the assistant CDO and SP Kedar Prakash Saud and informed them of the incident. I also talked with the chief warden before leaving the hospital and asked him to come to Bharatpur to talk to the local residents, the family of the deceased and chairman of the buffer zone user committee. But a few hours later, the assistant CDO called me to say the chief warden need not come. "We will handle the matter." The message was immediately relayed to the chief warden.

In the meantime, journalist Basanta Parajuli called to ask, "Why did you beat up a man so badly as to kill him?"

"I wasn't there," I told him. "From the post-mortem, we will soon know whether he died from beatings or from a brain haemorrhage."

Prabhakar Ghimire, a reporter with the *Kantipur* national daily, was next on line and wanted to know the truth. I gave him the same answer.

After I had slept for a while in Kasara, the chief warden called me at 4:30 in the afternoon. "We need to go to Bharatpur. Get ready soon," he said.

I got ready, and my son started crying. Whenever I got ready to go out, he would cry, insisting on coming along.

"Do I need to bring anything from the market?" I asked my wife.

"No vegetables in the kitchen," said she.

CONSPIRACY ALL AROUND

THE CHIEF WARDEN and I left for Bharatpur. We headed straight for the District Police Office to SP Saud's chamber. As soon as he saw us, he said, "You guys arrest people, and yet the rhinos keep dying. What's happening?"

I was shocked to hear him say so. In all my three years in Chitwan, the police had never done anything to mitigate the poaching problem. I was unable to understand why so suddenly the SP seemed so concerned about rhino conservation.

A few minutes later, some journalists and so-called human rights activists arrived on the scene. Inspector Ram Bahadur Shrestha entered the room and saluted the SP. "Seven ribs are broken," he said. "There are bruises all over the body. Broken ribs have pierced the lungs. The ribs must have been broken either by kicks from a boot or the hilt of a gun."

Upon hearing this, everyone started questioning us. We were stunned. The post-mortem report said exactly the opposite of what the doctor had told me. I had to believe the post-mortem report. There was no way I could protest. "Our boys made a mistake," I said. "We had no intention of killing him, but it has happened. Let us solve this problem."

But they were not willing to listen to us. "We informed you on June 8, but you ignored it, why?" members of the Federation of Nepalese Journalists shouted at the chief warden.

"Didn't you say that a little bit of beating is normal during an interrogation?" they asked me. However, no journalist had called me while Shikharam was in custody, and I had made no such comment to anyone.

The first report was on the SP's table. The assistant CDO also arrived. "What's in the report?" he asked.

"I don't know, I haven't read it either," said the SP.

None of us paid any attention to it. After a while, we decided to discuss the matter with the political parties the following day, on June 14. Just then, heavy rains accompanied by thunders and windstorm battered the city. Maybe Mother Nature too was not happy with what was happening. The SP requested that Ranger Ritesh Bhushan Basnet be called for the following day's meeting.

A tall, plump man with a beard, who looked like a Muslim, came in and demanded that the SP register the report and arrest the defendant. "Or else we will picket at the gate of the police office all night."

The SP was distressed. "They are right here, we will register the report tomorrow," he said. The man left, threatening to come with a rally of 5,000 people the next day.

We were asked to stay there and were taken to the quarter of the Deputy Superintendant of Police (DSP). We called several people on our mobile phones. We were hoping to talk to the political party leaders the next day to agree on an independent investigation of the case. We would also prepare a conducive environment for providing assistance to the family of the deceased.

Ritesh arrived in the morning. At half past eight on June 14, lawyer Krishna Bhakta Pokhrel arrived at the police office. The previous day, the SP and assistant CDO had praised him. "He is an understanding person. He can convince everyone, people listen to him," they had said. When he finally arrived, we felt as if God had arrived.

"I will take care of the matter, you people just hold your tongues. If you speak, it will only ruin the environment." We too agreed, as we just wanted the problem solved. I assumed he would help in providing assistance to the family of the deceased.

Quite a few representatives of the political parties had gathered. The bearded man from the previous day was there, too. The district secretary of the Communist Party of Nepal-Unified Marxist Leninist (CPN-UML) Bijay Subedi went out with him for a while.

The meeting started, and lawyer Krishna Bhakta talked first. A Janamorcha Party (communist party) cadre then said a few words. The chief warden was asked to express his opinion. He got emotional as he talked about conservation. The bearded man was trying to interrupt. A man in his thirties from Madi started chiding the chief warden, "Your speech reflects feudal arrogance."

The bearded man introduced himself. He was Arjun Thapaliya, head of Community Development Organisation, a Non-governmental Organisation (NGO). "Kamal Jung was the one who sent Yakche to Kathmandu," he said. "He jails everyone else in Bharatpur, but Yakche was sent to the Central Jail in Kathmandu. These days Yakche goes home to sleep with his wife."

I was shocked to hear his words. Later I learnt that the bearded man had appointed CPN-UML leader Bijay Subedi's wife as the head of his NGO's Chitwan branch.

"We arrested and jailed Yakche," said I. "But the jail management decides where to send the prisoner."

"Don't interrupt, let him speak," said Krishna Bhakta. OK, I thought, if our position is stronger by keeping silent.

Arjun was next, and he reminded everyone of the horn found in my bag in Simara. He accused Rangers Bed Bahadur Khadka and Bishnu Thapaliya and all other park staff for not allowing the people to gather *niguro* and not letting the Botes to fish in the river. He was trying to agitate the crowd that had gathered there by accusing me of quite a few crimes.

As soon as he finished, a short man beside him began speaking. "All this is Kamal Jung Kunwar's responsibility. We must punish him," he shouted. Later we learnt that he was Chhavi Prasad Neupane, a member of Arjun's NGO.

Just then, Tek Prasad Gurung, district chairman of the Nepali Congress Party, pointed at me and started shouting. He accused me of not letting him meet the rhino poachers and smugglers in park custody. Maoist representative Dandapani Poudel, too, advocated strict punishment to us and sided with the smugglers.

Some journalists, lawyers and so-called human rights activists too were venting their emotions.

After everybody had spoken, the SP proffered his opinion. "We should form a legal investigation committee and penalise the guilty," he said. Arjun pointed at him and started shouting, "I will bring in ministers, I will bring in the public." The SP and assistant CDO spoke no more.

After a while, all three of us were sent to the SP's chamber. But soon, the chief warden was called to the meeting hall. After the meeting, loud shouts of "Yes, Yes" were heard. Returning to the hall a few minutes later, we found the chief warden downcast.

"What happened?" we asked.

"They decided to punish us and left," said he. The major role in getting the other political parties to agree in punishing us was played by the Maoists.

That meeting, in fact, was just a formality. Everyone had already decided on what should be done beforehand. Some party representatives were angry that we hadn't released their people - rhino poachers - on bail; others resented taking away their livelihood, i.e., smuggling; and still others were frustrated by the conservation programmes that did them no good. The Maoists were agitated by the false, imaginary accusations made by the smugglers. The objectives of Arjun's NGO went against those of the parks and efforts at conservation. The so-called intellectuals did not see the parks as national treasures but vestiges of royal wealth, and conserving them meant strengthening the palace.

"It is only a matter of a few days, things will be alright soon," lawyer Krishna Bhakta tried consoling us. Out on the streets, Arjun led a rally of about 200 people. Poachers, smugglers, children, relatives and supporters of poachers and smugglers, thieves, robbers and timber smugglers were all there and shouting, "Hang the murderer! Kill this guy!"

It looked as if democracy benefitted only them, as if its main objective was to strengthen the partnership of the money minting NGOs and wildlife smugglers.

In Dolpa, for conducting trade in *Yarsagumba* Yakche pays more than $275,482 to the Maoists in taxes. Naturally, wouldn't he be dearer to the Maoists than people like us, who earn a salary of $124 per month and cannot give them anything?

It was 2005. While going to Kathmandu, a man that I had seen in Pokhara came and sat by me in the microbus. He was a member of the Maoist labour union and was known by his nom de guerre Basanta. Sometime later, he asked to meet me in a hotel at the Pokhara bus park in Narayangadh, and invited me to join the Maoist party. When I refused, he sought $689 in donations "to assist the revolution."

"I am in no position to give you that much," I said and gave him $124, a whole month's salary. After that, he began calling me from time to time, asking for more money. I thought maybe I could use them in anti-poaching operations and proposed, "I will pay you, but you must help me in conservation." He agreed.

I discussed the matter with the chief warden, and he sanctioned $248. In return, Basanta was to hang banners and distribute posters and pamphlets, with warnings that anyone found killing rhinos would be penalised by the Maoists. But he never did anything. The $372 that I gave him all went to waste. It was, thus, not surprising that smugglers who could give bags of money found favour with the Maoists. Why would Arjun's NGO side with honest people like us when smugglers, corrupt people, bribe givers, commission givers, thieves and robbers can give them everything?

Outside, the rally was raging. An inspector got us out of the hall and onto the roof. As soon as he saw us, Arjun excitedly ran to the front. Shikharam's son was threatening me with pointed fingers. He worked in the Nepal Army and supplied bullets to his brother and father to kill rhinos. He and his father had together hidden a horn. One other burly guy was denouncing us in excess. It was like a scene from the Hindi movies. As a Nepali proverb goes, the thief is treated to a rest while saints are hanged. I got all the more emboldened and vowed to fight the smugglers with all my strength.

We got down from the roof, and preparations were being made for us to undergo a medical examination. Just then, a ranger from the District Forest Office came running inside and asked for the arrest warrant.

"I have to fax it to the Ministry of Forests," he said. The warrant had not been given to us.

"The ministry will probably use the warrant to show it to the Home Ministry and release us," I assumed. Hence, we asked the police assistant inspector to prepare the warrant as soon as possible and give it to the ranger.

However, our assumption proved otherwise. The minister actually wanted the warrant to suspend us. The political parties, especially the district chairman of the Nepali Congress Tek Prasad Gurung (minister comes from the same party), CDO Narendra Prasad Poudel and the police had made a lot of negative comments to the minister about us. Why would he hesitate to suspend us? He was no ordinary minister either, he was the State Minister of Forests Gopal Rai, a favourite of Prime Minister Girija Prasad Koirala. Minister Rai had chastised the Forest Secretary, Swayambhuman Amatya, for trying to convince him of our innocence.

THE NEWS OF OUR arrest in the homicide case made headlines on the FM radios. It was front page news in the national and local newspapers. The mobile started ringing continuously. Relatives, friends, family, conservationists and colleagues called us. Given the tension they were in, we were forced to console them instead. "Don't worry, nothing will happen, we are fine," we said.

At that time, I was confident that nothing would happen to me. I had worked sincerely in the conservation of rare and endangered wildlife. So I held the belief that no matter who went against me, no one would able to harm me.

Prior to this, I had been arrested twice. First, in Pokhara for political reasons and second in Lukla in the course of conservation. In Lukla, I was arrested on December 30, 2002 when I was the officiating chief warden of the Sagarmatha National Park. I together with Ranger Nurendra Aryal and my friend's brother Krishna Sharma Poudyal were at Lukla airport, but the plane bound for Kathmandu looked like it wouldn't arrive due to bad weather. We then decided to inspect the buffer zone community forest. There had been complaints for a long time about the local residents voraciously cutting down trees. And true to the complaints, when we reached the forest, there was a long line of villagers entering the forest with axes and saws, and an equally long line of villagers exiting loaded with wood. Even a group of soldiers from the APF were entering the forest in their uniform and guns, and carrying saws to fell the trees. Politely, we requested everyone not to enter the forest and arrested everyone carrying wood.

We returned from the forest and talked to the local delegates. "Prevent the APF from cutting the trees, and we are ready to conserve the forests," they said. Then we went to meet the DSP, Neeranirakaran Shah, at his quarter. At first, it looked as if a quarrel would ensue. "These guys work hard to maintain security. If they prefer wood to kerosene, what's the harm in cutting a few trees?" said he. The APF received kerosene under a quota system. But the APF sold it and pocketed the money, while forests were being destroyed for fuel.

Again, we decided to have a meeting with the local social leaders and the police. At the meeting, it was decided that no one would enter the forests for two months, and during that period, the park would formulate a management plan for the forest and hand it over to the local residents as a buffer zone community forest.

We returned to the hotel in the evening. After a while, a group of APF personnel arrived and took us all, including an Amchi (Tibetan traditional herbal doctor) and his wife, with them. They also took Dawaphuti Sherpa, owner of the Paradise Hotel. At a helipad to the west of the airport, they searched us and had us standing there till 1 at night.

Our bodies had become rigid, what with having to stand in the open air at night in a place like Lukla (elevation, 2,800m/9,100ft), when it looked like it would snow. Besides, we were hungry and were surrounded by gun-toting policemen. They then ordered us to come to their office the next day. The next day, the DSP used foul language. It made my hackles rise, and my blood was boiling. But I restrained myself. "This is all for conservation," I thought. "If my pain can save even a single tree in the jungle, then it is acceptable to me."

When my mother heard news of my arrest for the third time, she fell ill. My brother's depression rebounded. My mother-in-law's health deteriorated. My brother-in-law Pradip Adhikari became ill and had to take medicine. My wife's worries and pain knew no bounds. And just then, my son also fell ill.

ON JUNE 16, 2006, we were taken to a government attorney, Omprakash Aryal, for a briefing. Sometime ago, I had arrested

Sanjaya Govinda Shrestha of Daldale, Nawalparasi, for smuggling timber. Omprakash's attempts to release him had failed, hence, he had a grudge against me.

Notorious rhino horn smuggler Phinjo Sherpa (Yakche's wife) had been charged with the same crime committed by her husband in the charge sheet. According to the National Parks and Wildlife Conservation Act 1973, there is a provision that says while filing a case before the adjudicating authority, the investigating officer may consult a government attorney. During that period, Omprakash had deleted Phinjo's name from the case file.

Omprakash asked me several questions, such as why we arrested Shikharam, when, where and on what basis. I responded to his queries. The police had actually been to Kasara the previous day and brought over all documents concerning the prisoner, including statement records, on the spot records and papers regarding his custody at the park. We had appointed Krishna Bhakta Pokhrel as our lawyer, who had been the legal advisor to the Chitwan National Park Buffer Zone Management Committee. He was with us while we gave our statements to the government attorney.

REVOLT AGAINST INJUSTICE

PEOPLE EVERYWHERE started to protest against our unjust arrest. Conservationists and nature lovers were on our side. Professional organisations like the Nepal Foresters' Association and Nepal Rangers' Association started nationwide protest movements. All the national parks, wildlife reserves and conservation area offices shut down. The DNPWC also closed down in protest. All organisations, departments and offices under the Ministry of Forests were shut down. Everyone participated in the picketing in front of the ministry. All officials at the Ministry of Forests - from the office helper to the joint-secretary - all put down their pens and closed the ministry. Such solidarity unseen previously was witnessed. Organisations like the Nepal Civil Servants' Association and Nepal Civil Servants' Union released statements to the press in support of us.

Likewise, the Central Regional Forest Director, Ram Prasad Poudel, also released a press statement supporting us. In Chitwan, several related organisations, like hotels, tourist businesses and community forests, joined hands with our colleagues to protest our arrest. Elephant rallies were taken out, and transport strikes were called. The District Administration Office was surrounded, but CDO Narendra Raj Poudel made his way into his office by kicking the protesters sitting in front of his office. In Bharatpur, there was a rally of hundreds of people.

On June 21, Minister Rai himself came to Chitwan. He heard the party representatives, hoteliers and conservation loving people. He assured the park officials that he would get us released. We were re-energised.

However, the minister proved immature and did not stand by his words. The CDO and SP refused to release us as the case was still in the process of investigation. It was a mistake on the minister's part not to take steps to coordinate with the Home Ministry through official procedures and halt the case proceedings. In Kathmandu, the ministry was closed, with the ministry officials on strike. He negotiated with the protesters and agreed to get us released within 72 hours, form a legal investigation committee and provide assistance to the family of the deceased.

The 72 hours passed, and yet the minister had done nothing. The protest movements had cooled down by then. It was a strategy of Minister Rai. He sent one protest committee member - chairman of the Rangers' Association of Nepal - to eastern

Nepal. Similarly, a member representing the DNPWC was sent to India to fail the movement. We were utterly disappointed.

Two weeks went by as we waited for our release. My mother would weep on the phone, and I would be very sad. I had made her cry a lot even as a child. While she was nursing her siblings, I was supposed to stay at home and cook for her. But while she was sleeping, I would sneak out to play. I would lose track of time as I played and return home scared of my mother. She would cry and tell me how offended she was that I didn't cook for her even when she was hungry and nursing a child. I would feel very bad to see my mom cry. I would then promise myself never to make my mother cry again. Twenty-six years had passed since I made that promise, and I was still making her cry. This time, however, I could tell her that I had done nothing wrong. "They are trying to frame us, but no one can do anything, nothing will happen to us," I tried convincing her.

Our case was still being investigated. The day we were to be presented in court drew near. I was worried about how the case would be presented. I expected many wildlife smugglers and poachers to be present when I appeared in the court, just to see what I would say. I made a resolve to speak confidently and say that I was a soldier of conservation and that smugglers were trying to frame me. I would not falter, and I would not allow smugglers to go scot free. Surely I wouldn't be punished for a crime I never committed?

The government doctor, Ishwarchandra Ghimire, who conducted the post-mortem at the Chitwan District Hospital, had reported that Shikharam had died because seven broken ribs had pierced his lungs. But is it possible that a man whose lungs had been punctured by broken ribs on June 11 could still be alive on June 13 without any medical assistance? There must have been a lot of internal bleeding, but the post-mortem made no mention of it.

The post-mortem, which should have been carried out in an isolated room, was performed outside in the open due to pressure from interest groups. When I got to know this, I asked my friend to get the X-ray and other reports as well as the death certificate of Shikharam from the private Bharatpur Medical College Hospital where he was undergoing treatment. But he was unable to access them despite great effort. There, it turned out, the doctors were under tremendous pressure to hold back the reports. There had been threats to torch the Bharatpur Medical College Hospital if they released the reports. In the X-ray taken in the medical college hospital, only one of Shikharam's ribs is slightly cracked, while his death certificate clearly states that the cause of his death is lack of oxygen to the brain, in other words, natural. But due to pressure and conspiracy on the part of smugglers, I could not lay my hands on these reports on time.

On July 1, national and international human rights activists came to interrogate us regarding the death of Shikharam.

We want the better for not just human beings, but all of nature. We are worried about the ecological balance. Human beings are just one small part of nature. There is benefit for humans only as long as there is balance in the ecology. In the end, ecological troubles will upset the whole of humanity. But these pseudo intellectuals were not concerned with these truths.

MURDER CASE

AT NOON ON JULY 9, Sunday, the case was registered in court. The chief warden and I were charged under section 17(3) of the Civil Act, and Ritesh was charged under section 13(3). Section 17(3) stipulates that the accused was present during the incident but did nothing to stop the course of action. Section 13(3) accuses one of murder.

On July 7, the file of the lawsuit was returned from the government attorney to the police office. Ritesh was told that since we had not been charged with homicide, we might be charged with accidental homicide instead - a lesser crime. His father too called him to say the same. But things did not happen that way, and the case was registered in court against us.

At half past one, Ritesh was asked to make his statement. We were in a different room in the court. The statement took nearly three hours. While he was giving his statement, a man called Madan Mahato, once arrested for killing rhinos, was shouting, "Shikharam was beaten to death." Actually, when a person is giving a statement, no one else is allowed to speak.

That day, there wasn't enough time to take my statement. After Ritesh's turn, we were all worried about what would happen. The chief warden was the most worried of all. He was lost in his thoughts and talked to himself. His face was easy to read, and his lips kept moving without a sound. We spent sleepless nights.

One evening, thinking we were asleep, the chief warden had called Colonel Ajit. Ritesh happened to hear him talk. "I did not do as you said, but please, you must release me. They can stay here, but I must get out, please get me out," he said on the phone. I was pained to learn that my chief warden had pleaded to the colonel.

A few days before, I had had a dispute with the chief warden over Game Scouts Yam Bahadur Khanal and Kedar Gurung, two of our staff members who had also been accused along with us. He wanted to present them to the police also. "We are already in custody, what is the point of calling the lower level staff here to have them arrested?" I had told him.

"We must get them here," he had insisted. But over the phone, I had asked them not to come, and he was angry with me about that.

On July 10, I and the chief warden were asked to give our statements. Different thoughts came to my mind. We were taken to the court on time. Several rhino smugglers, timber smugglers, criminals and other conspirators, relatives and other pointless people were there. Some of them were cadres of the Communist Party of Nepal (Maoist). They even took photographs of mine, perhaps to show them to their bosses involved in rhino horn smuggling. Also, I had heard rumours that should the court let me go, the Maoists were planning to harm me physically. Maybe the photo was for that purpose.

I spoke for nearly three and a half hours. I mentioned the importance of and the need to be sensitive towards conservation work and made it clear that Shikharam had died of natural causes. I also stated that I was in India the day the incident took place, and explained to the court why I had gone there. I presented to the court a cutting from the Indian newspapers *Amar Ujala* and *Kumaun Jagaran*, which had published accounts of my conservation work there with photographs on the front page. One of Shikharam's lawyers was stunned to see these and later was heard saying, "He wasn't even in Nepal that day!" The government attorney, Omprakash Aryal, who had first claimed that my travel orders were fake, was also dumbfounded.

After we gave our statements, we were put in vehicles to go to the District Police Office. Just then, I saw our lawyer Krishna Bhakta Pokhrel get on a motorcycle with plate No. 5280. I became immediately suspicious at seeing our lawyer, whom we had paid to plead in our favour, on a motorcycle with horn smuggler Gokul Panta's man.

In the evening, Ritesh mentioned something else. After I had given my statement to the government attorney, Krishna Bhakta had gone to his room and said, "I will see how Kamal Jung proves in court that Shikharam died of natural causes." Besides, Krishna Bhakta had tried to demoralise me once by stating that Maoist cadre Ramchandra Adhikari had killed the National Investigation police officer, Bharat Khadka.

When he was called to the District Police Office to plead for us, Krishna Bhakta had again mentioned Ramchandra and tried to terrorise me. That day, he had come to us at around 7 in the morning. We were talking about how to make the case stronger in the court when his cell phone rang.

"He is a good guy, he is our guy," Krishna Bhakta was saying. They were talking about me.

"That was Ramchandra," he said after hanging up. "He said Kamal Jung had just called him five minutes ago from the District Police Office phone."

I was suddenly angry. "I have been with you the past 15 minutes, how could I have called him five minutes ago? Moreover, I don't know his phone number and the police office does not allow us to use the office telephone. Is he mad or something?"

"He says you have been calling and teasing him for the past few days."

In the meantime, Ramchandra had apparently said, "I will go to the police station and take care of Kamal Jung."

Maybe this was Krishna Bhakta and Ramchandra's way of threatening me, or maybe this was a plan to demoralise me.

Due to many such incidents, it became clear that Krishna Bhakta was not on our side. Maybe we had made a big mistake by appointing him as our lawyer.

ASTONISHING VERDICT

THE 11th OF JULY was a holiday, as it was Teachers' Day. The next day, lawyers on both sides pleaded their cases. First, the plaintiff's lawyer Omprakash pleaded for nearly an hour and a half. This time, he had corrected his allegation that my travel order was fake. Then four private lawyers pleaded our case.

Since the district judge of Chitwan was on leave, the registrar in the District Court Narayan Prasad Regmi was officiating as the judge. Out on the streets, Somat Ghimire of the Community Development Organisation was leading a rally of rhino smugglers, timber smugglers and their friends. Apparently, Regmi was intimidated by the rally. After the lawyers finished, he entered his secret chamber. We waited with abated breath. After a while, an official with a file came and read the verdict. The verdict was astonishing.

The chief warden and I were accused under the same article of the act, but he was to be released on bail and I was to be detained on remand. All who heard the verdict were surprised. The Civil Act clearly states that if a jail term is less than three years, then the accused is either freed on bail or general bail while a judicial enquiry is underway. The same should have been applied to me. But the verdict overtook even the Civil Act. Ritesh too was to be detained on remand.

The chief warden's wife was in front of me when the verdict was announced. She looked at me and gave a wan smile. "Must be happy over her husband's release," I assumed. Who wouldn't be to have her husband saved from going to jail?

My mother-in-law Punya Prabha Adhikari, who was beside her, started weeping with her hands on my head as soon as the verdict was announced. "Don't cry," I told her, "it will only make those who want to see you suffer happy." Sameer Sherchan, who owned a saw mill at Hakimchowk, and who was shouting the loudest against us at the rally, was watching the drama closely.

Preparations were being made to take me and Ritesh to jail to stand trial. We knew there was a conspiracy to take us to the Bharatpur Jail. Several rhino poachers and horn smugglers that we had arrested were jailed there. They were glad to hear that we were joining them. Once in jail, they planned to break every bone in our body. Many others were also interested in keeping us at the Bharatpur Jail. But we cited safety reasons and refused to go to Bharatpur. The jail administration and police officials there also cited their inability to protect us. Hence, under the circumstances, another location had to be found for us. Bhimphedi, in Makwanpur, was the first choice, then Dang district. But we asked to be taken to Nawalparasi. Since we knew the District Forest Officer (DFO), we hoped to coordinate with the CDO and SP of Nawalparasi district so that instead of a jail, we would be able to stay in the police room.

On July 13, preparations were made to take us to the jail in Nawalparasi. I don't know why, but from morning, a sense of fear gripped me that something awful was going to happen to me. I had never been this scared earlier, even when the verdict was being read out.

After finishing the paperwork, we left for Nawalparasi at 10:30 in the morning, along with a police team and a clerk, Rambabu Shrestha, of the jail administration. My mind was greatly troubled. At Bardaghat, we had lunch. We reached Parasi, the district headquarters of Nawalparasi, at 2:30 p.m.

I first came here in February 1991. I was a young man of 22 then. Since I was from Pokhara, I found the weather in Parasi warm even though it was winter. I had come here to take up my job. There had been an advertisement in the papers for a temporary ranger, and I had been selected. That was a happy day. But things were different today.

I felt very desperate. I called the DFO of the Nawalparasi District Forest Office, Bijayraj Poudyal. "Go to the District Police Office and stay there, I am in a meeting and will arrive soon," he said. The assistant sub-inspector and junior clerk who had come with us, however, insisted on dropping us off at the jail.

"You can make arrangements later," they said. I asked them to take us to the District Police Office, as that was what the DFO had said.

As soon we got down from the vehicle, I was very glad to see Inspector Shobhit Bahadur Gurung, someone I knew. He had read about us in the newspapers.

The chief warden was also with us. He too was making efforts and requesting everyone to help us. Even after waiting for two hours, the DFO failed to return from his meeting. But thanks to his efforts, the CDO and SP arranged for our stay in a room of the District Police Office. We were greatly relieved. After a while, SP Ramesh Kumar Pandey met us. "We are making things easier for you as you are government officials," said he. I expressed my gratitude.

A few days back, a prisoner had escaped from Nawalparasi jail, and the jailers, police and administration were afraid we might also run away. We assured them that this would not happen. I really thanked the moment for receiving such helping hands. The fear I felt in the morning was also gone.

Jail Diary

IT WAS THE FIRST DAY of our jail life. Ranger Ritesh's nephew Keshav Basnet was an inspector there, too. He said we should eat together. It was like manna from heaven. We had brought along our mattress, bed sheets, pillows and quilts. We also had our cell phones with us.

The SP advised us to keep a low profile. "If journalists find out you are in our office room instead of in jail, then you will be in the news all over, and we will have trouble."

He had asked for our cell phones, but I joined my hands and requested, "We will not call anyone, and won't receive phone calls either." He did not insist.

The day after we were jailed, on July 14, the Nawalparasi CDO Keshar Bahadur Baniya, came to meet us. We thanked him for making arrangements in the police office.

We heard on July 23 that the district judge was back in office. We were glad that now there would be a hearing. In the evening, we learnt that the hearing would be on August 1. Everyone was surprised that the date was pushed back. Later we learnt that the chief warden, in coordination with the lawyers, had pushed the date far. The reason was that lawyer Krishna Bhakta was in Pakistan, and he would help smoothen matters once he returned. What an irony!

Was the judge giving his verdict based on law or the atmosphere? Is the crime judged on the basis of rules or lawyers?

If there is a rally of a hundred smugglers, then are we to assume that justice will be denied to us? If so, then why do we need a court? We could just take out rallies to penalise or forgive those we want. The law gives us semi-judicial rights, and we make our decisions based on laws not on the atmosphere or people. What do judges of full judicial organisations base their decisions on?

We decided to request a preponement of the hearing, but we were not successful. In the meantime, the prisoners of Nawalparasi jail, where we were supposed to be accommodated, torched and vandalised the building, demanding a general pardon. There were 36 men and two women in the jail.

THURSDAY, JULY 27

I WAS FEELING sad with bitter memories haunting my mind. I had asked to be transferred from Chitwan quite a few months back. I worked with all my heart to save the rhinos as part of the Anti-poaching Unit for three years. During this period, I arrested more than 150 poachers, brokers and smugglers. I confiscated more than 10 home-made guns and hundreds of bullets. I also confiscated five horns, four tiger skins, 20 kilos of tiger bones, mobile sets, jeeps, cars, motorcycles and more than $68,870 from the poachers and smugglers.

Rhino poaching and smuggling of horns had decreased by nearly 80 per cent in comparison to the last couple of years. Even though times were very tense due to the Maoist conflict, I went about my duties not caring for my life. I never turned away from my responsibilities, despite the difficulties, rough patches, problems and threats. I intended to tell all this to the Ministry of Forests and Soil Conservation Secretary Swayambhuman Amatya while requesting for a transfer to the Bardia National Park.

But before I could speak, he had posed me a question: "Did you guys arrest Yakche without evidences?"

I was stunned to hear this. What an irony! Just because a smuggler's accomplices come to see them in shining cars and say, "My man is innocent and was framed," the top secretaries and ministers of the nation are ready to believe them and end up insulting their officials and encouraging smugglers? By doing this, they are trying to win the favour of smugglers as well as the county's bigwigs.

Even though these thoughts were coming to my mind, I told him politely, "Sir, I have no personal enmity with Yakche that I should want to frame him. He admitted to selling 20 rhino horns when a journalist asked him at a press conference. Nepal Television had broadcast the clip, I can get it to you if you want. Yakche has not just one but five cases registered against him. Why would anyone need to frame him?"

I had expected him to congratulate me on my work and arrange for my transfer, but he refused.

FRIDAY, JULY 28

WE HEARD THAT poachers had again shot and injured a rhino, and I felt very sad. Also, today there was a news report in the *Kantipur* daily about the death of two rhinos in a week. I felt awful on reading it. We never cared for the time or the dangers simply so that we could save the rhinos. But today, smugglers and poachers were walking about freely, almost arrogantly, while conservation activists were rotting in jail.

One rhino had been poisoned at Piprahar of Rajahar village, Nawalparasi. A picture accompanied the news. Another rhino that had just given birth to a baby had been killed in the Chaturbhuj Community Forest of Tikauli, Chitwan. The baby apparently runs around crying, looking for its mother. Another rhino too was apparently shot. Maybe that one is running around bleeding in the forest, looking for help. Those who say that parks cannot save rhinos and should be handed over to the communities must answer as to why rhinos are dying in the community managed forests.

What has the naïve animal done to you? You think you are the best animal, but you are terrible, appalling, mean and demented. You give sorrow, pain, tears and heartache to the animals. You broke their swimming pools and turned their beautiful meadows into fields. How blissfully she would have swum with her young ones in the muddy pools? How happy the rhino would be roaming freely amidst the *Khayar* and *Sisau* trees? It could cross the Narayani unhindered. No one would dare stop it. But today, your selfishness has destroyed its ancestral home. You ruined the forest, visited the courts and offices and gave bribes, just to make its land yours. What heights of evil did you not scale to deprive it of its natural rights and privileges? As if this was not enough, you still continue to kill her, stealthily like a thief from behind, sometimes for its horn and sometimes with a ready excuse of protecting your crops. Shame on you!

We were hoping for good news, but right from the morning, there was only bad news. Later in the day we got to know that the state minister of forests had met Yakche's wife Phinjo. So worried the minister was about a horn smuggler! It is shameful that a minister should go and meet Phinjo, a smuggler herself.

In the evening, my friend Diwakar Chapagain, who worked at the DNPWC, informed me over the phone that *subba* Uttam Prasad had been transferred to the Chitwan National Park Office again.

It only showed how active the well wishers of the smugglers were!

SATURDAY, JULY 29

THE CHIEF WARDEN told me on the phone that gunshots had been heard in the Chitrasari Community Forest the previous day and poachers had killed a rhino and taken the horn.

That explains why they had gone to such lengths in the first place! The conspiracies, rallies and influence over the court, they were all for killing rhinos in safety. The sad thing was that the leaders too were present in Chitwan to praise the smugglers simply because the smugglers had paid them a small amount. What an irony that the Maoists who call themselves the builders of a New Nepal were patronising smugglers! What would become of the country if the Maoists really got into the government and ran the show? What would they do to those who disagreed with them? Wouldn't there be a new Pol Pot then? Wouldn't Nepal become a collection of terrifying stories which the world community dreaded to hear?

I have been seeing good omens in my dreams for the past few nights. In one dream, I saw someone garlanding me and taking me around town. It seemed like a sign of freedom. In another dream, I was sitting in a strange place. A familiar inspector sat nearby. Just then, the same inspector was taking my friend Ritesh Bhushan along as he walked. There was a river between us. This dream seemed that I would be released. In yet another dream, I had met my mother and was chatting with her. She was in a fresh mood. These dreams raised hopes that the court would release me on bail or on guarantee. The chief warden too informed us that the atmosphere was better now, and things were looking more positive.

SUNDAY, JULY 30

THE DEATH OF A RHINO in her 15th month of pregnancy in the Chitrasari Community Forest made headlines in the papers and on the radio. Pregnant rhinos usually come out of the national park and enter other forests. They prefer smaller jungles during this period to save their calves from the tigers and other dangerous animals and also because they can get grass easily outside the park during the summer. It is a golden opportunity for poachers and smugglers.

MONDAY, JULY 31

GUNSHOTS WERE HEARD at 5 in the evening at the Khageri irrigation canal in Chitwan. A rhino had been injured and had run away bleeding. If these incidents of injuring rhinos happen too often, it means that there is a new gang of poachers. They are still learning and are not sharp shooters yet. That is why they just manage to injure the rhinos. A wounded rhino does not stand a chance of surviving for more than two or three months.

TUESDAY, AUGUST 1

TODAY WAS TO BE our court hearing. We went to Bharatpur from Parasi early in the morning in our office vehicle sent from Kasara. We had our food and reached the Chitwan District Court at 11. Our friends had already arrived, and the chief warden was quite excited.

The hearings started at noon. Our lawyers pleaded the case on our behalf. The assistant district government attorney presented the case on the plaintiff's behalf. There were four private lawyers on their side. The District Judge was Hari Kumar Pokhrel.

The hearing lasted until 4 o'clock. Like the last time, there were rallies in the streets this time, too. The rally was regarding some other issue, but the timing was perfectly orchestrated. The rally reached the court's gate just when our lawyer Krishna Bhakta was pleading the case, and his whole style changed after that.

After the pleadings, we chatted with friends for an hour and a half, waiting for the judge's verdict. At 5:30, a court official came out from the judge's chamber with a file and called us to hear the verdict. The verdict of July 12 given by the officiating judge was endorsed. Later Krishna Bhakta told us, "The rally influenced the verdict."

We were disappointed. My father-in-law Ganesh Bahadur Adhikari had come from Chainpur, and he looked very sad. I consoled myself and smiled. "This is life, anything can happen. One day I will surely find justice," I said.

As the chief warden came out of the government attorney's office he was asked to hear the court decision also. After hearing the verdict, he said, "I know no court, we will just bring elephants and destroy it," he said. I had to cool him down. "We are protectors of nature, and nature will protect us," I told him.

I reassured my friends, but for a long time I could not bring myself to call my mother and my wife, Pramila. What could I say? Slowly I gathered strength and called my mother, but the mobile was switched off. Thank God, the situation was averted for a while.

My wife's phone was also busy. "Someone else must be giving her the bad news," I assumed.

The phone got connected only after a while. I had just said hello, when Pramila burst into tears at the other end. No words, just sobbing. Seeing his mother weep, my 14-month-old son also began crying. Sounds of their wailing on the phone left me shaken for a while. I somehow managed to compose myself before addressing her. "If you weep, I will become weak. I will be even more demoralised. Calm yourself," I told her. Slowly she began speaking.

"Don't worry, everything will be fine," I said to her.

"OK," she said unhappily. The way she said it shattered my heart, and my eyes welled up.

Then I called my mother and consoled her, too. I called friends and relatives to give them the bad news.

It was 10 at night when we reached Parasi. Pramila called me on the phone. "Come to see me tomorrow," I said. We were tired from the journey. We lay on our beds after our meal, with worry, confusion, anger and thought of revenge playing in the mind till we fell asleep.

WEDNESDAY, AUGUST 2

PRAMILA ARRIVED AT 1 in the afternoon. My uncle, Purna Bahadur Kunwar, friend Sarita, Bishnu Ghimire and his wife Nirmala accompanied Pramila. Purna uncle carried my son. I stared at my little son who was wearing a sky blue T-shirt. He was fair and slim. He recognised me from afar. His eyes were alert and tried to come to me. I felt like crying on seeing him.

I took my son on my lap and kissed him. He was very happy. He turned his questioning eyes towards me, as if to ask, "Why papa, why are you here in a strange place, leaving me alone?"

"*Teetit*," he said, meaning a car, and started playing with me. As usual, he took my cell phone and put it to his ear. Some dirty liquid was oozing from his ear.

"Take him to a good doctor," I told Pramila.

When it was time for them to leave, my son refused to go. He was instead waving his mother goodbye. I had to hand him over to his mother by force. He was crying as he wanted to stay with me. The god in me must surely have been cursing those villains.

FRIDAY, AUGUST 18

TODAY *MUKHIYA* RAMCHANDRA SHRESTHA arrived from Kasara. We were supposed to file a case with the Appellate Court, therefore, we needed to sign some papers. Our lawyer and the chief warden would be going to the Appellate Court in Hetauda the following week.

The chief warden called to say that the seven political parties had held a meeting with the objective of bringing rhino poaching under control. According to him, there was unanimity among the representatives of the political parties that staff members trying to free us from custody should be penalised.

"It is not true that the rhinos are dying, they are just rumours spread by the park officials, and they should be penalised," a Maoist leader is said to have told the gathering. "On the contrary, the rhino smugglers serving sentences in jail are innocent, they should be released."

The chief warden was certain that it was the Maoists who had influenced the judge in preventing our release on bail.

There were only two options left with us: either the government withdraw the case or we appeal to the Appellate Court. We learnt that the prime minister had ordered Home Minister Krishna Prasad Sitaula to withdraw the case. But again we learnt today that the files needed to begin the process were not ready. For a week, we had been hearing rumours that our case would be presented in Monday's cabinet meeting. But the copy of the decision made by the Chitwan District Court had not yet reached Kathmandu even after 20 days, and without this document, the process to withdraw the case could not start.

Monday, August 21

While we were in custody, a committee comprising representatives from the Home Ministry (Madhav Regmi), Ministry of Forests (Anil Pandey) and the Attorney General's Office (Pushparaj Koirala) was formed. The chief warden told us by telephone that the committee coordinated by Pushparaj Koirala had presented a report that was not in our favour. Later I got hold of that report. The committee had interacted with many organisations and individuals, including Dr. Nataraj Prasad, Dr. S.P. Patwari and Dr. Bhojraj Adhikari from the Bharatpur Medical College.

The statement given by Dr. Bhojraj, who was involved in the Shikharam case, was as follows: "The patient's right side was paralysed, oxygen shortage in all parts of the brain, no progress even with oxygen pipes. The major cause of death was lack of oxygen to the back of the brain. The post-mortem report does mention that seven broken ribs had pierced the lungs, but there is no mention of internal bleeding. If a patient stops breathing, a doctor may have to press his chest several times to restart his breathing. In the process, a weak rib of a patient might break."

Even though this was the truth, the report concluded that we had arrested and beaten to death an innocent man.

Everyone was trying to frame us.

As I continued to think, I began to pity them. And in no time, the panic had vanished. When I contemplated the behaviour of the country's so-called bigwigs, I felt proud, not bad, to be in jail. I was much greater, more patriotic than these leaders, ministers, secretaries, CDOs, policemen, judges, lawyers and all others.

FRIDAY, SEPTEMBER 15

I WAS EAGERLY waiting for our hearing at the Appellate Court, Hetauda that was scheduled for September 15. I was hoping we would at least be released on bail. Just then the chief warden called to say it had been postponed for the following Friday, i.e., September 22.

I remembered my mother, Pramila and my small kid. How could I console them? I have extended the date of my release many times now. I had told them I would be released the following Friday... after three days... a week... a fortnight. I had then told them I couldn't be released because the judge was absent or the file was not ready on time or the case was being withdrawn by the government. I had consoled them by saying nothing would happen to me. For how long was I to keep on lying to them and disappointing them?

In the meantime, DFO Bijay Raj Poudyal sent us a novel 'Palpasa Cafe'. Before this, I never had the time to read, what with meeting informers, the investigation process and all the running around. Now we had time enough. Ritesh read the book first and gave it to me. I found it interesting; we seemed to have visited the places described in the book. It used a language that we spoke daily, and the scenes resembled those from our own villages.

FRIDAY, SEPTEMBER 22

A HEARING WAS scheduled for today, but Chief Judge Govinda Prasad Parajuli decided not to have it three days before the start of the *Dashain* festival. Our dreams of celebrating *Dashain* with our family were shattered.

Just then, Buddhi Bahadur Praja called to say that he and 12 others, including Ramsaran B.K., who were in jail for poaching rhinos had been offered a pardon by the government at the initiative of then Home Minister Krishna Prasad Sitaula. Ramsaran B.K. had been arrested in October 2011 for smuggling rhino horns by the Chitwan National Park with the help of the CIB of the Nepal Police. Now Buddhi Bahadur Praja is in the most wanted list.

SATURDAY, SEPTEMBER 23

ON THE 3 P.M. news bulletin, the radio channels reported that a helicopter had gone missing at Ghunsa of Taplejung. The area lay inside the Kanchanjanga Conservation Area. In the helicopter were several dignitaries who had gone to hand the conservation area over to the local communities. I was especially worried to hear that many conservationists were in the helicopter.

MONDAY, SEPTEMBER 25

THE SEARCH FOR the helicopter on Saturday and Sunday was hindered by the difficult geography and inclement weather. Today on the 1:30 p.m. news bulletin came the report that the helicopter had crashed, and everyone in it had died. The slim hope that they might be found alive vanished, and I was shocked.

Former Director-general of the DNPWC Tirthaman Maskey had come to visit me just a week ago. I had informed him that I was keeping a diary, and he had said, "We must publish it as a book."

"You know everything, you should write, it will be a guideline for everyone. I am proud of you," he had said, and I had beamed with pride. I found a great emptiness after his death. My wish to include his suggestions in my book would never be fulfilled now.

FRIDAY, SEPTEMBER 29

TODAY WAS *PHULPATI*, the seventh day of the *Dashain* festival. Pramila called in the morning. I asked her about our son. To my boy, all TV characters looked like his father, and he called them papa. Whenever he saw someone on the road wearing a shirt like mine, he would say, "There goes papa."

MONDAY, OCTOBER 2

I WAS BORN IN the month of October. I was hoping that this month would be a favourable one for me. I spent my days reading the *Mahabharata* and *Bhagavad Gītā*.

It was the day of *Tika*, the greatest day of the 10-day festival. In the morning I talked to my mother, mother-in-law, Pramila and elder sister Devi K.C., younger brother Kulendra, sisters Sita and Bishnu over the phone. My uncle and aunty from Sarangkot also called me.

Mostly we were free to watch television in the police inspectors' mess. We used to pass the time watching movies on the TV set. On the day of *Tika*, I watched "Rang de Basanti", an Indian flick. The movie's message was that to bear oppression quietly was akin to living a dead man's life. It seemed to say that it was better to die having done something for the country and society. There were extra shots in the film which showed scenes from real life. One of them included the story of an official from the Indian Oil Corporation who had refused to accept a commission and tried to stop the adulteration of oil. As a result, he was shot dead for his honesty.

FRIDAY, OCTOBER 13

WE HAD WAITED for this day very eagerly. This was the first Friday after the long *Dashain* holidays. News from everywhere seemed positive. The chief warden as well as the lawyers said that they were quite sure of a positive verdict that day. I, too, had firm belief in such a verdict.

At 3:30 p.m., Ritesh looked at his watch and said, "They must be pleading our case."

I had called a ranger from the Parsa Wildlife Reserve. He told me that the hearings were over and that he was on his way to drop our lawyer at the airport.

Assuming that the verdict had been given, I called my mother-in-law, but she could not be contacted on the phone. I became suspicious: the verdict must have gone against us, that is why mummy went her way without calling us. Then we called lawyer Krishna Bhakta. "The previous decision of the District Court was upheld again," he said.

I was stunned.

I later contacted my mother-in-law. She was in Parsa Bazaar, Chitwan. She wept over the phone, saying she could do nothing.

I tried consoling her.

After some time, I called home to give the bad news and to console them. My mother picked up the phone. She had already heard the news, and she was sobbing. Pramila, too, was crying.

On the night of October 12, I couldn't sleep for a long time, bothered as I was by the verdict. When I did, I dreamt that I was going somewhere in the night. I had a small vehicle shaped like a jeep and also like a motorcycle. It was packed with people. After going a short distance, the headlight stopped working. In anger, I started hitting it. A friend sitting in the back said, "A broken headlight isn't going to work simply by hitting it." Just then I saw a huge mound on the road. I was trying to drive over it when I woke up. I took the dream to be a bad omen.

Due to the increasing conspiracies around us, the feeling of revenge was high in me. My heart told me again and again - you must take revenge against the conspirators. If such upsetting verdicts continued, then I would have to take tough steps. If God were to order me to destroy all smugglers, poachers and their supporters, I would gladly do so.

My heart told me that God was deliberately creating situations where my patience would cross the limits so that He could destroy all tyrants through me, like Arjun in the *Mahabharata* war.

THURSDAY, OCTOBER 19

FROM MY UNCLE Purna, I got information that poachers had killed a rhino at old Padampur, one kilometre away from the army post. They took not only the horn but also the hooves. What confidence the thieves suddenly had that they could operate near the post! A similar incident had taken place at the Khoriya Muhan last year. Those poachers were from Meghauli village and were later arrested.

FRIDAY, OCTOBER 20

IN THE EVENING, I asked Ritesh to call Kathmandu and find out regarding the withdrawal of our case. After the phone call, he told me that the prime minister had reprimanded Home Minister Krishna Prasad Sitaula for not implementing the order, and he had promised to carry it out after the *Tihar* festival. This news provided me great relief.

WEDNESDAY, OCTOBER 25

IN THE MORNING, there was news that poachers had electrocuted a rhino at Jagatpur and taken away its horn. This was the first incident in which smugglers had electrocuted a rhino to kill it. Previously, locals would electrocute animals to protect their crops, not to obtain their horns. A week ago, a rhino had been killed by electrocution at Dibyanagar, but the horn wasn't taken. The FM stations had aired the news day and night. As a result, smugglers got to know that electrocution was another method of killing rhinos and had used it successfully at Jagatpur.

TUESDAY, OCTOBER 31

TODAY WAS MY birthday. I got up early and after washing, listened to the sermons on the TV for some time. Today was also *Thulo Ekadasi*. "Every organism faces favourable and unfavourable times," said preacher Asharam Bapu on an Indian television channel. "During favourable times, it spreads widely. But during unfavourable times, it shrinks and might even die."

During his sermon, he also mentioned that Bhishma became a great man due to his adherence to the truth. And that is why celibacy, truth, compassion and kindness made Mohandas Karamchand Gandhi a great man.

Since my cell phone was not working, I asked Ritesh for his, and called my mother at home to remind her of her happiness in going through the labour pangs 37 years ago. But her mobile was switched off. I tried many times but could not contact her. Then I called Pramila in Chitwan.

"Happy birthday," she said, "I sent you a message on the mobile." We exchanged greetings for happier days soon.

Today the newspapers carried a report which said, for the first time, a woman had been arrested for killing rhinos. But that was not correct. Eight years ago, a woman had been arrested at old Padampur for killing a rhino. She had been jailed, too. There are many women involved in rhino smuggling! Evidences have been found against Yakche's wife Phinjo, and cases have been registered against other women, too.

Today a meeting of all the parties was held to discuss the conservation of rhinos. In 2000, there were 544 rhinos in Chitwan, but there remained only 372 in 2005. In the first two years, in 2001 and 2002, many rhinos had been killed by poachers. After that, there was a 75 to 80 per cent drop in rhino poaching. We couldn't stop it completely, but we were successful in greatly reducing it. The Maoist terror and faulty government policies were other reasons for the decrease in the number of rhinos.

What could a bogus meeting accomplish, anyway? Even while a meeting was being held and big plans were being formulated, a rhino was killed at Kali Khola in the Jaldevi Community Forest.

Wednesday, November 22

TODAY THE HOME MINISTER was supposed to work on our file, but he apparently did not go to office. The file had reached the ministry a month ago from the Chitwan District Administration Office, but it was stuck there. The newly appointed acting CDO of Chitwan, Shambhu Prasad Koirala, and legal officer Ram Prasad Sharma had forwarded our file to the Home Ministry without delay. The minister, apparently influenced by smugglers, was holding the file. Otherwise, he wouldn't have dared to hold the file when the prime minister had ordered him to process it.

Personally, I am satisfied with what I have accomplished in the past three-and-a-half years. It was a challenging time for wildlife conservation. I am proud of my work. People are jailed for so many reasons: crime, politics, social reasons. We must be the only two people jailed for conserving wildlife.

Another reason for the proliferation of poaching activities is the lack of coordination among the concerned agencies. There is not much probe into the criminals arrested by the District Forest Office, and the national park is not informed about them. As a result, in many cases, only the middlemen and brokers get arrested or penalised, while poachers continue with their activities unhindered. For example, five horns were found in Aaptari, Chitwan but no investigation was conducted to find out where they came from or who the poachers were. Finding horns is not a great thing, the important task is to penalise the poachers and reduce poaching.

Strict policies must be implemented immediately to control poaching. Country representative of the WWF Nepal Programme had discussed organising an awareness raising concert with singer Amrit Gurung. *The Kathmandu Post* had given a lot of prominence to the programme in an article. But we have only two options at hand to stop poaching: first, patrolling and collecting information so that on their basis, criminals could be arrested and punished as per the law. Awareness raising is good in theory but unworkable in practice. Poachers, brokers and smugglers are like poison and can be cured only by strict laws and immediate action. By the time the people are made aware, the rhinos might become extinct.

Whenever the country is unstable, the smugglers become particularly active. In times of trouble, the army is focussed on the trouble. Security posts are left unmanned, and poachers seize the opportunity to kill the rhinos unhindered. If we do not have a mechanism in place to save the rhinos during times of trouble and use guesswork to get by, rhinos conserved over the centuries with great investment will be destroyed in only a couple of years. It is definitely more important to conserve them during chaotic times, anyone can save them during peace times.

In the Kaziranga National Park, India, the park manager is the security manager as well. As a result, he can work towards fortifying the protection and, therefore, has a higher chance of actually conserving wildlife. In Nepal, the park plays no role in managing the protective wing of the armed soldiers. The park warden does not have the authority to increase or decrease the number of army posts. It can neither order a patrol nor use arms. How then can rhinos be saved during times of trouble? Hence, armed protection should be managed by the park.

Posting soldiers in the park means the establishment of a military regime there. It is against the nature of the army to be in direct contact with civilians. Besides, if the army with modern technology and training is not able to handle poachers armed with ordinary home-made guns, it shows the army's incompetence. It only proves that they lack military strategies, dexterity, up-to-date plans and professionalism.

The country has been maintaining 7,000 troops in conservation for years. The army has been in the national parks since 1975. Back then, it was very effective, but now, times have changed. In the changed context, it is essential to formulate new strategies and follow new models. The nation needs to take firm decisions on effective conservation practices. If such a decision is taken, then conservation may need only half the resources it now consumes.

Saturday, November 25

Pramila and my brother Narayan arrived in the evening with my son.

My son wanted to spend the night with me. He cried, and I felt sad. By the time he reached the District Forest Office guest house, all of Parasi bazaar had heard his wailings. They stayed in the District Forest Office guest house for two days. My son would be with me all day. Having had his fill of daddy's company, he returned with a heavy heart on the third day.

Monday, November 27

SP Ramesh had gone to Triveni. Upon returning, he talked of Kamalnayanacharya. I remember going to Triveni on a mission to stop the construction of the Triveni-Dumkibas road. If that road had been built, it would have had a negative impact on the conservation of crocodiles and many other animals. The crocodiles in the Gajamoksha area need to be protected. But Kamalnayanacharya was intent on destroying the environment in the name of development. In fact, in the tenth chapter of the *Srimad Bhagavad Gītā*, Lord Krishna clearly states that among the water creatures, He is the crocodile. What sort of a yogi is then Kamalnayanacharya who is hell bent on destroying these crocodiles?

Home Minister Krishna Prasad Sitaula had still not begun processing our files. He ignored the requests from many leaders as well as the prime minister himself. This is a clear proof of how wide and pervasive the smugglers' nets were. But what could the home minister gain from them and what could he possibly do to us?

I had been reading the *Srimad Bhagavad Gītā* and *Mahabharata* for five days and finished reading the epics. When I was a very young child, aged around 6-8 years, I used to sleep with my father. When he woke up early in the morning, he chanted *Hare Kṛṣṇa, Hare Kṛṣṇa, Kṛṣṇa Kṛṣṇa, Hare Hare/ Hare Rāma, Hare Rāma, Rāma Rāma, Hare Hare*. When I woke up, I would sit on the bed and listen to his chantings. He told me many stories from the *Mahabharata* epic in the evening before going to bed.

When I was in grade 3, our teacher Khagendra Thapa had told us many stories from the epic. At home, there was an old volume of the *Mahabharata* whose front pages were missing. I had read it when I was in grades 5 and 6. The second reading refreshed memories of the epic.

It helped to calm me down. My sufferings are miniscule compared to those borne by the Pandavas and other kings, sages and saints. Is God testing me? Can I pass this test?

Hence, floating in the sea of knowledge, that is the *Bhagavad Gītā*, makes your soul carefree and light. When I read the *Bhagavad Gītā*, I realised that birth and death are not under our control. Hence, worrying about them is a waste of time. Desire, anger, greed and attachment make us sad. I should shed my greed and attachments. In order to etch my version of history, to fight against smugglers, I must strive to shed those things. Punishing sinners and evil-doers is the noblest deed. Until and unless I do not immerse myself in my task and prove myself in this test of fire, my life will remain unfulfilled, and this book of mine will also remain incomplete.

The one who is scared of death never achieves anything. Jail sentence, underground life and reclusion only refine and develop a person. If a person is unwilling to spend a life of struggle, he can forego any dreams of achievement. We must lose something to gain something. A drab life without any milestones is of no value. As you keep struggling in your path of duty, ups and downs, praises and insults, successes and failures, will all become a part of your life. Only then can you feel the meaning of life, and that's the gist of life.

My soul would not have been able to embrace this mystery of life had I not been in jail. I understood life only because of this. If I hadn't been jailed, I would not have read the *Bhagavad Gītā*. I understood life by reading the *Gītā* with great concentration and feeling. I received unimaginable knowledge about the origin, continuity and end of life. I was able to view life, society and the individual through the lens of knowledge. I was very lucky to get the opportunity.

A story in the *Shiva Purana* goes like this: When it did not rain on earth for 12 years, sage Gautam and his wife decided to undergo severe penance. Pleased with their penance, Lord Varun created an everlasting pond for them. Wives of other sages became jealous of this and instigated their husbands into destroying sage Gautam. The sages prayed to Lord Yagyadev. When he appeared, they asked that Gautam be destroyed. Yagyadev refused to grant it, but upon the sages' request, he agreed to transform himself into an old cow and pretended to die in Gautam's courtyard. Accordingly, the other sages arrived after the cow died and accused Gautam of *gauhatya*. Sage Gautam was forced to admit to a crime he did not commit and went into further penance. Similarly, ringed in the smugglers' conspiracy, I too am forced to go through a punishment for a crime I did not commit.

I wanted to fight the ring leaders of the smugglers. I arrested many people, and yet I felt like I never really fought a powerful smuggler. It would have been such fun to wrestle with a real don. The so-called heads of smuggling rings, like Yakche and Tamling, are also commissioned by other higher ups.

In the war between right and wrong, it is a great honour to fight on the right side. As a descendant of the brave ancestors, it is my duty to fight the traitors and smugglers, and defeat them. It is a golden opportunity offered by God. In the *Bhagavad*

Gītā, Lord Krishna says:

Yadṛcchayā copapannaṁ svarga-dvāram apāvṛtam
Sukhinaḥ Kṣatriyāḥ pārtha labhante yuddham īdṛśam
(2.32)

O Partha, happy are the Ksatriyas to whom such fighting opportunities come unsought, opening for them the doors of the heavenly planets.* [2]

hato vā prāpsyasi svargaṁ jitvā vā bhokṣyase mahīm
tasmād uttiṣṭha Kaunteya yuddhāya kṛta-niścayaḥ.
(2.37)

O son of Kunti, either you will be killed on the battlefield and attain the heavenly planets, or you will conquer and enjoy the earthly kingdom. Therefore, get up with determination and fight.*

Just as injustice crossed the limits in the *Mahabharata* and became the reason for Arjun to fight, the injustice meted out to us is inspiring me to fight. In the latter days, I even wished they would give me more pain. Extreme pain, which would fan the flames of revenge even more, and encourage me even more to fight. The tiger is Goddess Mahakali's vehicle, the elephant is Lord Ganesh's incarnation, and every living thing like the rhino is a form of Lord Krishna himself. Having made wildlife conservation my only aim, it is slowly dawning on me that Lord Krishna is motivating me, like Arjun, to give up everything and enter a war of righteousness.

nainaṁ chindanti śastrāṇi nainaṁ dahati pāvakah
na cainaṁ kledayanty āpo na śoṣayati mārutaḥ.(2.23)

[2]   BHAGAVAD GĪTĀ, AS IT IS : His Divine Grace A.C. Bhaktivedanta Swami Prabhupāda

The soul can never be cut to pieces by any weapon, nor burned by fire, nor moistened by water, nor withered by the wind.*

It is one of the basic duties of a nation to prevent a person from rebelling. It is necessary to understand that the results of hurting an individual's psyche and not respecting it properly might be terrible. Any intelligent mind will revolt under the circumstances and say, "It is the Lord's order that you destroy traitors and tyrants! Wake up! Get up! How long will you silently endure this pain? Why do you hesitate? Get rid of your fears of death! No one can kill the soul. The soul is immortal. You are not your body, but your soul. Who can kill you?"

My father Chitra Bahadur Kunwar never lowered himself before anyone. He never treated anyone unfairly and did not tolerate such treatment either. He was very courageous and was devoted to the cause of forest conservation. He had gone to the Supreme Court to fight a case against forest encroachment. He devoted his entire life to the conservation of the forests as a member of the forest conservation committee. As long as he was alive, no one dared think of cutting trees in our community forest. He would motivate and unite the people to save the forests and spent a lot of money in the process. As a result, sometimes there were quarrels with my mother. But my father always said that the forest is a great thing. "We get wood, grass, leaves, fire wood, all from the jungle. As long as there are forests, man will never need anything." Maybe I was influenced by him on my journey of conservation.

Thursday, December 14

Pramila came to meet me alone today. I missed my son very much. That night Pramila reached home late. My mother-in-law called to tell me that the kid was looking for his mother.

He talked to me on the phone. When he said, "Papa," my heart nearly broke. "Son, your mom is coming in the *teetee*..., and she is bringing some *papa* to you. Stay well," I said.

Two days back, another rhino had been killed in broad daylight at Syalbas of Meghauli village.

TUESDAY, DECEMBER 26

AT THE SECOND international elephant race organised in Sauraha, Hotel Association Nepal Sauraha Chapter and Mrigakunja Buffer Zone User Committee honoured me with a conservation prize. I was unable to attend the programme, so on my behalf, Pramila attended it and received $344 and a certificate from the minister for culture, tourism and civil aviation.

A Maoist cadre had also attended the programme. He and Pramila were sitting next to each other on the stage. "Maoists have filed reams of complaints against Kamal Jung, and if he makes a request to us, we can investigate the case," he said. Poor guy, he did not know that I would never ask the Maoists for help, not even if I had to die.

From the fourth week of December 2006, Nepal Television's comedy tele-serial *Tito Satya* began screening a story similar to ours. The park officials work diligently, even to the point of loving their rhinos more than their children and family, but at the end, it is they who are framed by the smugglers.

Conservers of Mother Nepal,
keep at it continuously
Soon the golden morning will come,
how long can the night stay?

Pure aim, indomitable courage is yours,
move forward always
Truth is always victorious,
millions support you.

- Raj Kumar Bhatta
Former Chairman
Lothar Buffer Zone User Committee

The Lothar Buffer Zone User Committee family, Surdevi and Parewashwari Community Forest User Committee and Machan Wildlife Resort of Sunachuri gave us a combined letter of appreciation with these loving and inspiring words on January 24. This letter gave us great consolation and encouraged us. Friends from the Meghauli Buffer Zone User Committee also expressed their solidarity with us. They greeted us with flowers and a letter of appreciation. Many relatives, family members, friends, colleagues and conservationists met us in jail and encouraged us.

GOVERNMENT CORRECTS ITS MISTAKE

TUESDAY, FEBRUARY 27, 2007

A CABINET MEETING was scheduled for today. Since the Maoists would be joining the government in a few days, it was important that our case be withdrawn today. If not, our withdrawal might be stalled by the coalition government.

To withdraw the case, the home minister had asked for official letters from the two major parties - the Nepali Congress and CPN-UML. Accordingly, both had submitted the letters. Ritesh's father Chhatra Dhoj Basnet's lifelong contribution to the Nepali Congress helped in getting a consensus letter to withdraw the case while my friends Kiran Poudyal,

Madhav Khadka and others played a huge role to get a similar letter from the CPN-UML.

I had participated in the 1979/80 revolution at the age of 10. During the referendum on whether to continue with the partyless *Panchayat* system or go for a multi-party polity in May 1980, I had worked hard in the village, requesting everyone to vote for the blue colour, or multi-party system. In the 1990 people's movement that reinstated multi-party democracy in the country, I was very active in the protest rallies and other programmes. I battled the police in the streets. Once, when arrested friends, unable to bear the torture, told the police that I was their leader, I even had to go into hiding.

The police at Hemja had even passed an order to "shoot Kamal Jung at sight". While the order caused me extreme anxiety, it caused greater anxiety to my mother. After the re-establishment of democracy in 1990, though I was busy with my office work for a long time, I again became active in the second people's movement. Since the decisive revolution was to start from April 16, 2006, I had taken leave on April 15 and gone home to Hemja from Chitwan. Taking part in the democratic revolution meant facing a lot of obstacles from the royalists. I am proud to have played an active role in both the movements.

After both the parties had agreed to withdraw the case against us, the home minister came up with another excuse. He demanded a consensus letter from the Parliamentary Environment Committee. Just two days remained for the parliament to dissolve and a new one to take its place. The parliament was meeting for the last time. It was clear why the home minister wanted written letters of authorisation. But since the Environment Committee consisted of the Nepali Congress and CPN-UML members, they heard the matter carefully and also gave the required reference.

What is interesting is that Sujata Koirala, the prime minister's daughter, was trying her best to prevent the withdrawal of our case. Her intention was to free Yakche instead. I had heard that from colleagues that Yakche had offered to donate $206,612 through Journalist Narayan Dahal to her Sushma Koirala Memorial Trust. That's why she was so keen to free Yakche. As part of the plan, the State Minister for Forests Gopal Rai had appointed Gopal Upadhyaya the chief warden of Chitwan. In the third week of January 2006, the chief warden implemented the first phase of the plan - using his discretion on one of the five cases filed against Yakche, he sentenced Yakche to five years in jail.

After he awarded an equal number of years to both Chandra Bahadur Praja, a man who received a paltry $41 from a poacher, and Yakche, a notorious smuggler, there was a huge public outcry against Gopal Upadhyaya. As a result, he was suspended from his post before he could judge the second case. His dream of releasing Yakche and becoming the acting director-general of the DNPWC with Sujata's support remained a dream.

The home minister did not process the file even after the environment committee provided its reference. Then Ritesh's father went to the prime minister along with then Vice-president of the Nepali Congress Sushil Koirala. It was only after this that the home minister sent our file to the cabinet.

The cabinet usually asks permission from the Ministry of Law to withdraw cases. But after Gopal Upadhyaya's unjust decision over Yakche's case, the ministry had a negative view of park officials. Hence, the file was stopped again. When they got wind of this, hoteliers from Sauraha, conservationists immediately left for Kathmandu. When our well-wishers had made the matter clear to the minister, he approved the file, and it reached the cabinet for the final decision.

We were very hopeful that the cabinet would withdraw our case on February 27, 2007. But there was also a fear that the proposal might be rejected for some reason. Our breath nearly stopped in anticipation of the results. I was watching TV, not fully knowing what I was watching.

Suddenly Ritesh came in and said, "They have decided to withdraw the case today."

What news could have given me more happiness?

I shook hands with him, with a feeling of great happiness and victory. It was around 3 in the afternoon.

We started sharing the good news with our family and well-wishers.

Today the day had finally arrived after continuously promising my mother and my wife many times that it would arrive some day and soon. First of all, I relayed the news to them. Their happiness knew no limits. I was even more elated by the happiness they were undergoing.

Technicalities remained though: even after the government had withdrawn the case, the court where the case was filed would have to give permission. The Attorney General's Office, Kathmandu would inform the District Attorney Office, Chitwan of the withdrawal, and then the District Court would have to be notified. Ritesh's father asked for a fax letter to be sent from Kathmandu to Chitwan, and he himself went to the District Attorney Office to submit the letter.

He had fallen ill from all the stress. Ritesh's mother had been equally worried and galled by her youngest son's misery.

One day, Assistant Government Attorney Baburam Adhikāri called me to say that the court might not agree with the withdrawal.

My blood boiled. "Then we too are ready to go to any length," said I.

That was not just a momentary emotional outburst on my

part. Disappointment and pessimism were ringing me from all sides, and I had formulated a plan. I planned to fight against injustice, even if it meant breaking out of jail. If my case hadn't been withdrawn, then I would probably have been fighting corruption and smuggling in the country with a gun in my hand.

But on March 3, 2007, we were taken to the Chitwan District Court, and after some formality, we were released. My son and Pramila were there to welcome me. My son was very glad to see me. Many relatives, well-wishers, colleagues and conservationists had gathered there. After we were released by the court, they welcomed us with flowers and vermilion powder. Glad that victory had finally won, we returned to Kasara.

AFTER BEING RELEASED FROM JAIL

AT KASARA, TOO, our colleagues welcomed us with flowers. The new lieutenant colonel of the army was there too to welcome us. We then headed for the party organised by our friends from Sauraha. The next day, I went to Chainpur to meet my in-laws and started for Hemja. I badly wanted to meet my mother.

It was evening by the time we reached home. My cup of happiness was full when I met my mother. It was a result of her patience, a gift of her prayer. I bowed down to her and saluted her prayer and patience.

My mother had fallen ill while I was in jail. A lady doctor from the Fishtail Hospital, Pokhara, had referred her to the Bharatpur Cancer Hospital, Chitwan. On March 8, I took my mother to Bharatpur. Preliminary diagnosis showed Stage 3B cancer of the uterus. A senior official from the hospital called me aside. "Your mother will not live long, don't have high hopes," he said. But I was not swayed, I was fully confident my mother would be well again.

While my mother was undergoing a check-up, I received a phone call from the Ministry of Forests and Soil Conservation on March 10. "The ministry has decided to appoint you the acting chief warden of the Chitwan National Park. What do you say?" said the joint-secretary.

I discussed it with a few friends and accepted the offer the next day. The ministry was probably appreciative of my work and trying to show it through this gesture, but I was not really keen on staying in Chitwan. Since I would anyway have to stay in Bharatpur for a few days because of my mother's health, I accepted it.

My role changed once I became the chief. Instead of going out on field work, I was confined to the office. My job entailed leading the conservation work and giving verdicts on cases as a semi-judicial court. With similar enthusiasm and motivation, Assistant Warden Ananath Baral and other friends took up the field work.

Even after persistent efforts, I had been unable to arrest the dangerous poacher Hari Bahadur B.K. from Dumarwana, Bara. While I was in jail, I had received a call from Kasara that said a rhino had been killed in the island area. "What type of bullet did you find during the post-mortem?" I had asked.

"SLR," was the reply.

"You must arrest Hari Bahadur," I had said. Our team had gone after him in coordination with the Bara Armed Police Force, but he had managed to run away from his home. Friends had given chase and captured him near a small stream. I was very glad when I heard this news in jail.

Pilot Ramesh Pokhrel was later arrested on the basis of his statement, and a case was filed against him on March 11, 2007. A junior army officer stole SLR bullets from the army barracks at Adhavar and gave them to Ramesh, who, in turn, gave them to the notorious poacher Hari Bahadur. Ramesh sold the horns he got from the poachers to a Manange, Tashi, who passed them on to Kalu Gurung aka Kalu Manange. Like Yakche and Tamling, Kalu Manange was also a top class smuggler.

I worked in Chitwan as chief warden from March 2007 till the third week of August. More than 33 poachers and smugglers were arrested during this time.

Rhino poaching decreased dramatically. Eight rhinos were killed the previous year, that is, between March and August 2006, and one was killed when I was the chief.

Poachers and smugglers kept trying to spin webs of conspiracy around me and trip me up, but I was satisfied in being able to motivate and enthuse my friends. In the meantime, I started the tradition of open debates in the park office.

Following the chemo and radio therapies, my mother regained her health after three months. After she left for home, I was eager to compile my experiences on rhino conservation into a book. Hence, I asked the Ministry of Forests and Soil Conservation for a transfer to Kathmandu.

The Web of Rhino Horn Smuggling

WHY RHINO HORN SMUGGLING?

WHY WOULD ANYONE smuggle rhino horns? Where do the horns go? Where are they used? According to the book "Convention on International Trade on Endangered Species of Wild Fauna and Flora (CITES) Implementation in Nepal: Introduction and Identity, (2002)", written by Diwakar Chapagain and Janardan Dhakal and published by the Department of National Parks and Wildlife Conservation, rhinos are killed for their horns. The horns are transported to illegal international markets, where they command the highest prices.

According to the book, all species of rhinos are nearing extinction due to poaching. The horn of the Asian rhino weighs on average between 800 to 1,000 grams, and its price is 5-10 times more than that of the African one.

In many oriental traditions, including Chinese Medicine, the rhino horn is used as an aphrodisiac and in the treatment for asthma, fever and disorders of the lungs and the digestive system. In Arab countries, it is used to make the hilt of knives and small swords. Also, it is set in metal to be worn as a ring as a lucky charm.

All nations of the world have made poaching of and trade in wildlife articles/trophies illegal. In 1975, Nepal became a signatory and a party to CITES and prohibited the poaching, buying and selling, transportation and use of all wildlife products. Despite the legal provisions enacted to prevent the trade in wildlife products in most countries, still the annual trade is worth more than US$ 20 billion, 3 per cent of which (US$ 500 million) is illegal. The book by Chapagain and Dhakal mentions that a kilo of rhino horn is sold for more than US$ 26,000, or Nepalese Rs. 2 million.

How much does a horn cost in Kathmandu? A guess can be made from the statements given by arrested poachers and smugglers. After killing a rhino, poachers cut off the horn, along with the surrounding flesh, and boil it thoroughly. The flesh detaches itself from the horn, and when polished, it is ready for smuggling out. Many hand over the horn to the local brokers at a predetermined price. Some poachers also take it to Kathmandu and sell it to other brokers or take the horn straight to the big smugglers. Those who sell it in Chitwan, Nawalparasi and Makwanpur get $826 - $964 for 100 grams, and $8,264-9,642 if the horn weighs a kilo. Those who take it to Kathmandu get a higher price. By the time it passes through the hands of two or three brokers, its price goes up by around $2,755. Traders in Kathmandu who export it to Tibet have been known to make a profit of $4,132 - $6,887 on the price. If we calculate thus, we see that a trader who exports a hundred horns from Kathmandu earns $413,223 - $688,705. Recently, a gang of poachers had stated that they had sold a horn weighing 400 grams for $13,223, which tells us that the price of a horn is not fixed.

Hence, a horn sold by a poacher at $8,264 in Chitwan is valued at $9,641 - $11,019 by the time it reaches a broker in Kathmandu, and upon exiting Kathmandu, its price might be as high as $16,529 or sometimes even $20,661. When the horn reaches the end user through Khasa (Tibet), a kilo of horn might be worth as much as $41,322.

Mostly Tibetan refugees and Nepalese of Tibetan origin are involved in the horn trade. Why? This is because Tibet and China are the major consumers of the horn and other wildlife products. Because the language, culture, traditions and lifestyle are similar, it is easier for Tibetan refugees and Nepalese of Tibetan origin to engage in the business. Hence, they have a near monopoly in the business. Though other people might work at the lower level, it is not easy for them to climb up the ladder of the business. However, helping the smugglers and protecting them are several so-called high-class people of Nepal, Royal family members, political leaders, traders, high-ranking officials, police and army officials and prominent members of the civil society who do everything in their power to help them succeed and make some money for themselves. A few major incidents should make this phenomenon clear.

AAPTARI INCIDENT

ON JULY 13, 2004, the army arrested four people along with five horns, a Grand Vitara jeep and $826 during a check. I was in Kathmandu at that time. The chief warden called to inform me of the incident and said, "I have asked the colonel of the Bharatpur Battalion to hand over the arrested people and horns to us."

I was curious to know from where they got so many horns. But when I returned to Kasara, I learnt that those men had been sent to the army headquarters in Kathmandu, while the colonel himself was riding the jeep he had confiscated.

The chief warden had told him, "You can keep the vehicle, just hand over the men. We will give $689 as a reward to the army immediately and will take steps to ensure more rewards." But the colonel would not surrender the men to the park or to the Chitwan District Forest Office.

A little later, when I enquired about the matter in Kathmandu, I found that those arrested had been released. When I met the assistant forest officer of the corresponding Kathmandu District Forest Office, he told me, "The army sent those people to us after 40 days. One of the five horns proved to be fake. Since two of the boys were college students, we released them. We had registered a case with Dawa Lama and Pemba Sherpa as defendants, but the DFO released them on bail". He instead told me, "You guys don't speak up even when things get so bad!"

When these people were arrested at Aaptari, Colonel Rameshraj Mahat, who was stationed at Bharatpur, had immediately organised a press conference as if something great had been accomplished. When all television channels and newspapers started giving news of Dawa and Pemba's arrest with the horns, the head smugglers became active. The army had ignored the legal provisions that say an arrested suspect should be presented to the concerned authority handling the cases within 24 hours of the arrest. Instead, the boys were taken to the army headquarters and not handed over to the concerned authority for 40 days.

Was there a personal interest of the then Chief of Army Staff, Pyarjung Thapa, in initiating the process? Or did some higher power force him to take such steps and involve the whole army in illegal tasks? Which was the force that used such great powers to free these big smugglers?

Saman Bahadur B.K., who was arrested in September 2005 and later committed suicide, had mentioned in the third week of June 2004 that he had given two horns to Hari B.K. of Dumarwana, Bara.

"To whom does Hari give the horns?" we had asked Saman.

"He gives them to his neighbour, pilot Ramesh Pokhrel," he said. Dawa Lama and Pemba Sherpa, arrested in the same month at Aaptari, Chitwan, had also mentioned that they had brought horns from Birgunj, Parsa. If we assume that Saman Bahadur gave the horns to Hari, and Hari gave them to Ramesh, who then gave them to Dawa and Pemba?

If we examine the statement given by them - after the army finally surrendered the men to the Kathmandu District Forest Office after 40 days - it certainly looks doctored, as if it had been written by law experts. The report makes no mention of the persons who gave them the horns nor of the people to whom the horns were destined.

Again, the actions of Kamal Bhakta Shrestha, the DFO of Kathmandu, were suspicious. Dawa and Pemba were remanded on bail by him. How could he ignore the legal provisions which state that if the jail duration is for more than three years, the accused should be questioned in jail while awaiting trial? On whose initiative or support did he take such drastic steps which could prove very harmful to his career?

Meanwhile, as the whole government was earning a bad reputation because of the Aaptari incident, the forest minister of the royal regime appointed an investigation committee. However, the higher power was determined to save the smugglers and prevented the committee's recommendations from being implemented. The file was just transferred from the Kathmandu District Forest Office to the Chitwan District Forest Office. Though the files arrived, the culprits did not appear on the due date to face trial.

At that time, the District Forest Officer, Imamuddin Ansari, was transferred to Rupandehi district from Chitwan. But even after a new official had been appointed, Imamuddin released two smugglers found with four horns with just a small fine, while the law clearly states that such culprits shall be punished with a fine ranging from \$689 - \$1,377 or an imprisonment ranging from five years to 15 years or both. Not just that, Imamuddin even decided to give back the Vitara jeep confiscated from the smugglers. This was another stark example of the powers that tried their best to save the smugglers.

State Minister Gopal Rai was the one who asked Imamuddin to take such decisions. He would meet Yakche's wife Phinjo at his own home, and even take her around in his vehicle. He had called Tikaram Adhikari, the chief warden, and said, "I am sending my personnel assistant Rajababu over, please release Yakche by any means." When Tikaram refused to do so, the minister sent Gopal Prasad Upadhyaya to Chitwan as the new chief.

Such incidents of powerful people siding with the smugglers are common place, and they demoralise the park officials as well as everyone involved in conservation work. All such incidents should be investigated, the secrets disclosed and the guilty ones punished, no matter how powerful they are. Only then can conservation work be truly effective.

Horn Smugglers and Maoists

When Pemba Lama aka Yakche was arrested, he confessed to being a trader of *Yarsagumba*, too. A few years ago, we had received news that Maoists had confiscated *Yarsagumba* worth \$826,446 in Dolpa, a Himalayan district in western Nepal. During interrogation, Yakche revealed this. Also, he spoke of how he had met Maoist leaders Pushpa Kamal Dahal 'Prachanda' and Baburam Bhattarai many times to get back the *Yarsagumba*, and how he had also travelled to Delhi, India, to meet them. Later, Narayan Dahal, a journalist who acted as his advisor, had come to escort him when he was being moved from the Bharatpur jail to Kathmandu.

"I was there with Yakche when he met Prachanda and Baburam in Delhi," Narayan claimed.

The Maoists were against me because I coordinated the team that arrested Yakche, who was close to the Maoists.

Yakche and his men had no difficulty in manipulating the administration. One day, the personnel assistant of Chitwan's CDO Narendraraj Poudel phoned me to say that the CDO wanted to see me immediately. When I reached there, he ordered tea and called Narayan. Narayan rebuked me. "What are you doing, guys? Framing a guy like this? I have known him for several years, he is not a criminal at all," he said.

"We have found evidence," I said. "He himself admitted to journalists that he had sold 20 horns. Five cases are registered against him. Our records show that he has sold more than a hundred horns. How can he be innocent?"

But he started arguing with me. "You both talk to each other inside," said the CDO.

We went to his secret room. "We have evidence against Yakche's wife Phinjo, too," I told him. "We only left her then on humanitarian grounds because Yakche said she was seven months pregnant."

Then he faltered. "You can arrest her any time you want," he said. "Yakche is ill, his liver is not functioning properly, you must release him on bail as he needs to see a doctor, undergo examination and have good care or else he will die," he insisted.

"The jail management decides such things, and besides, it is the doctor's job to refer sick prisoners and prescribe medicines to them."

"Will you guys just let him die?" he started shouting and called the CDO in.

The CDO came in and shouted at me. "You must release him on bail because he is ill!"

The CDO then called the jailer. As soon as the jailer arrived, he too started shouting at me that Yakche was ill and must be sent to Kathmandu immediately.

Despite the combined pressure from these three people, I refused Yakche's release on bail or his transfer to Kathmandu. The CDO himself then went to Kathmandu and made the arrangements for his transfer. When we met later, he revealed, "Yakche's family and mine have close relations. I must do it anyway."

And when he was the CDO of Parsa district, he not only backed rhino horn smugglers but also supported Indian criminals. On November 21, 2006, *Kantipur's* reporter, Sujit Mahat, wrote that the CDO had released Indian criminals found possessing illegal weapons on a bail of just $14 due to political pressure and after accepting a bribe. At that time, crimes flourished in the Terai region, but culprits were released from jail with help from the political leaders and also the corrupt administration of the CDO.

On November 5, 2006, the *Kantipur* had published news that Maoist Chairman Prachanda had stayed at Kalu Gurung's (Manange) house. And the Maoist party had held its central committee meeting in Kalu Manange's hotel. Prachanda shifted to Naya Bazaar from there.

Who is Kalu Manange? Apart from dealing in drugs and running other illegal trades, he was also a notorious smuggler of horns. A case was registered against him in the Chitwan National Park Office on March 11, 2007. He was arrested in January 2012 by the Chitwan National Park with the help of the CIB of the Nepal Police, and now he is in jail.

Smugglers like Kalu Manange and Yakche have great influence on the Maoist party since they can provide luxuries such as expensive vehicles, motorcycles, fridges, TV sets, money and even good food, according to the receiver's status. In Chitwan, a Maoist cadre, Om Prakash Wagley, was trying his best to have Til Bahadur Gurung - a broker of rhino horns and tiger skins - released. Later they managed to free him on bail.

Another Maoist activist, Ramchandra Adhikari, also siding with the smugglers, was strongly against us. When I was in jail, he was the one who had threatened the district judge, Hari Kumar Pokhrel, that he would shoot me to death if I was released from jail. The language, behaviour and objectives of the Maoists and smugglers are the same. The Maoists are against people who are against smugglers. This makes their bond clear. Five months before I was transferred from Sagarmatha to Chitwan, the army had shot dead a few Maoist cadres in Chitwan. Just to make the smugglers happy, Ramchandra and other Maoists had blamed the incident on me and proceeded to condemn me.

LEADERS IN HORN SMUGGLING

HARI KUMAR SHRESTHA and Gunaraj Pathak, Members of Parliament in the *Panchayat* era, were notorious horn traders of Chitwan. Even after the *Panchayat* system was dismantled, leaders of many parties continued to be involved in this trade.

Hari Kumar was a feudal landlord of Jagatpur, Chitwan, and was fond of poaching. Bhagaur Chaudhari, a *subba* (senior elephant keeper) from Chitwan, had once shared an interesting anecdote with me: Once he had gone to Sitamadi in India to buy elephants. (Back then, the park bought domesticated elephants from India). There, Hari Kumar had taken him to the house of a *zamindar*. When they were about to leave, the *zamindar* requested Hari Kumar, "When you get home, send me five or six of those stuffs, people here are looking for them."

To this Hari Kumar had said, "OK, I will send them with the people who come this way, don't worry."

A few days later, *subba* Bhagaur happened to go to Sitamadi again on official business. At that time, the *zamindar* had asked him, "Didn't Hari Kumar send anything with you?"

"I have no idea, did you order anything?" asked Bhagaur.

"As he was leaving, I asked him to send a few horns. I thought he would send them with you."

"I do not have them," Bhagaur replied. He then requested Bhagaur when he got back to remind Hari Kumar.

Hari Kumar was very daring since the horn business had become quite lucrative. When Tirthaman Maskey was the warden, he took steps to reduce poaching. Then, Hari Kumar himself had gone to Kasara with his henchmen to beat him up. Tirthaman escaped with his life by running out of the back door. His wife Laxmibadan Maskey mentions this incident in her book "Tiger Warden". More about this incident can be leant from the former chief warden of the park, Rampreet Yadav.

The elderly locals still remember how Gunaraj Pathak used to exchange a horn for a few *pathis* of millet. A case was registered against him in 1974 after Campa Kaila, a man who had killed a hundred rhinos, was arrested and told Warden Tirthaman Maskey and then Ranger Rampreet Yadav that he had given all the horns to Gunaraj. But in 1977, when he won the *Panchayat* elections on the strength of money and goons, the case was withdrawn by the government on the orders of the Royal family members. Thereafter, though his smuggling continued, no case was registered against him.

Smugglers played a crucial role in getting both Hari Kumar Shrestha and Gunaraj Pathak elected as members of Parliament. Since they had open political support, both continued with their poaching and smuggling activities all their lives, and earned immeasurable wealth for themselves and their masters. If you want to know more about the activities of Hari Kumar and Gunaraj, go to their village and just ask anyone in his fifties, and you will have the details.

The process did not stop even after the autocratic *Panchayat* system ended. Even after the country became democratic, Member of Parliament Santa Kumar Chaudhari of Chitwan, who was also an assistant minister at a point, was arrested along with a horn. Lal Bahadur Jhankri, arrested for selling horns, revealed many things about local Congress leader Tek Prasad Gurung. According to him, local Congress leader Purna Bahadur Gurung and former chairman of the Kalabanjar Buffer Zone User Committee Ambar Bahadur Tamang gave horns to Tek Prasad. Lal Bahadur himself is a local Congress activist. Now Amar Bahadur Tamang is in Bharatpur Jail.

Tek Prasad had apparently said to Prem Dhoj Basnet, a Congress leader: "Look for horn buyers, and you will earn a lot." But Prem Dhoj replied that he did not engage in such work. Prem Dhoj's nephew Ritesh told me this while we were in jail together. But wanting to hear it from the horse's mouth, I had asked Prem Dhoj when I met him in Kathmandu: "Is it true that Tek Prasad said such things to you?"

"Yes, for a long time I have known many people involved in this trade. It is the official trade of many so-called bigwigs and landlords of Chitwan and Nawalparasi," he said. "This was also the major source of income of Hari Kumar and Gunaraj. The Rayamajhis of Nawalparasi are also into it".

I was startled to hear this. Now I understood why Govinda Prasad Parajuli, Chief Justice of the Appellate Court, Hetauda did not even bother to explain when he failed to appear in court in a case against Landlord Lekhjung Rayamajhi of Nawalparasi. Tek Prasad and Purna Bahadur Gurung refused to accept allegations made against them by their own local Nepali Congress activists.

Smuggling Rings

In the course of his statements, poacher Birman Praja had named quite a few people. He seemed pretty scared while naming some of them. According to him, he took the horns straight to Gyamjo and Tamling. Gyamjo had once taken him to Hetauda to a fat, bespectacled man's place. The fat man had asked Birman to shoot rhinos with his automatic gun. It must have been a lucky day of the rhinos as Birman was not comfortable with the automatic gun and returned it.

In July-August of 2002, Gyamjo died. A little before this, Anil Ghising and Jhalendra Gurung had been arrested and killed. According to Birman, they were Gyamjo's right hand men. They ran the entire smuggling ring from the Chitwan National Park and its surroundings viz Sauraha, Padampur, Dumariya, Meghauli, Island, Kawasoti, Koluwa and Tamaspur, and were responsible for hiring poachers, providing them money and guns, and buying and selling horns.

When the park arrested Anil and Jhalendra, the Devidutta Battalion of the Nepal Army interrogated them in custody. The army got to learn a lot about the smuggling rings through them. The two also revealed the smuggling honchos, some of whom were powerful, wealthy and belonged to the so-called high social strata. When this news was leaked by the army, it created a hullaballoo in the upper echelons of the smuggling rings. And then, according to the smugglers' plans, Anil, Jhalendra and seven others were killed. They were said to have been shot dead while trying to flee. The poor guys' only fault was their knowledge of the smuggling rings and their heads. On the orders of the same smuggling leaders, the army did not maintain a written report of their statements. Rangers Madhav and Rupak were stunned when the army insisted on killing them, while they had been steadfastly avoiding it until the previous day.

HORNS AND THE ROYAL PALACE

BEFORE APRIL 9, 1990, i.e., before the reinstatement of multi-party democracy, the horns and hooves of all rhinos that died of natural causes were handed over to the Royal Palace. In the 40 years between 1950 and 1990, nearly 400 horns were submitted to the palace. The park officials themselves had to take the horns to the palace, which would be recorded by the officials at the Narayanhiti Royal Palace. The recorded documents are still with the park's head office at Kasara. The question is, where are the horns? Are they still in the palace or somewhere else?

On the one hand, the Royal family played a major role in establishing the park and developing it, but on the other hand, they had a monopoly on its wealth and profited from it. So much so that in 1988/1989, when a tiger died in the park, there was an order to take the carcass to the palace in a vehicle sent to the national park to bring the dead tiger. The Royal family and its close associates were directly or indirectly involved in every type of smuggling. It was they who had arranged to free Pemba Sherpa and Dawa Lama, arrested with four horns at Aaptari, Chitwan.

At that time, no one dared to go against them since those were the days of the autocratic *Panchayat* political system and Royal regime. But the times have changed, and so have the people. The people now have the strength to speak up and fight against injustice. Hence, my friends and well wishers are speaking up against the smugglers and are active, too. I am fully confident that the war against the smugglers will heat up in the days to come. And the day is not far when their power in the country will end. Wildlife smuggling will end, and nature can rejoice without interference from anyone. That is my dream and aim.

Rhinos in Nepal and Attempts to Conserve Them

CONCEPT OF NATIONAL PARKS

UP UNTIL 1951, when the 104-year-old family rule of the Ranas came to an end, the Chitwan Valley was a hunting preserve of the British and Nepalese royalty as well as the Ranas. The Ranas frequently invited the British royalty visiting India on hunting trips to Chitwan in a bid to appease them. The Kasara building - the first concrete structure to be built in Nepal and now the office of the Chitwan National Park - was built in 1939 for the very purpose of hunting. A close study of history reveals that the British and Nepalese royalty and the Ranas were the first hunters of rhinos in Nepal.

Prime Minister Chandra Shumshere Rana invited King George V of Britain to Chitwan in 1911. History records that he had then hunted 37 tigers, 19 rhinos, four bears in addition to lesser game. The Prince of Wales and his party had similarly killed 17 tigers, 10 rhinos, two leopards and two bears in 1921. Another devastating hunt took place in 1939, when Prime Minister Juddha Shumshere Rana invited the British Viceroy - Victor Alexander John Hope, Marquis of Linlithgow - to Chitwan. The viceroy as well as princes and princesses of Europe, including those of Britain, had on a single hunting trip killed 120 tigers, 38 rhinos, 27 leopards and 15 bears.

The concept of national parks first developed with the

establishment of the Yellow Stone National Park in America in 1873. Initially, many such protected areas were established in North America. Gradually, such areas were set up in European countries, Australia, New Zealand and other countries. In the 1970s, national parks also got established in South Asian countries, including Nepal.

After the fall of the Rana regime, the Malaria Eradication Programme and Rapti Valley Settlement Programme were introduced simultaneously, which encouraged the clearing of forests to make room for new settlements in Chitwan. As a result, the population of Chitwan grew three-fold in the 1950s.

In 1957, the area between Tikauli and the Mahabharat range was declared a "rhino sanctuary", and this was the first step towards wildlife management. Also at this time, *Gaida Gasti*, or armed "Rhino Patrol", was put into operation to protect the rhinos. Due to heavy deforestation and rampant poaching, there was a sharp drop in the number of wild animals during the 1950s. Given this alarming situation, E.P. Gill, on behalf of the Flora and Fauna Preservation Society (FFPS) Mission to Nepal, in 1959 proposed setting up a national park to the north of the Rapti River and a rhino sanctuary to the south.

He again visited Chitwan in 1963 as a representative of The World Conservation Union (IUCN) and FFPS. This time, he suggested that the area to the south of the Rapti River also be converted into a national park. In 1963, the area to the south of the Rapti was declared a rhino sanctuary. In the same year, a national-level committee for land reform was instituted. The then assistant minister was also a member of the high-level committee which was given all rights to expel people who had illegally encroached upon government land and settled down. The committee found that 20,000 people had illegally occupied government land and were removed. Out of the 20,000 illegal occupants, 4,000 had captured land belonging to the rhino sanctuary.

In 1970, a wildlife conservation specialist was appointed with the help of the United Nations Development Programme/ Food and Agriculture Organisation (UNDP/FAO). He too proposed that the area to the south of the Rapti be declared a national park. By April 1971, the borders of the national park were fixed by a survey team whose coordinator was Bishwo Nath Upreti. But the national park actually started functioning only after WWF provided substantial assistance to the park in October 1971. Thus, Flora and Fauna Preservation Society, IUCN, UNDP/FAO, WWF and other organisations played prominent roles in the establishment of the Chitwan National Park.

In 1973, the National Parks and Wildlife Conservation Act was passed. That same year, the Chitwan National Park was declared the first national park of Nepal. Its area was increased from 540 sq. km. to 932 sq. km. in 1977.

This step proved to be a milestone in the annals of conservation. With assistance from FAO and UNDP, the government founded the National Parks and Wildlife Conservation Project and even appointed a game warden. The first warden of the park was Tirthaman Maskey. The project was initiated in 1976, and 18 guards and two assistant wardens were appointed. The project set up the necessary infrastructure like guard posts, warden quarters, drinking water, roads, forest paths and fences, and handed them over to the government.

It is generally believed that during the partyless *Panchayat* System and after, the royal family played an important role in the initiation and sustenance of wildlife conservation efforts. But it should be noted that at that point of time, the need for conservation was felt throughout the world, and there was a corresponding wave of establishing national parks and other protected areas. Several conventions of a global level had accepted proposals regarding the matter and had started implementing them. In Nepal, several locations noted for their biodiversity, like the Chitwan Valley, were slowly being destroyed. In such a scenario, the declaration of protected areas was a pressing necessity for the nation, regardless of the regime in power.

Protected Areas in Nepal

Chitwan, Bardia and Banke National Parks, and Shuklaphanta, Parsa and Koshi Tappu Wildlife Reserves are located in the Terai (lowland), Inner Terai and fragile *Chure* regions. The 10 national parks, three wildlife reserves and one hunting reserve cover a total area of 13,157 sq. km. Koshi Tappu is actually a frequently flooded plain of the Koshi River. Major parts of the Parsa Wildlife Reserve fall within the *Chure* hills and in the dry *Bhawar* regions. Major parts of the Chitwan National Park lie within the *Chure* hills and *Duban Chhetra*, the flooded land of the Narayani, Rapti and Reu Rivers in the summer. Parts of the Bardia and Banke National Parks lie in the *Chure* hills and parts in the summer flooded land of the Karnali and Babai Rivers. Many parts of Shuklaphanta also lie in the summer flooded land of the Mahakali River and so the parks and reserves areas are not suitable for agriculture or for human settlement.

Most of the remaining protected areas lie in the mountains and Himalayan regions. However, 15,425.95 sq. km. of land attributed to six conservation areas also include agricultural and residential areas. In these areas, the local communities participate in programmes for the conservation and management of biodiversity as well as sustainable development. Similarly, 5,422 sq. km. of communal forest, marginal lands, agricultural and residential area have been declared as buffer zones.

Thus, protected areas occupy an area of 34,185.62 sq. km. in total, which accounts for 23.23 per cent of Nepal's total area. The protected areas in the Terai and Inner Terai, ranging from the Koshi Tappu Wildlife Reserve to the Shuklaphanta Wildlife Reserve, occupy an area of 3,429 sq. km., of which 50 per cent can be used for agricultural or residential purposes.

In the past, certain rights-based non-governmental organisations had attempted to disparage the conservation efforts by claiming that protected areas occupy 23.23 per cent of the country's total area. However, in truth, protected areas only cover 1,714.5 sq. km. of arable and residential land (in the Terai and Inner Terai) which is about 1 per cent of the country's area.

ASIAN ONE-HORNED RHINO

CURRENTLY, FIVE TYPES of rhinos are found in the world. Of them, two species, black and white, are found in Africa, two - the Javan and Sumatran - are found in Indonesia, and the remaining Asian one-horned rhinoceros is found only in South

Asia. Its scientific name is *Rhinoceros unicornis*, which is made up of Greek and Latin words. In Greek, the word 'rhino' means nose, and 'ceros' means horn. Similarly, in Latin, 'uni' means one and 'cornis' means nose. This rhinoceros, known as the Asian one-horned rhinoceros, is a peculiar animal and is found only in Nepal, India and Bhutan. The highest concentration of this animal is found in the three protected areas of Nepal and in some protected areas of north-eastern India.

There were 544 rhinos in Chitwan in 2000 (total 612 in Nepal), of which only 372 remained in 2005. According to the rhino count of 2008, there are 408 rhinos in Chitwan, 22 in Bardia and five in Shuklaphanta: in total, 435. The census conducted in 2011 has, however, revealed an increase of 99 rhinos since the last count in 2008. The Chitwan National Park was found to have 503 rhinos, while 24 reside in the Bardia National Park, and the Shuklaphanta Wildlife Reserve protects seven. Thus, Nepal's population of the greater one-horned rhinoceros has increased to 534. The rhino is a very rare and endangered wild animal, and it is a huge mammal. Its natural habitats are the riverbanks and grasslands. The one-horned rhinoceros is the second biggest animal among the land animals. In Eastern civilisation, it is considered a holy animal, and our religious texts like the *Vedas* and *Puranas* also make mention of it.

The rhino is a part of the Rhinocerotidae family. Studies of the rhino's ancestors show that 50 million years ago, they branched from the Equidae family. The one-horned rhinoceros was previously found in many countries of Asia like Burma, Pakistan, Bangladesh, Bhutan, Nepal, India and China. By mid 20th century, it died out in many places due to habitat destruction and massive and rampant poaching, and rhinos survived only in some parts of Nepal and India.

Though male and female rhinos look alike, male rhinos are

slightly larger. A male rhino's average weight is 2,000-3,000 kgs (4,900-6,600 pounds), and a female rhino weighs about 1,600 kgs (3,500 pounds). Their height varies from 1.7 to 2 metres (5 feet 7 inches to 6 feet 7 inches). The male and female both have a single horn. The horn is a bunch of hairs that grow on the rhino's nose. The baby rhino does not have a horn. The average length of a horn is 25 cm (9.8 inches), however, horns of 57.2 cm (22.5 inches) at most have also been recorded. The average weight of a horn of an Asian one-horned rhinoceros varies from 800 to 1,000 grams. The horn is not connected to the head or skull in any way. The horn continuously grows throughout the life of the rhino, and if lost, it grows back.

The rhino has a thick skin, silver-brown in colour, and is pinkish where the skin is folded. The male has a thicker skin at the neck compared to the female. There is very little hair on the skin, with some hair on the eyes, ears and tail. Rhinos have very big and strong legs with three hooves.

Rhinos like to live in the wetlands or grassy lands, but sometimes they are found in the forests or riverbanks. They usually like to roam alone. However, they like to be in a group while wallowing in water. The baby rhino remains with its mother until it is four years old. The male remains with the female only while mating. Each has a home range of 2-8 kilometres. Sometimes the home ranges overlap. When this happens, there are dangerous fights between the male rhinos. There are also fights between dominant males and new males looking for mating partners. These fights are very deadly. During the fights, they strike each other with their teeth that are as sharp as swords. The horn does not play any significant role in the fights. Female rhinos can also charge fiercely if they have babies with them.

Rhinos can make up to 10 different sounds. If a male rhino feels that it is in danger from external forces, it throws urine to a distance of 3-4 metres. Rhinos have the strange habit of walking backwards to the same spot to defecate every time. Due to this habit, until a few years ago, poachers would look for the place where a rhino regularly defecated and dig ditches on the way. The poachers would kill the rhino with spears after it fell into the ditch.

In summer days, rhinos like to wallow in the lakes, ponds, rivers and marshy mud holes. They can swim very well. While they are young, they face danger from the tigers and not so much from other animals. They can run at a speed of approximately

55 km per hour. They also have keen senses of smell and hearing. However, they do not have good eyesight. They can hardly see a hundred metres. The cattle egrets that sit on top of the rhinos eat small insects from their body and warn them of any impending dangers. They have a mutual relationship.

Rhinos are herbivores. Their major food is grass, but they also consume plants, leaves, branches and fruits in or near water. They set out in the morning and evening for food, and graze all night. Sometimes, they eat crops from the nearby farms.

In zoos, female rhinos are ready to give birth by the age they are four, but in a natural setting, they are usually ready to reproduce only at the age of six. Their pregnancy normally lasts for 16 months and sometimes can extend up to 19 months. They give birth to one baby at a time. They give birth to another calf only when one is fully grown.

The male rhino is ready to mate at the age of five. In a zoo, a rhino gets to mate easily when it is of age. In a natural habitat though, it might not get to mate even in an advanced age because of the dominance of stronger males. The new male only gets a chance if it can defeat the dominant rhino in a fight or if the latter dies. A recent study has shown that, typically, a rhino needs to be 15 years old before it can defeat the dominant rhino. Though rhinos do not have a specific mating season, they normally mate between February and April.

Challenge to Rhino Conservation

Currently, poaching is the biggest challenge to rhino conservation. Rhinos were hunted in large numbers in the 18th, 19th and 20th centuries. With the beginning of the Rana regime, hunting and poaching became the major causes of the rhinos' destruction in Nepal. The most prolific hunters were the British and Nepali royalty. Records reveal that as many as 39 rhinos were killed in one hunting trip in Nepal, and one army officer killed 200 rhinos in Assam of India. In 1950, there were still 800-1,000 rhinos in Chitwan whereas there remained only 12 rhinos in India, and they had become extinct in the western (Bardia) region of Nepal.

But deforestation due to increasing pressure of the migrants from the hills and poaching would lead to the death of more than 700 rhinos between 1950 and 1970 in Chitwan. By 1970, there were only 70-100 rhinos in Nepal. The rhino had thus become extremely rare and endangered.

The establishment of the Chitwan National Park in 1973 saw a pause in poaching for about a decade. However, 20 rhinos were poached between 1984 and 1991, and 18 more were killed in just one year in 1992. In 1995, poaching was under control for a short period, but again between August 1996 and October 1999, 20 rhinos were killed. In December 1999, one rhino was killed.

The following year in 2000, poaching increased dramatically. That year, 34 rhinos died. Of them, 25 had died of natural causes while seven were shot, one was poisoned and one was found dead in the rice fields of the buffer zone.

It is unfortunate that even at the beginning of the 21st century, the poaching of rhinos continues unabated in Nepal. Since horns are used to make traditional Chinese Medicines, they command a good price in the international market. Rhinos are also dwindling due to the destruction of their habitat.

In 2001, 26 rhinos were found dead. Of them, 11 had died of natural causes while 15 had been shot by poachers. In 2002, a total number of 51 rhinos had died, of which 13 had died of natural causes while 35 had been shot dead. Besides, two rhinos were electrocuted to death and one was poisoned.

I was deputed to the Chitwan National Park at the beginning of 2003. The task of conserving rhinos was truly challenging then. Rhino poaching was at its peak. On the 24th, 25th and 26th

of February 2003, one rhino was found dead every day.

In 2003, of the 35 rhinos found dead, one had been electrocuted and 21 had been poached. As in the previous year, only 13 had died of natural causes.

In 2004, 27 rhinos were found dead. Of them, 10 had been poached, two poisoned while 15 had died of natural causes. In 2005, 22 rhinos had died, of whom 13 had been poached and one electrocuted. That year, only eight rhinos had died of natural causes. The following year, 20 rhinos died - 11 were shot, one was poisoned and one was electrocuted, while seven had died of natural causes. Luckily in 2007, not many rhinos met an untimely death through poaching and natural causes. Only two rhinos were killed by poachers while seven had died of natural causes.

EFFORTS AT CONSERVATION

IN 1846, JUNGA BAHADUR RANA, Nepal's first Rana prime minister, had labelled the rhinos as 'royal game'. Through a declaration, only the royal family and the Ranas were entitled to hunt rhinos. Anyone else found poaching the animal were to be strictly penalised.

The Wildlife Protection Act was passed in 1958. The rhino sanctuary was founded on the basis of this very act. In 1973, Flora and Fauna Preservation Society had provided financial assistance to help control the pressing problem of rhino poaching. The then warden Tirthaman Maskey had utilised this fund by announcing a reward of $27.50 to anyone providing information about poachers. Former Chief Warden Rampreet Yadav says that this decision was pivotal in controlling poaching. Persons who were involved in poaching turned informers in the hope of earning some money. As a result, 17 rhino poachers and smugglers were arrested in just three months.

After 1984, when rhino poaching increased again, the park tried to strengthen its surveillance network. However, from 1988, the government discontinued the funds for informers. As reported by Kenyan journalist E.B. Martin, the control over rhino poaching slowly weakened as the funds dried up. E.B. Martin has shown concern for the rhinos in Nepal for a long time.

The fourth amendment (in 1992) to the National Parks and Wildlife Conservation Act, 1973 decreed that any person who illegally kills or injures, sells, purchases or transfers or obtains rhinos, and purchases or sells rhino horns shall be punished with a fine ranging from \$689-\$1,377 or imprisonment ranging from 5-15 years or both. After this amendment, there was a reduction in the poaching activities for fear of the heavy penalty.

Significant efforts were made at conservation at the beginning of the 21st century. But between 2000 and 2006, poaching increased because the 33 army posts were merged and reduced to just seven during the state of emergency that was imposed to bring the insurgency raged by the Communist Party of Nepal (Maoist) under control. However, many criminals were apprehended during this period and penalised. As a result, poaching slackened. Without this timely intervention, the rhinos in the Chitwan National Park and its vicinity could well have been extinct by now.

In the first half of the first decade of the 21st century, the TAL Programme - with financial and technical support from WWF Nepal Programme - and the UNDP-funded TRCP provided financial assistance for poaching control. In 2003, the TAL programme provided \$2,879, while the TRCP provided a total of \$9,917 per year, at the rate of \$496 per month.

After the TRCP ended in 2005, interest accrued from the fund deposited for conservation has been used for various programmes of the Chitwan District Forest Office, the Nepal Army at Kasara and the Chitwan National Park. Total interest earnings from the fund amount to $2,066 per year. Since 2004, the TAL programme has provided anywhere between $8,264 and $11,019 every year for poaching control. In January 1991, the UK-based ITNC provided $27.50 per month to an informer. This amount was later (2003) increased to $413 per year for each of the informers. In total various agencies have been providing $11,019 to $13,774 each year for poaching control. If necessary, funds are also available from the Buffer Zone Management Committee of the Chitwan National Park. As a result, poaching control became more effective.

Funds thus received are used to provide a monthly salary to the informers, buy information from them and manage the living and transportation costs involved in the process of collecting information. The funds also cover expenses for fuel, motorbike and vehicle repair, and camping and sweeping operations inside the park. Also, this fund pays for the medical expenses of the employees and for emergency financial assistance if needed by them. It also rewards any individual who has worked hard. Every year, 50 to 60 poachers, brokers and smugglers are nabbed.

The conservation process became more effective after the army became involved. The army has been a part of the conservation efforts since 1975. In the beginning, 200 army personnel were posted in the Chitwan National Park. Soon after, such arrangements were made in other protected areas as well. At present, except for the Dhorpatan Hunting Reserve, six conservation areas and the Makalu Barun National Park, there are army barracks in each of the other 12 protected areas. After the army was posted in the Chitwan National Park in 1975, not a single rhino was killed until 1984.

Biodiversity and Eco-tourism

The Chitwan National Park is the habitat of 50 species of mammals, about 568 species of birds, 49 species of amphibians and reptiles, four species of turtles and about 120 species of fishes. There are three different types of vegetation, namely sal and mixed forest, riverine forest and grasslands. Within these vegetation types, there are seven types of forest and six types of grasslands.

Inside the park area, the Tiger Tops was established in 1965. The resort was modelled after the world-famous Tree Top Hotel in Kenya. The 40-bed resort hotel occupied an area of 160 acres in the beginning. Later in 1973, a 15-bed tented camp was also added. Between September 1973 and June 1974, 4,000 visitors had stayed at the Tiger Tops.

Presently, more than 100,000 tourists visit Chitwan annually. Calculating the economic returns, even if each of the tourists were to spend on average just $ 100, the Chitwan National Park would stand out as one of the largest industries in Nepal. Apart from this, thousands of domestic tourists also visit the park every year. This way, the tourism industry plays a crucial role in the economic upliftment of the local people.

The UNESCO has listed four World Heritage Sites in Nepal. The Kathmandu Valley, listed in 1979, and Lumbini, the birth place of Lord Buddha, listed in 1997, are cultural sites. The Sagarmatha (Mt. Everest) National Park, listed in 1979, and Chitwan National Park, listed in 1984, are natural sites. These parks have been conserving not just the wild flora and fauna but also the landscape, wetlands, and monasteries and temples in their respective areas. Thus, national parks and conservation areas have been playing an important role in promoting our peculiar identity to the international community.

Glossary

abeer - vermilion powder

asala - snow trout *(schizothorax richardsonii)*

Asoj - sixth month of Nepali Calendar which falls in September-October

Astami - the eighth day of the lunar fortnight

baba - a word used for an ascetic or old person; father

babu - small boy or brother or small son

bakkhu - a typical Nepali wear of Himalayan people

banko kafal banko charilai - a Nepali folk song meaning 'the wild box myrtle for the wild birds'

Bhagavad Gītā - sacred writing in verse devoted to the exposition of religious and theosophical doctrines

bhailo - a practice or a song sung during the fourth night of Tihar festival

Bhawar - a low lying land, foothill, a hot valley in southern Nepal

Bhote - literally, a person or ethnic group from Bhot, that is, Tibet; most people living in the northern part of Nepal (of different ethnic groups)

Biharis - people from Bihar State of India

Bishwokarma/B.K. - a caste or class of people who were traditionally black smith's or iron smith's. The term Bishwokarma in mythology is Gods' smith or engineer. He is worshipped every year.

Bote - an ethnic group that lives mostly by the riverside

Brahmin - a caste group whose traditional occupation is to conduct rites during religious occasions

chaubandi - a piece of female's upper garment with four gussets

chautari - a platform under a tree or at crossroads, resting place

Chepang - an ethnic group that lives mostly in the vicinity of Chitwan

chhetra - area

Chhetri/Kshatriya - a caste of people who are traditionally regarded as warriors

chhyang - home-made beer

chowk - a yard, a courtyard, a marketplace, a square, a crossroad

Chure/Churea - youngest mountain/fragile low mountain lying in the southern part of Nepal

dai - one's elder brother; a word of respect used for any elderly male

Dashain - the great festival observed in honour of Goddess Durga in September or October

daura suruwal - traditional Nepali national dress

didi - one's elder sister

dohari - a duet (song competition)

doko - wicker basket

duban - flooded (area)

ekadasi - the 11th day in a lunar fortnight observed in honour of God Vishnu

gaida gasti - rhino patrolling

gandharva - a celestial musician (an ethnic group whose profession is singing Nepali folk songs)

gauhatya - cow slaughter

ghat - a place for securing boats

ghyampo - a huge jar made of clay or metal for storing grain or liquid

geet - a song, lyrics; a tune

gumba - a monastery; Buddhist temple

guru - a teacher, a master, a tutor, a preceptor

hattisare - elephant keeper

Holi/Phagu Purnima - the festival of Holi, the great festival of colours observed in the month of March

jaggae - an altar, oblation, site of religious performance

jamdar - head of soldiers, a person on guard, junior level army officer

janai - the sacred thread that is donned by Brahmin and Chhetri males

Janai Purnima - the day on which the Hindu Brahmin and Chhetri people wear the new sacred thread

Janmat Sangraha - referendum

jeri - a kind of sweetmeat

Kali Pare Dai - a Nepali folk song

katuwa pistol - home-made pistol

kharkhadai - thatch, dry grass (act of harvesting it)

khayar - cutch tree

khola - a small river, stream, rivulet

khukuri - a Nepalese knife

laddu - a spherical sweetmeat

lahure - Gurkha soldier in the Indian or British Army, a Gurkha soldier trained in Lahore (formerly)

Mahabharata - eastern epic, the 5th Veda (which tells of the war between the Kauravas and Pandavas)

Majhi - an ethnic group that lives mostly by the riverside

mama - uncle (mother's brother)

Manange - a person from the district of Manang that lies to the north of Nepal

Mandale - a person who used to support *Panchayat* system

mandir - temple

mit - a formal friend; to enter into formal friendship

momo - Dumplings filled with minced meat or vegetable

mukhiya - a non-gazetted third class rank in the civil or other service (junior clerk in government job)

Mushahar- a group of under privilege people

musuro - lentil

nahar - irrigation canal

namaskar - greeting, salutation, greeting (Nepali style by joining both hands together)

namaste - I bow to thee, salutation to you; to greet, to salute, to say hello

niguro - a kind of green wild vegetable of the fern species

om mani padme hoom - a prayer, a Buddhist mantra

paan - betel leaf enclosing betel, lime, catechu and other ingredients and is chewed

Panchayat - an autocratic partyless system which lasted 29 years until 1990

papa - sweet bread or biscuit (child language)

pathi - a vessel measuring eight manas or about 4 kilos (of grains)

phariya - traditional women's wear, a saree, a skirt

Phulpati - flowers brought in for the Durga Puja

Pipal - bodh tree

puja - reverence, worship, prayer

Puranas - eastern epic (Hindu)

Purnima - the full-moon day

raja - a king, a monarch

sarangi - a Nepali traditional and indigenous stringed musical instrument made of wood and played especially by the Gandharvas

sarkar - government

Sati - widow burning

sauji - a trader, a merchant; a shopkeeper (male)

shikari - a hunter, a hound

Shivaratri - the day in February when Lord Shiva is worshipped

Sisau - rosewood

siwalik - youngest mountain (fragile mountain, low mountain)

subba - senior clerk (government employee)

tal - a lake

tauwa - haystack

teetee/teetit - blow of a horn (in child's language)

Terai - land at the foot of the hills, the plains in southern Nepal

thulo - big, large, great

Thulo Ekadasi - an auspicious day that falls on the 11th day of the lunar fortnight in October-November

Tihar - a five-day festival of lights that falls during half of November

tika - red colour mark on the forehead

tito satya - bitter truth

Vedas - the divine knowledge, holy write

Yarsagumba - spores of the cordyceps mushroom that settle on the heads of caterpillars that live underground. It is a rare and unique herb that grows in the meadows above 3,500 metres (11,483 feet) in the Himalayan region of Nepal.

zamindar - landlord

Acronyms

APU	-	Anti -poaching Operation Unit
APF	-	Armed Police Force
BISEP-ST	-	Biodiversity Sector Programme for the Siwalik and Terai
CBI	-	Central Bureau of Investigation
CIB	-	Central Investigation Bureau
CDO	-	Chief District Officer
CIAA	-	Commission for the Investigation of Abuse of Authority
CPN-UML	-	Communist Party of Nepal-Unified Marxist Leninist
DNPWC	-	Department of National Parks and Wildlife Conservation
DFO	-	District Forest Officer
FFPS	-	Flora and Fauna Preservation Society
FAO	-	Food and Agriculture Organisation
ITNC	-	International Trust for Nature Conservation
IUCN	-	The World Conservation Union
SLC	-	School Leaving Certificate

SLR	-	Self Loading Rifle
TAL	-	Terai-Arc Landscape Programme
TRCP	-	Tiger Rhino Conservation Project
TCN	-	Timber Corporation of Nepal
UN	-	United Nations
UNDP	-	United Nations Development Programme
UNESCO	-	United Nations Educational, Scientific and Cultural Organisation
VDC	-	Village Development Committee
WWF	-	World Wildlife Fund